PRENTICE HALL

HISTORY OF MUSIC SERIES
H. WILEY HITCHCOCK, editor

MUSIC
IN THE
CLASSIC PERIOD

third edition

MUSIC
IN THE
CLASSIC PERIOD

REINHARD G. PAULY
Lewis and Clark College

PRENTICE HALL, ENGLEWOOD CLIFFS, NEW JERSEY 07632

Library of Congress Cataloging-in-Publication Data

Pauly, Reinhard G.
  Music in the classic period.

  (Prentice-Hall history of music series)
  Includes bibliographies and index.
  1. Music—18th century—History and criticism.
I. Title. II. Series.
ML195.P38 1988   780'.903'3   87-14497
ISBN 0-13-607623-8

For my Konstanze—
and for Deborah, Rebecca, and Michael

Cover art: Interior of Salzburg Cathedral,
engraving by Melchior Küsell, c. 1680. Museum Salzburg

Printed in the United States of America
20 19 18 17 16 15 14 13 12 11 10 9 8 7 6 5 4 3 2 1

 © 1988, 1973, 1965 by Prentice Hall
A Division of Simon & Schuster
Englewood Cliffs, New Jersey 07632

PRENTICE-HALL INTERNATIONAL (UK) LIMITED, *London*
PRENTICE-HALL OF AUSTRALIA PTY. LIMITED, *Sydney*
PRENTICE-HALL CANADA INC., *Toronto*
PRENTICE-HALL HISPANOAMERICANA, S.A., *Mexico*
PRENTICE-HALL OF INDIA PRIVATE LIMITED, *New Delhi*
PRENTICE-HALL OF JAPAN, INC., *Tokyo*
SIMON & SCHUSTER ASIA PTE. LTD., *Singapore*
EDITORA PRENTICE-HALL DO BRASIL, LTDA., *Rio de Janeiro*

FOREWORD

Students and others interested in the history of music have always needed books of moderate length that are nevertheless comprehensive, authoritative, and engagingly written. The Prentice-Hall History of Music Series was planned to fill these needs. It has succeeded: revised and enlarged second editions of books in the series have been necessary, and now a new cycle of further revisions exists.

Six books in the series present a panoramic view of the history of music of Western civilization, divided according to the major historical periods—Medieval, Renaissance, Baroque, Classic, Romantic, and Twentieth Century. The musical culture of the United States, viewed historically as an independent development within the larger Western tradition, is treated in another book; and one other deals with music in Latin America. In yet another pair of books, the rich folk and traditional musics of both hemispheres are considered. Taken together, these ten volumes are a distinctive and, we hope, distinguished contribution to the history of the music of the world's peoples. Each volume may also, of course, be read singly as a substantial account of the music of its period or area.

The authors of the books in the Prentice-Hall History of Music Series are scholars of international repute—musicologists, critics, and teachers of exceptional stature in their respective fields of specialization. Their goal in contributing to the series has been to present works of solid, up-to-date scholarship that are eminently readable, with significant insights into music as a part of the general intellectual and cultural life of man.

H. WILEY HITCHCOCK, *Series Editor*

PREFACE

Other volumes in this series—especially those on Medieval and Renaissance music—deal with periods which the general listener discovered only fairly recently. The present volume concerns itself with music of the late eighteenth and early nineteenth centuries, much of which has enjoyed virtually uninterrupted popularity since then. In this period the works of Haydn, Mozart, and (to some extent) Beethoven assume a central position. Studies of their lives and works are far more numerous than works about the Classic period in general. In this small volume I attempt to trace and describe the evolution of musical style through the Classic period, and to clarify its main characteristics as expressed in the chief categories of Classic music: symphony, sonata, concerto, opera, chamber music, and sacred music.

Several periods of residence in the region—particularly Austria—where musical Classicism flourished have made this music more meaningful to me. A fairly extensive chapter on the background of the Classic period has been included in this volume in the hope that some acquaintance with the historical and cultural setting will similarly add to the reader's understanding and enjoyment.

Since this book first appeared, many compositions of the late eighteenth century that were previously unavailable have been published in both scholarly and performance editions. A great deal of musical research has been done, often in connection with these editions, all of which has added to our knowledge of the Classic period. Such activity illustrates two points: that we are still learning much about the music and musicians of this "well-known" period, and that the music of the Haydn-Mozart age continues to hold a secure place in the affections of today's public—even more so, perhaps, than a generation ago. The tastes of professional and amateur musician, of concert-goer and record collector, confirm that many compositions from the Classic period continue to be "classics" in one sense of the term discussed in the opening chapter of this book.

This third edition is again revised; it is also somewhat enlarged. I have attempted to take into account recent scholarship by reference to important publications, in the text, footnotes, and bibliography. The literature on the Classic period has grown enormously, partly in observance of important anniversaries of major composers. These references therefore make no claim to completeness. In the *Bibliographical Notes* at the ends of chapters the emphasis is on publications in English. Readers should keep in mind that *The New Grove Dictionary of Music and Musicians,* published in 1980, incldues among its many outstanding features extensive bibliographies and detailed lists of works for many composers and topics related to the Classic period.

Other factors account for the greater length of this edition. In my own teaching I have often found that categories of Classic music which may be considered "peripheral" by some[1] are vitally important to today's students and informed amateurs of the history of music. In recognition of this I have added sections on some of these genres, including solo song, organ music, and guitar music. The extensive repertoire of music for wind instruments has also been given some consideration. The extent to which these topics are discussed does not imply their greater or lesser importance in the overall picture of Classic music. The song repertoire, for instance, is treated in some detail because it has tended to be neglected and is little known by students and even by professional singers.

When this book first appeared, terms such as "period instruments" and "authentic performance" were unfamiliar and certainly were not applied to the Classic period. These and other subjects related to so-called "early music" are complex and may be controversial, but they have had

[1]See p. 9.

much bearing on how we hear Classic-period music today. They are taken up briefly at the conclusion of this volume.

Even with these additions, the present edition, like its predecessors, claims to be no more than an introduction to the music of the Classic period. Such an introduction, if it is to result in real understanding, needs to be supplemented by extensive study of the music itself, in its written form, through live performances, and on recordings. Happily, because of the greater availability of the music, this can be done even more easily today than when this book first appeared.

In preparing this edition I was helped by many colleagues: performers, teachers, librarians. Among the latter I should like to extend special thanks to Dr. Otto Biba and his staff (Gesellschaft der Musikfreunde, Vienna) and to Frau I. Pechotsch-Feichtinger (Music Division, Austrian National Library). Professor William S. Newman was most generous and helpful in providing many excellent suggestions for this revision. The book also owes a great deal to my students, past and present, who were exposed to much of its subject matter. Their responses and suggestions often helped me to decide what material was relevant and how it might be presented.

R.G.P.

CONTENTS

ABBREVIATIONS

DT   *Denkmäler deutscher Tonkunst* (Leipzig, 1892–1931)

DTB   *Denkmäler der Tonkunst in Bayern* (Braunschweig, 1900–38, rev. ed. Wiesbaden, 1962–)

DTO   *Denkmäler der Tonkunst in Österreich* (Vienna, 1894–)

Grove 6   *The New Grove Dictionary of Music and Musicians* (London: Macmillan, 1980)

GMB   *Geschichte der Musik in Beispielen*, ed. Arnold Schering (Leipzig, 1931)

HAM   *Historical Anthology of Music*, ed. A. T. Davison and W. Apel (Cambridge, MA: Harvard University Press, 1950)

Hob   *Joseph Haydn: thematisch-bibliographisches Werkverzeichnis*, ed. A. van Hoboken, 3 vols. (Mainz, Schott, 1957–78)

JAMS   *Journal of the American Musicological Society* (1948–)

K   *Chronologisch-thematisches Verzeichnis sämtlicher Tonwerke Wolfgang Amadé Mozarts* (first published by L. v. Köchel, Leipzig, 1862; 6th ed. Wiesbaden, 1964)

HD *Harvard Dictionary of Music*, ed. Willi Apel, 2nd ed. (Cambridge MA:Harvard University Press, 1969)[1]

MC *The Mozart Companion*, ed. H. C. R. Landon and D. Mitchell (NY:Norton, 1956; 2nd ed. 1965)

MGG *Die Musik in Geschichte und Gegenwart*, ed. F. Blume (Kassel, 1949–)

MQ *The Musical Quarterly* (1915–)

NMA *W. A. Mozart, Neue Ausgabe sämtlicher Werke* (Kassel, 1956–)

NOHM *The New Oxford History of Music* (London: Oxford University Press, 1954–)

SBE William S. Newman, *The Sonata in the Baroque Era* 4th ed. (New York: Norton, 1983)

SCE ————, *The Sonata in the Classic Era*, 3rd ed. (New York: Norton, 1983)

SMH *Source Readings in Music History*, ed. O. Strunk (New York: Norton, 1950)

[1]References are to this edition. See also *The New Harvard Dictionary of Music*, ed. Don M. Randel (Cambridge MA: Harvard Univ. Press, 1986).

MUSIC
IN THE
CLASSIC PERIOD

part one

The Evolution
of Classic Style

ONE

"CLASSICISM" IN MUSIC

VARIOUS MEANINGS OF "CLASSICISM"

When we use terms that refer to periods of history and of style, we are dealing with generalities, not with neatly circumscribed stretches of time. It is the nature of any historical development—especially in the arts—to move now gradually, now suddenly; to show precocious starts but also to contain stubborn lingerings; to produce startling, avant-garde results in one region or country while the status quo still reigns in another. In the arts we frequently deal with the hard-to-define; terms such as "Baroque," "Classic," and "Romantic" can be useful if they are recognized as simply laborsaving devices—terms that suggest (in an admittedly general fashion) the chief stylistic qualities of an era, qualities that were widespread and prominent during a period, though by no means restricted to it. Nor does a period necessarily include exactly the same time span in different arts.

Romanticism in literature, for example, covers a far shorter number of years than Romanticism in music.

Modern historians are far more style-conscious than their predecessors. Political history today tends to be presented as the unfolding of many kinds of human experience rather than as a succession of birth or death dates, or great battles won by famous men. Cultural history, including the history of music, likewise shows more concern with the imprint that greater and lesser men have made *through their works*. This approach has led to a need for such stylistic terms as "Baroque" or "Classic," and it is significant that only in the twentieth century have they come to be generally accepted as referring to periods. For instance, "Baroque" has entered our vocabulary as a term referring to style in all the arts during the seventeenth and early eighteenth centuries; it has been so generally accepted that to the general reader it means either this or nothing at all. It has lost its earlier meanings, which were mostly derogatory: As used by eighteenth- and nineteenth-century writers, "baroque" was frequently synonymous with "exaggerated," "unnatural," "confused," "absurd," "stilted," "bizarre." (Similarly derogatory meanings were attached to the term "gothic" well into the nineteenth century.)

While "Baroque," especially when spelled with a capital *B*, has lost its earlier variety of meanings, general usage of the word "classic" (or "Classic," or "Classical") continues to be ambiguous, particularly in the field of music. Since the general and musical uses of "classic" are related, a look at definitions given in a general dictionary may provide a useful point of departure. *Classicus* referred originally to classes in Roman society, especially to the highest class, not only of people but of things and achievements in many fields. High achievement ordinarily implies permanence of some kind—lasting value and validity. In this sense a remark or speech may be "classic," as may be an achievement in science or sports, or a particularly brilliant solution to a chess problem. A motion picture is spoken of as "a classic" if it has lasted longer than run-of-the-mill pictures.

In order to have this lasting appeal, a work of art must have universal qualities. It must speak to us directly, on a generally valid human level; it must be timeless in that its eloquence must not depend on the accidental, the local, or the conventions of an age or place.

"Classic" was used by eighteenth-century writers on literature and aesthetics to describe a work that was exemplary—a model. Finscher cites examples of this use of the term. This sense of the term was only rarely applied to music, and then chiefly to the Palestrina style.[1]

This general meaning of "classic" has its obvious musical application. When we talk about "classical" music in a general way, we may not have

---

[1]Ludwig Finscher, "Zum Begriff der Klassik in der Musik," *Deutsches Jahrbuch der Musikwissenschaft für 1966*, 11 (1967), 9–34.

any precise definition in mind but we may think of music that has stood the test of time. By another widespread but inconsistent definition any music is considered classical that is not "popular." The inconsistency is obvious: *Some* popular tunes do achieve what the trade likes to refer to as immortality. There *are* classics of jazz. At any rate, a Tchaikovsky symphony qualifies for the label "classic" in the general meaning of the term: It has achieved lasting popularity. But suppose there was a Tchaikovsky symphony which had been a dismal failure at its first performance and therefore was withdrawn by the composer. If it were resurrected today, it probably would still be called classical music by most people, simply because it is a symphony. This shows that questions of category, form, and style affect even the general meaning of this troublesome term.

CLASSICAL MUSIC AND CLASSICAL ANTIQUITY

Nothing has been said so far about "classic" in relation to the civilizations of antiquity, especially of ancient Greece and Rome. Here again usage varies greatly, with music being a special case. Qualities of balance, proportion, clarity, moderation, and serenity have been generally admired in the art of these civilizations. When, in the course of the eighteenth century, a decided return to classic style took place in architecture, painting, and other fields, many original examples of ancient classicism were still existing, though often in ruins. To distinguish the revival from the original, the term "neoclassicism" eventually was coined and widely applied to the visual arts of the late eighteenth and nineteenth centuries. Why, then, do we not refer to music of the same age, especially of the age of Haydn and Mozart, as neoclassic? The reasons are easy enough to see: Our knowledge of the music of antiquity—classic music in a more specific sense—is woefully inadequate today, in spite of much recent musical scholarship, and it was far more limited in the late eighteenth and early nineteenth centuries. While a good deal is known about the place and function of music in ancient Greece, and while important theoretical and philosophical writings have been preserved, the music itself is lost except for a few short melodic fragments. Charles Burney, while collecting material for his own history of music in 1773, was already aware of this:

> Poetry, painting and sculpture . . . have a standard in the remains of antiquity, which music cannot boast. There are classics in poetry, sculpture, and architecture, which every modern strives to imitate. . . . But who will venture to say, that the musician who should compose or perform like Orpheus, or Amphion, would be deservedly most applauded now? Or who would be

bold enough to say, *how* these immortal bards *did* play or sing, when not a single vestige of their music, at least that is intelligible to us, remains?[2]

The term "Classic," then, as applied to a period in music history, refers to the music of the second half of the eighteenth and the beginning of the nineteenth centuries. For the period from about 1730 to about 1770 the term "pre-Classic" has often been used, indicating that musical Classicism was not established before the mature works of Haydn and Mozart. (See also p. 37.) In this way we speak of musical Classicism largely by analogy from the fine arts, avoiding the term "neoclassic" since music of the Classic period in no direct sense represents a revival of the music of antiquity.

An added reason exists for attaching the label "Classic" to the music of this specific period: much of it incorporates to a high degree the general aesthetic qualities associated with classicism, among them universality of meaning and appeal. To have such universal meaning music must be simple: This requirement is voiced again and again by the eighteenth-century writers on music, including some of the musicians themselves; by Gluck, for instance. Music must also show balance and order. The function of music is no longer imitation of nature but symbolic expression of the highest order. Significantly, this concept is related to the views held by some philosophers of antiquity. Equally significant is the way in which similar concepts have been expressed by some mid-twentieth-century musician–philosophers to whom the function of music is not the expression of personal emotions (as was frequently claimed during the Romantic age) but is simply a presentation of organized sound.

Balance and order are qualities that most listeners today find prominent in late-eighteenth-century music. This may become apparent in discussions of specific works below. That these qualities were no longer considered of paramount importance in Romantic music can easily be seen. Blume[3] points to the changing emphasis in the Romantic symphony, beginning with Beethoven: The concept of climax rather than balance is manifested in the greater importance of the last movement. It now often represents a high point (in terms of emotional intensity and excitement), creating a feeling of victory after struggle, of apotheosis, rather than providing a happy and "unproblematic" conclusion as was typical of the earlier Classic symphony.

"Classic" in the sense of universally valid: This requirement also

[2]Charles Burney, *The Present State of Music in France and Italy* (London, 1773; facsimile edition New York: Broude, 1969) pp. 34f.

[3]Article "Klassik" in *MGG*. An English translation of this article, by M. D. Herter Norton, forms part of Blume's *Classic and Romantic Music* (New York: Norton, 1970).

loses importance for the Romantic artist, who frequently is introspective, subjective, and self-centered. The change is outwardly manifested in the composer's greater concern with exact expression and communication of personal feelings. To make certain of this he writes far more detailed performance instructions into his music than had been the custom in the eighteenth century. The word "adagio" alone no longer suffices; "molto espressivo" may be added, or further instructions, frequently in the vernacular, along with metronome markings which have since Beethoven's time been widely used to convey as precisely as possible the composer's wish—to insure that the work will be performed at *his* tempo.

NINETEENTH-CENTURY USES OF "CLASSIC" AND "ROMANTIC"

That no clear-cut definitions of the terms "classic" and "romantic" are possible appears from the many different ways in which they occur in writing from these periods. Before they were generally accepted in the *historical* sense they were widely used to describe *style* characteristics of a composition regardless of the time it was written. Thus E. T. A. Hoffmann could refer to Bach's *B Minor Mass* as "one of the few classic sacred works which . . . reached a larger audience,"[4] meaning, presumably, that it was a work of lasting significance and value. In the same journal, a few years earlier, Haydn's instrumental works had been called "an entirely new genre of romantic tone paintings." Ambiguous statements (by our standards) can be found in early nineteenth-century music dictionaries: Gerber, in the second edition (1812) of his *Lexikon der Tonkünstler*, speaks of Bach and Handel as "gray[i.e., old-fashioned] *Kontrapunktisten* of the Gothic age"; other writers considered Palestrina to be Gothic and Handel to be Classic. To some of the early Romantics the term "classic music" represented a contradiction: All music, by nature, was romantic since it dealt with emotions, but other writers were not at all bothered by the alleged contradiction—the terms were too vague in their application to music to be mutually exclusive.

The label "classic," to be sure, was applied to works by Haydn and Mozart during their time. A few days after Mozart's death an obituary appeared in a Prague paper, stating:

Everything he wrote carried the clear stamp of classical beauty. . . . [His music] will always please for it will always seem new—the advantage of being a

[4]*Allgemeine Musikalische Zeitung*, 1814.

classic. His operas furnish proof: don't we hear them for the eightieth time with as much pleasure as we did the first time?[5]

A few years later, Niemetschek praised his operas, concertos, quartets, and other works; to him their classic value was proved by the fact that one could listen to them again and again without tiring.[6] To Niemetschek Mozart's genius had produced works comparable to the masterworks of Greek and Roman art which "grow" on us with repeated study and contemplation. Niemetschek admired the happy combination of "technical skill" (*Kunst des Satzes*) and "grace and charm," of form and content, so often considered an outstanding characteristic of classic art; he then applied these general observations to specific works as well. He referred, for instance, to the "simplicity" and "silent grandeur" (*stille Erhabenheit*) of Mozart's opera *La clemenza di Tito*—thus using the very terms which, through Winckelmann,[7] became widely accepted as describing the essence of Greek and Roman art.

THE "VIENNESE SCHOOL"

Before the present-day general acceptance of the label "Classic period" for the age of Haydn and Mozart (and, in part, of Beethoven), the term "Viennese school" was favored in some quarters. Historically and geographically it must be considered misleading: Of the three composers none was Viennese by birth, and only Beethoven spent the major portion of his creative life in Vienna. Confusion may also arise from frequent references to the twentieth-century "Viennese school" represented by Schoenberg, Berg, and Webern. Confusion does not end there: Two books published some time ago are entitled *The Golden Age of Vienna* and *Vienna's Golden Age of Music*—but while the former deals with the Classic period, the latter describes Vienna's musical life at the time of Brahms and Wagner. In spite of these reservations it is true that in the late eighteenth century Vienna did become the musical capital of Europe: Vienna, the city to which Mozart went with high hopes for the last ten years of his short life, gladly leaving behind provincial Salzburg; Vienna, the city to which Haydn often looked with longing from Eisenstadt, wishing that his princely employer would spend more time there; Vienna, the city, finally, to which Beetho-

[5]Quoted in *Mozart, die Dokumente seines Lebens. . . . , Addenda and Corrigenda* (Kassel, 1978), p. 75.
    [6]Franz Niemetschek, *Leben des k.k. Cappellmiesters Wolfgang Gottlich Mozart . . .* (Prague, 1798).
    [7]See below, p. 68.

ven journeyed in 1792, full of hopes that he would receive there "the spirit of Mozart from Haydn's hand."

WERE THERE ALWAYS "CLASSICS" IN MUSIC?

Returning once more to the term "classics" in its general meaning—works that have established themselves, that have become standard repertory—the questions arise: Was this always so? Were there "classics" during the period with which this volume deals? The answers to these questions can be found in a study of concert programs of the time. Although public concerts were then relatively new, the available statistics will surprise those of us today who are accustomed to the idea of a standard repertory in symphonic, operatic, and other music. Eighteenth-century audiences did not expect, want, or tolerate music that had been performed many times before. They went to the opera or to an "academy," as public concerts frequently were called, in order to hear "the latest." In the field of opera this had already been true in the early eighteenth century: The average Venetian in Vivaldi's day would not think of hearing last year's opera again, though the "new" opera might well be another setting of a well-known libretto and might include some arias borrowed from earlier works. This situation still prevailed in the late eighteenth century. In 1798, Niemetschek could point out that Mozart's *Don Giovanni* "even now" was being widely performed, though all of ten years old—a "classic," we might say, and much the exception then. Similarly, concerts given under Haydn's direction at Esterháza consisted for the most part of music written for the occasion; an academy given by Mozart in the Augarten in Vienna was bound to include one or several substantial new works, and the rest of the program in all likelihood would consist of works not more than ten years old. The statistics given by Carse[8] are fascinating and reveal the same situation at many musical centers: Not only were the majority of works performed "contemporary," but most of them were written not by the few whom we consider the great composers of that time (our "classics") but by hundreds of now forgotten composers, usually the local Kapellmeister whose main function it was to compose "such music as His Highness may command," as Haydn's contract stipulated. At semi-public events such as opera or concerts in a prince's residence the audience was a select one and thus might be expected to be fairly conversant with the latest styles. The

---

[8]Adam Carse, *The Orchestra in the Eighteenth Century* (Cambridge: Heffer, 1940), pp. 5–15. Carse gives additional statistics for the period 1830–39 in *The Orchestra from Beethoven to Berlioz* (Cambridge: Heffer, 1948), p. 8. See also William Weber, "The Contemporaneity of Eighteenth-Century Musical Taste," *MQ*, 70 (1984), 174–94.

programs of public concerts, however, attended as today by an anonymous, admission-paying public, show the same absence of "classic masterworks"— of the concerto that has stood the test of time, of the symphony so well known that the chief interest of many a listener lies in the conductor's interpretation. In the field of sacred music, taste traditionally changed somewhat more slowly, but even here contemporary music was the rule. Burney makes special mention of having heard in Vienna "some admirable old music, composed by Fux,"[9] music which then may have been fifty years old. Imagine someone today referring to Schoenberg's *Kammersinfonie* as "admirable old music!" Yet the same attitude accounts for the "Concert of Antient Music," a society established in London in 1776 for the purpose of performing music that was more than twenty years old—"antient" by the standards of the time.

Thus, we must think of the Classic period as a period without classics. Not until well into the nineteenth century did the public concert acquire the typical program makeup with which we are so familiar: works which are 50 to 150 years old making up the bulk of the repertory, with a sprinkling of older and newer works rounding out the program.

EXTENT OF THE CLASSIC PERIOD— SCOPE OF THIS BOOK

The statement was made earlier that stylistic periods cannot be defined by exact dates. For the Classic period this means that numerous manifestations of the new music outlook and style appeared before the Baroque had spent its force. Johann Stamitz and Handel were contemporaries; in fact, Stamitz, the most famous representative of the "pre-Classic" Mannheim school, died two years before Handel did. The death of Bach in 1750 has often been chosen to symbolize the end of the Baroque era, but by the time Bach had composed the *Art of Fugue* his son Carl Philipp Emanuel had already written keyboard sonatas in a distinctly new style. All through the first half of the eighteenth century the aesthetic conventions and musical traditions of the Baroque were being challenged. One of the results was a great amount of music displaying a purposely light, pleasing, and entertaining quality—music that expressed the Rococo spirit. Since this development took place before the end of the Baroque era, it seems appropriate to think of Rococo style or spirit rather than of a Rococo period. The ingredients of this style will be examined in the following chapter; the complex ways in which they are related to pre-Classic and Classic music should

[9]Charles Burney, *The Present State of Music in Germany, the Netherlands, and the United Provinces* (London, 1773), p. 239.

make it clear why a beginning date for the Classic period is difficult to establish. Today some scholars, mindful of the stylistically complex nature of mid-eighteenth-century music, avoid the terms "pre-Classic" and "Classic" altogether.[10] J. P. Larsen has suggested the following terminology:

1. Late Baroque, until about 1740;
2. Mid-century style (he prefers this to "pre-Classic"), ca. 1740–70;
3. Classic style, ca. 1770–1800;
4. Early Romanticism, from about 1800.[11]

Similar difficulties beset us at the end of the period. Should Beethoven be discussed in this book? He died in 1827, and there are many ways in which he represents Classicism, in the general as well as the narrower chronological sense. To some, a book on the Classic period may be unthinkable without a prominent place given to Beethoven; yet we consider Schubert a representative of Romanticism, for equally valid reasons, in spite of the fact that he died within a year of Beethoven's death. Nothing could better demonstrate the overlapping of stylistic periods than the music of these two composers. Beethoven's music is briefly discussed in this book, chiefly in its relation to Classicism, leaving a more detailed treatment to the next volume in this series.[12]

This volume will have the music of Haydn and Mozart as its core. Since it is not a comprehensive history of music, many important composers cannot be discussed. Geographically the emphasis will be on those countries in which the Classic style was most clearly and brilliantly formulated. The given limitations of space demand that those categories of music be omitted that are peripheral—that do not materially affect the total picture of Classic style. For Mozart, these include Blume's *Nebengattungen* (in his article "Mozart" in *MGG*): dances, marches for piano, many separate arias and songs, canons, and so forth. The general aim will be to deal with categories of special importance for each composer: symphony and string quartet for Haydn; opera, concerto, and sonata for Mozart. Concentrating on the music of Haydn and Mozart has the practical advantage that most of the music is readily available in printed form and on recordings.

[10]See "Sources of the Classical Idiom" in *International Musicological Society: Report of the Eighth Congress, New York 1961* (Kassel, 1962), II: 135ff. During this symposium Blume expressed the opinion that, from the point of view of stylistic unity, there was no "Classic period" except, perhaps, the 1770s, "one decisive period of stylistic confluence."

[11]"Some Observations on the Development and Characteristics of Vienna Classical Instrumental Music," *Studia Musicologica Academiae Scientiarum Hungaricae*, 9 (1967), 123ff. Barry Brook, also dismissing rigid periodization, stresses the appearance of classic and romantic traits throughout the period 1750–1850 in other arts as well. "Sturm und Drang and the Romantic Period in Music," *Studies in Romanticism* 9 (1970), 269ff.

[12]Rey M. Longyear, *Nineteenth-Century Romanticism in Music*, 2nd ed. (Englewood Cliffs NJ: Prentice-Hall, Inc, 1973).

Despite the small size of this volume, an attempt has been made to discuss the music in its proper frame by dealing with the historical and general intellectual background and, in particular, the musical life of the period. Admittedly much of the music speaks to the present-day listener directly and forcefully, yet some knowledge of the conditions under which it was written and heard can do many things for us: It can increase our sensitivity to the music itself; it can clarify the composer's objectives; and it can prevent us from looking into Classic music for qualities (including aspects of musical form) that cannot possibly be there.

BIBLIOGRAPHICAL NOTES

In addition to the literature quoted in the preceding pages, the reader may wish to consult the following: Hans Engel, "Haydn, Mozart und die Klassik," *Mozart-Jahrbuck* (1959), pp. 46ff.; Ludwig Finscher, "Zum Begriff der Klassik in der Musik," *Deutsches Jahrbuch der Musikwissenschaft für 1966* (Leipsiz, 1967), pp. 3ff.; Wilhelm Fischer, "Zur Entwicklungsgeschichte des Wiener klassischen Stils," *Studien zur Musikwissenschaft*, 3 (1915), pp. 24ff.; and Charles Rosen, *The Classic Style*, New York, 1971. How to set a date for the beginning of musical Classicism was the topic of one session at the Tenth Congress of the International Musicological Society in 1967: "Critical Years in European Musical History 1740–60," *Report of the Tenth Congress, Lubljana, 1967* (Kassel, 1970), pp. 159ff.

TWO

LATE BAROQUE
AND ROCOCO STYLE

The development from Baroque to Classic style is complicated and full of crosscurrents. That there are distinct differences between, say, a Handel concerto grosso and an early Haydn symphony is obvious to many listeners, whether or not they know these works were written within twenty years of each other. The differences, in fact, are so pronounced that we would be hard put to explain them purely in terms of chronological development. The matter becomes less enigmatic when we examine examples of what is generally referred to as Rococo style—a phase of expression, in the visual arts as well as in music, which occurred simultaneously with the end of the Baroque era.

Rococo art is still essentially art of the aristocracy. To understand its meaning and flavor one should be mindful of political developments in the early eighteenth century, especially in France, where the Rococo saw its greatest flowering. Louis XIV, powerful and absolute monarch, died in 1715 after a reign which had seen the creation of many lofty works of art

Madame Favart, Marie Justine Benoît Duroncerey (1727–72), French actress and singer, who in 1745 married Charles Simon Favart, Director of the Opéra Comique. The Metropolitan Museum of Art, Bequest of Isaac D. Fletcher, 1917. The Mr. and Mrs. Isaac D. Fletcher Collection.

embodying the high Baroque style. In a sense his reign personified the grandeur and power of the Baroque. The successor to the throne being a minor, a regent was appointed: the Duke of Orleans, an aristocrat with a far less conscientious outlook on the responsibilities of government but with a great talent for enjoying the privileges and prerogatives of his position. During the regency, which lasted until 1723, the formalities of court entertainment and ceremony gave way to a more casual, informal atmosphere. Playfulness and wit were considered the desirable attributes of social intercourse in an environment that saw the gradual lowering of social barriers between the monarchy and the lesser aristocracy. Members of the royal family mingled more freely with those of lower status and even participated in performances of opera, pastoral plays, and other diversions. Similarly, the social life of the aristocracy tended to move away from the large palace to the less formal and imposing town house—the intimacy of the salon seemed preferable to the formal halls of Versailles. This movement away from formality continued after the regency; Louis XV preferred to spend more time at the smaller residences and lodges in the country than in Paris or Versailles.

Rococo art likewise was more playful and intimate than Baroque art. To be sure, it still belonged to a court milieu with its conventions of etiquette (now somewhat relaxed). In this art the extremes of emotion so often expressed in Baroque art were considered out of place and in bad taste, while wit, charm, and sentimentality were cultivated and appreciated.

The term *"Rococo"* is derived from *rocaille*, meaning "rock work" or "shell work," a favorite motif in the decorative art of the time, which stressed purely ornamental, light, casual, irregular design. In architecture, painting, sculpture, and furniture making, Rococo design pleases rather than moves—by stressing grace and elegance. The forceful, exuberant colors of Baroque art give way to lighter, delicate shades in painting as well as in fabrics.

In spite of the lessening of court formality, the world in which Rococo art unfolded was artificial and unrealistic—a world of make-believe, of game-playing. It was characterized by, among other things, sentimentality, including a sentimental and artificial view of nature. The pseudo-rustic *hameau* (hamlet) within the park of Versailles was the typical setting; it was populated by courtiers playing at being shepherds and shepherdesses, or dressing as milkmaids without going so far as to do the milking themselves. While the artificiality is obvious, it can be understood as an effort to overcome the even more formal and stiff setting of the previous age. The parks and gardens themselves furnish excellent examples of the change. Baroque pomp and formality linger to this day in the parks surrounding many royal palaces from the time: carefully, symmetrically planned, with straight paths, clipped hedges; with statues, pavilions, and benches carefully placed; with circular or oval ponds and elaborate fountains. Gardens of this type, ostentatious and severe, impressed on the visitor the need for a large staff of gardeners and other servants; in this way they testified to the glory and power of the sovereign. Eventually a more genuine appreciation of the beauties of nature made itself felt, reflecting the philosophical and aesthetic views of Rousseau's age.

Around the middle of the century the "English garden" became fashionable on the continent, with its less formal, more natural impression. In 1775, Louis XVI, tired of the sight of artificially clipped hedges and trees, ordered them cut down; in doing so he was expressing the same sentiment voiced by Hirschfeld, a contemporary writer on what we call landscape architecture, who wrote in his *Theorie der Gartenkunst:* "Nowhere do we find art more distasteful than where it attempts to impart artificiality to natural objects."

In painting, Rococo style saw a turning away from the life-size, formal portrait by which earlier aristocrats liked to be immortalized, with stern expression and elaborate dress. The smaller portrait, suitable for display in a more intimate room, gained favor in the early eighteenth century. A friendly mien, and more relaxed and natural position also characterize Rococo portraiture. In other types of painting the *fêtes galantes* also symbolize the Rococo spirit: courtly entertainments such as garden parties with ladies and gentlemen engaged in games and dances or represented in playful and frequently coquettish or amorous poses. There are so many canvases of this kind that one might speak of a cult of love in a pastoral setting as typical subject matter. Watteau's *L'embarquement pour Cythère* is one of the better-known examples, Cythera being a mythological island of love. That many paintings by Boucher, Watteau, Lancret, Fragonard, and others were reasonably accurate representations of the court life of the time is confirmed by contemporary descriptions of such *fêtes*.

Nymphenburg Castle, Munich (François de Cuvilliés, 1695–1768, architect. Painting by Canaletto, engraving by Jungwirth, 1766). The New York Public Library.

In architecture, the Rococo spirit manifested itself in a similar turn-ing from the grandiose to the casual, from the awe-inspiring to the pleas-ing. The era of great castles and palaces came to an end; instead, the infor-mal summer residence and hunting lodge were favored. The German term *Lustschloss* and the French *maison de plaisance* indicate the change both as to function and aesthetic impression of these structures—they were to give pleasure. A French architect, François de Cuvilliés (1695–1768), brought this style to the Bavarian court about 1725. From then on it flour-ished all over southern Germany and Austria. This is the period when many Austrian palaces and churches acquired their present-day appear-ance, both exterior and interior, providing together with sculpture

Microscope, eighteenth century, showing the application of Rococo ornamentation to a scientific instrument. Vienna, Kunsthistorisches Museum.

and painting the setting, the backdrop as it were, for music during the Classic era.

Along with other manifestations of interior design, furniture showed qualities of lightness and prettiness, of elegance and smaller size, with ornamentation frequently based on the shapes of natural objects (other than *rocaille*), leaf shapes in particular. White and gold were favored colors for decorating these three-dimensional ornaments. The enthusiasm for embellishment seemed boundless and its application extended even to scientific instruments like microscopes. China figurines, book illustration, and many other artistic endeavors also reflect the appreciation of the small and delicate.

ROCOCO AND STYLE GALANT IN MUSIC: OPERA AND BALLET

After Lully's death in 1687, his lofty and serious style in opera *(tragédie lyrique)* and ballet gave way to a lighter approach. Entertainment rather than the stirring of strong emotions was now stressed, and the new category of the *opéra ballet* became symbolic of the change—employing music throughout but lacking a continuous plot; in it, drama was clearly sacrificed for display. Campra's *L'Europe galante* (1697) began the vogue of the *opéra ballet;* the title of this work is significant for the new orientation. To be sure, the tradition that Lully had built was not abandoned. Many of Rameau's operas, though textually and hence dramatically weak, contain music that is expressive and compelling, serious in purpose and effect. But even among Rameau's works, the *opéras ballets* increase numerically toward the end of his career. Perhaps this represents a capitulation to the trend of the times by a composer whose earlier aim had been to maintain the *tragédie lyrique*. Rameau's arias show a significant increase in melodic ornamentation over that in Lully's style, where clarity of diction had been of utmost importance.[1] Fondness for embellishment, as in the visual arts, became one of the main style characteristics of the musical Rococo, both in vocal and instrumental music.

That the *style galant* of this age stressed the pleasing, entertaining, and unproblematic is further shown by the increasing popularity of comedy of all descriptions, musical or other. The development of Italian *opera buffa* (comic opera) out of comic intermezzos performed between the acts of an *opera seria* took place during this period. Plots were simple, characters few and uncomplicated; certain stock characters were much in evi-

---

[1]Rameau's operas, and his significance in other areas, are discussed in Claude Palisca's *Baroque Music* (2nd ed., Englewood Cliffs, NJ: Prentice-Hall, Inc., 1981), pp. 230ff.

dence: the flippant chambermaid, the suspicious and crotchety old doctor, the blustering captain. These maintained their popularity for easily a hundred years, to the time of Rossini's *Barber of Seville*. Instead of listening to gods and emperors reflecting on *virtù* and *magnanimità* in elaborate coloraturas, audiences delighted in watching in an *opera buffa* people of their own kind engaged in real-life situations and complications, speaking their own language—and frequently in local dialect. The music of intermezzo and *opera buffa* was correspondingly simple. Arias were shorter and simpler in structure, vocal ranges were modest, and melodic lines frequently suggested folk song or popular air. The bass voice became part of the ensemble, after having been virtually excluded from Baroque *opera seria*. Accompaniment tended to be light so that the melodic line would stand in no danger of being obscured even if given (as was frequently the case) to a protagonist who was primarily an actor rather than a singer.

Giovanni Battista Pergolesi (1710–36) stands near the beginning of this development; His *La serva padrona,* first performed in 1733, soon achieved great popularity and has a modest place even in today's repertory.

French opera from its beginnings had been close to and sensitive to Italian influences and competition. For some time the Italian theater had been banned in the French capital or had lived an unsteady existence at the fairs and in the suburbs. After Lully's death the Italian theater again opened its doors, and in time the attractive if light fare performed there caused great dissension among Parisian audiences. This was the period when the relative merits of Italian and French opera were argued at great length in journals, pamphlets, and books, as well as in the salons of society, leading to few conclusive results but providing entertainment and subject matter for conversation—the same commodities that the music itself was expected to supply.

La serva padrona had reached Paris in 1746 and was performed without creating much of a stir. But when a traveling company included it among other Italian operas in Paris during the 1752–54 seasons, it caused a different reaction, touching off one of the more celebrated controversies in the history of opera, the *War of the Buffoons*. Once more sides were taken for or against the Italians and their music.

Among those proclaiming the superiority of Italian music was Jean Jacques Rousseau (1712–78), whose *Le devin du village* (The Village Soothsayer), an *intermède*, appeared in 1752. The little song-play by the philosopher-essayist-musician[2] embodies many of those qualities expressive of the Rococo spirit. To a simple and sentimental pastoral text Rousseau provided continuous music, as in the Italian models, in the form of recitatives

---

[2]He contributed articles to the great *Encyclopédie* of d'Alembert and Diderot (first part published 1751) and was the author of a *Dictionnaire de musique* (1768).

and short airs, romances and duets, as well as orchestral interludes, dance scenes, and pantomimes, all in a style that avoids grand gestures or extremes of emotion and frequently reminds one of the pseudo-rustic milieu which those in the audience delighted in imagining as a setting for their own lives.

Around 1750 Charles Simon Favart was successful as a writer of texts for *opéra comique*. Gradually the genre became "respectable": After 1762, it was no longer restricted to the suburbs but played in the city, in the Théâtre Italien, renamed Salle Favart. Works by Philidor and Monsigny were among those performed there.

ITALY: OPERA SERIA

By the beginning of the eighteenth century, *opera seria* had acquired some dramatic and musical characteristics that became quite firmly established and lasted well into the latter part of the century. While in its earlier stages comic scenes had infiltrated into much serious opera, reforms advocated by Apostolo Zeno (1668–1750) and other dramatists largely did away with them and generally restored greater dramatic persuasiveness to *opera seria*. Further changes took effect when opera found a poet of eminent stature in Pietro Metastasio (1698–1782), whose librettos were set by countless musicians throughout the century up to and including Mozart. We can obtain an idea of Metastasio's leading position by examining the list of operas based on his *La clemenza di Tito*. Before Mozart composed this text in 1791 it had been set to music by many composers, among them Caldara (1734), Hasse (1738), Jommelli (1753), Galuppi (1760), and Anfossi (1772). Metastasio is said to have remarked that he never wrote words for an aria without having imagined its musical composition. His sensitivity to the musical requirements of Baroque opera accounts, of course, for some of his success and the veneration accorded him throughout Europe,[3] but his fame also rests on purely literary grounds. Some of the "abuses" that had been so scathingly criticized by Benedetto Marcello (*Il teatro alla moda*, 1720) and others were abandoned in Metastasian opera. Plots were tightened by eliminating superfluous characters and scenes. The dramatic conflicts, stereotyped as they may seem to us, became the center of gravity since fewer distractions were provided by elaborate stage machinery, extras, animals, and the like. Except for these simplifications and improvements, *opera seria* of the eighteenth century as a medium of dramatic ex-

---

[3]Burney, in his description of Vienna, devotes some fifteen pages to "the admirable poet Metastasio." *The Present State of Music in Germany . . .*, I: 223ff.

pression was essentially fixed. Many later composers continued within the tradition without altering it in any significant way. Others, including Francesco Algarotti, made recommendations for further improvement. In his *Saggio sopra l'opera in musica* (1756), Algarotti voiced concern with the formalism of *opera seria* as shown in the rigid succession of recitatives and arias, resulting in a string of loosely connected musical "numbers." Chorus and dance should be part of the dramatic action, not merely an additional entertainment sometimes borrowed from another opera. Historical subjects should be treated in a less superficial manner and based on better knowledge of the historical background. Likewise, the music should express the poetic ideas (rather than meanings of individual words) in a more than superficial way.

Some composers did attempt to bring new vitality to *opera seria*, regenerating it from within rather than abolishing its forms and conventions. Niccolò Jommelli (1714–74), one of the Italians who earned their greatest successes abroad, was able to infuse *opera seria* with dramatic vigor and excitement before its ultimate decline set in. He paid careful attention to the orchestral accompaniment, according it much independence through contrapuntal writing and attention to instrumental color. His dynamics are careful; a score dated 1749 includes the indication "crescendo il forte." His favoring of accompanied over *secco* recitative also speaks for his concern with dramatic expressiveness. Numerous ariosos further interrupt the traditional sequence of *secco* recitatives and da capo arias, and there are sections of an act in which the "number" concept is lost sight of altogether. Instead, Jommelli supplies a freely constructed scene in which arioso texture is interrupted by a few measures of accompagnato, flowing again, without break, into a florid aria.[4]

That Jommelli should have been called "the Gluck of Italy" may be historically untenable since Gluck approached operatic reform from different literary and musical premises, discarding much of what Jommelli had tried to improve and save. Yet other composers showed much greater reluctance to vary the time-honored conventions of *opera seria*. Johann Adolf Hasse (1699–1783), a German who had studied with Alessandro Scarlatti and Porpora and who had thoroughly assimilated the Neapolitan idiom, reaped tremendous successes all over Europe. Still, only in his late operas do we find attempts to overcome the traditional number opera. Under Hasse's leadership the orchestra at the Dresden court became one of the best in Europe; but, while he insisted on great precision in performance, the orchestra in his operas does not rise to the importance it enjoys in Jommelli's works.

---

[4]For example, *Fetonte*, 1768, Act 3. Published in *DTB*, vol. 32–33.

ITALY: OPERA BUFFA

The beginnings of *opera buffa* in the early eighteenth century have been mentioned above as one manifestation of the Rococo spirit: a reaction to the pompousness of serious opera, a delight in smaller forms and simple homophony, a concern with less lofty subject matter. For some time it kept its newly found identity apart from *opera seria*, achieving great popularity by 1750. In the second half of the century the separation of the two genres became less distinct. As it lost its purely slapstick, farcical character, *opera buffa* acquired greater substance. Although still comical, or at least humorous, it now expected to be taken seriously, as drama. Librettists, among them Carlo Goldoni (1707–93), one of the foremost eighteenth-century dramatists, introduced *parti serie* (more serious and frequently sentimental roles) into *opera buffa*. Piccinni (1728–1808) achieved special success in this sentmental genre with *La buona figliuola* (1760). *Buffo* elements likewise appeared once more in *opera seria,* preparing the way for the merger of the genres that we know best from Mozart's *dramma giocoso, Don Giovanni.* Parodies of *opera seria* continued to be popular throughout the Classic era; yet the popular *opera buffa* never replaced the older genre altogether. In Italy especially it lingered, relatively immune even to the successes (on the other side of the Alps) of Mozart's masterworks. Some composers, including Jommelli, managed to be successful in both the serious and comic fields. Baldassare Galuppi (1706–85) excelled in the latter but also composed many of the former.

Opera buffa differed most decisively from serious drama of the Metastasian type by its delight in human characterization, its creation of lifelike (though light) plots. Hence, for greater realism and contrast, the inclusion of *parti serie;* hence the absence of the (unrealistic) castrato voice and the return of the previously neglected bass voice. Arias were simple in structure; melodic lines consisted of many short fragments that were repeated, just as individual words or text phrases tended to be repeated.[5] Light accompaniment was still preferred; unison passages for voice and orchestra were frequent, especially at the opening of an aria and in cadential passages. Instrumental introductions to the arias either were shorter than in *opera seria* or were altogether absent. Some comic operas continued to employ very small casts (Pergolesi's *La serva padrona* has only two singing roles), but gradually the number grew, thus allowing greater variety in ensemble writing. Much attention now was given to the finale of each act. Unlike the traditional *opera seria* finale which consisted of a brief, perfunctory chorus, *opera buffa,* beginning with works by Nicola Logroscino

[5]For an example, see the bass aria from Galuppi's *Il filosofo di campagna, HAM,* No. 285.

(1698–1765), contained increasingly complex finales in which the action continued to unfold. Galuppi's works contain sectional finales of this type; here again we can trace a development that culminates in the remarkable finales of Mozart's *Le nozze di Figaro* and *Don Giovanni*.

THE OPERATIC OVERTURE

Italian opera contributed in an important way to instrumental music of the Classic period through the *sinfonia avanti l'opera*—the overture which gradually rose from a modest fanfare or call to order at the time of Monteverdi to a substantial composition of several contrasting sections. By 1700, the so-called Italian overture was becoming established, especially in Neapolitan opera; it consisted of three sections in fast-slow-fast sequence. Of these the first was most extensive, amounting often to a separate movement in binary form, occasionally with several themes. When all three sections increased in length, a *sinfonia* was often performed apart from the opera, as an independent orchestral composition. This was natural, especially since an overture was seldom related, either through general mood or actual music, to the opera for which it had been composed. As we shall see, many eighteenth-century overtures acquired lives of their own, appearing on concert programs simply as, for example, *sinfonia del Sigr. Bach* and omitting any reference to their particular operatic origins.[6]

Before the middle of the century this practice quite naturally led to the composition of orchestral works which contained three movements as described above but which were no longer related to any opera—symphonies in our sense of the word. This development, in which non-Italian composers eventually rose to prominence, will concern us in the next chapter, along with some other antecedents of the Classic symphony.

FRANCE: INSTRUMENTAL MUSIC

Baroque music had among its chief underlying principles the "doctrine of the affections"—the concept that a specific and rationally definable affection or mood can be expressed through specific musical devices, and further that *one* basic affection should prevail in any work of music such as

[6]Similarly, an opera score might contain not only an overture but also other instrumental music which was later used in symphonies (in the modern sense) by the same composer. See B. Churgin, *The Symphonies of G. F. Sammartini, Vol. I: The Early Symphonies* (Cambridge, MA 1968), pp. 6, 210ff.

an aria, or in a single movement of a suite, sonata, or the like. One of the major musical characteristics of the eighteenth century is that it overthrew the doctrine of the affections and substituted for this essentially rationalistic concept the idea of music as an art of more delicate expression. Music, in the Rococo setting, became the art of sentiment par excellence, with the avowed purpose of eliciting response from feeling rather than from reason. It preferred to speak in subtle tones, to evoke gentle moods with restrained means.

Instrumental music reflects the Rococo spirit particularly well, and it comes as no surprise that the delicate tones of the harpsichord *(clavecin)* inspired some of the most representative music of the *style galant*. French composers had been partial to the harpsichord for some time before; for this reason it is illuminating to compare the works of seventeenth-century clavecinists with those of a later generation, among them Louis Nicolas Clérambault (1676–1749), Jean François Dandrieu (1684–1740), François Couperin (1668–1733), and François d'Agincourt (1714–58). The earlier composers had cultivated larger (multiple-movement) forms as well as the descriptive genre pieces typical of the early and mid-eighteenth-century composers. Among these François Couperin was to acquire the greatest fame, as well as the appellation "LeGrand," the latter to distinguish him from other members of this musical family. Active in many fields of composition, he achieved his greatest success with keyboard works. They include several books with sets of clavecin pieces called *ordres*, the French equivalent of the Italian or German suite except that the French collections contain many more dance movements than the fairly standardized late Baroque suite. More often than not Couperin's titles were fanciful and precious, both in his programmatic ensemble sonatas *(Le parnasse ou l'apothéose de Corelli*, a *grande sonade en trio)* and in the four books of *Pièces de clavecin. Le rossignol en amour (HAM*, No. 265) comes from one of the latter collections; its title is typical, as are its performing instructions ("*Lentement et très tendrement*"; later, "*accens plaintifs*"). In these *galant* miniatures the sweep and continuous motion of Baroque melody is no longer found; instead, we have an abundance of short melodic phrases with much repetition and profuse ornamentation.

From the many Baroque dances, the minuet emerged as the most favored. Since it is a refined, courtly dance with many small steps and gestures, it might again be considered symbolic of the Rococo spirit. Of the many dance movements in the suite it was the only one to maintain its place in music during the Classic era, when it established itself firmly in symphony, divertimento, and other instrumental music. On the other hand, a dance such as the musette, with its stylized bagpipe effects so dear to the Rococo, disappeared with that age.

Instrumental music for string or wind instruments in addition to the keyboard was characterized by similar style and titles. Louis-Gabriel Guillemain (1705–70), an accomplished violinist and composer, published a set of six sonatas with the subtitle *Conversations galantes et amusantes entre une flûte traversière, un violon, une basse de viole et la basse continue* (1743). The composer himself stated that he considered *délicatesse* the main characteristic of his music. A set of his clavecin pieces, written a few years later, has an added violin part "to conform to the taste of our day," but the violin part is optional and musically not essential. A similar collection by Jean-Joseph de Mondonville (1711–72) had appeared about ten years earlier. Pieces of this kind, including some by Rameau (*Pièces de clavecin en concerts*, 1741), were significant in that they provided the point of departure for the Classic violin sonata, to be discussed later.

The trio sonata, one of the chief instrumental forms of the Baroque, continued to be cultivated during the early Classic period. Some sonatas have typically *galant* titles: Jean-Marie Leclair's (1697–1764) *Première récréation de musique d'une exécution facile, composée pour deux violons* (1737), or Chédeville's *Les galanteries amusantes, sonates à deux musettes* (1739). As a standard instrumental grouping, however, the trio sonata gradually disappeared to make way for the new chamber-music combinations of the Classic era.

Can music and the other arts during this period be viewed as parallel developments, as manifestations of the same aristocratic outlook on the function of art? The question is raised by Blume[7] and others who hold that the parallels frequently drawn are not tenable. According to this view the *style galant* in the other fine arts is a direct continuation of Baroque style, but in music it is separated from the older style by a chasm. This argument seems open to question when we remember that elements of the *style galant* can be found in the works of Telemann and others whom we associate primarily with Baroque music. The *galant* dance music of French composers was studied assiduously in Germany; it is reflected in suite movements by Bach and others. More convincing is Blume's argument that in music Rococo style flows into Classicism whereas in the fine arts neoclassicism represents a decided contrast and reaction to Rococo style. All of this brings us back to the dilemma of terminology, especially to the many meanings of the term "classic." In a later chapter the intellectual background of Classicism will be touched upon—what it means and what it does not mean as to the interrelation of the arts—but for the earlier eighteenth century the examples show that the term "Rococo" has meaningful applications in all the arts.

[7]Article "Klassik" in *MGG*.

GERMANY: EMPFINDSAMER STIL

During this period, the cultural life of Germany continued in many ways to reflect French influences. French language, manners, and dress rated high with the aristocracy; the written German language was permeated with French words. Frederick the Great considered his native language coarse and unfit for literary use, an opinion which caused him to invite Voltaire to the Prussian court and to do most of his own writing in French.

French *galant* music likewise made its imprint on the German musical scene. When one considers along with this the virtually undisputed reign of Italian music in most of Europe, one understands why German music had not yet acquired any significant international reputation. The gradual rise in esteem of German music began during this period; it can be said to coincide with the rise of Classicism.

How popular taste turned from Baroque to Rococo style is well exemplified by the fate of Bach's music. In his later years Johann Sebastian Bach became more and more isolated from musical developments of his time, so much so that by 1750 or even earlier the mention of the name Bach to most people would suggest not the cantor of Leipzig but one or another of his sons, especially Carl Philipp Emanuel Bach (1714–88), a composer whose music represents the new spirit in many ways. Father Bach's music was little known even within Germany and was considered old-fashioned by many. In 1737, an attack on his music appeared in Johann Adolf Scheibe's *Critscher Musikus* in which the author deplored the lack of "naturalness" in Bach's works, many of which he considered "bombastic and confused"; Bach's music, he continued, would be more widely performed if it contained more "pleasantness" instead of involved polyphonic writing. Scheibe had been Bach's pupil, and his critical remarks may have been colored by some personal animosity; they resulted in several rebuttals.[8] It is significant to us, in retrospect, to note that naturalness and pleasantness now were viewed as the more desirable qualities of music. Almost fifty years later, similar attitudes toward Bach's music continued to be voiced. J. F. Reichardt had great admiration for Bach's profundity and knowledge of harmony—but when he chose a Bach fugue for publication he gave these reasons: Its special merit is the expressive melody with which it speaks to us.

---

[8]Arthur Mendel refers to the affair as a "tempest in a teapot." *The Bach Reader*, rev. ed. (New York, 1966), pp. 237ff. See also G. Buelow, "In Defence of J. A. Scheibe against J. S. Bach," *Proceedings, Royal Music Association*, 101 (1974–75), 85ff.

Bach may have composed many fugues that are busier and more learned, but few that are so beautiful and touching. When I first came upon it I had to play it again and again. It stirred in me feelings both sad and sweet.[9]

In spite of strong French and Italian influences, German music of the generation after J. S. Bach displayed some distinctive features which are often referred to collectively as the *empfindsamer Stil*. The German word *Empfindsamkeit* can be translated as sensitivity, sensibility, or sentimentality. Before we investigate its application to German music of this age it should be pointed out that sentimentality, during the mid-eighteenth century, was generally present in European art, including French and English literature (Richardson, *Clarissa*, 1750; Sterne, *Sentimental Journey*, 1768; the title was translated by Lessing as *Empfindsame Reise*). This was an age of tears—both musicians and audiences were often moved to shed them copiously and, presumably, enjoyed it. Forkel, in his *Musikalisch-kritische Bibliothek* of 1778, describes a rehearsal at the *Concerts des amateurs* in Paris at which first one, then all the musicians were so moved that "they put down their instruments and gave free rein to their sorrow." In painting, this spirit is effectively captured by Jean-Baptiste Greuze (1725–1805), whose canvases often show sentimental, moralizing subjects taken from middle-class life. This is not yet the stern morality on a political rather than personal level that characterizes French painting of the revolutionary age.

In music, the *empfindsamer Stil* was characterized by an emphasis on subtle nuances or shadings, on the expression of a variety of sentiments, often in rapid succession, within one movement of a composition. To achieve this variety, phrases tended to be short; dynamic and rhythmic patterns changed frequently. The style is most clearly represented in the works of C. P. E. Bach, the third son of Sebastian. After spending some years studying law, C. P. E. Bach entered the service of the Prussian crown prince, who became king in 1740 and eventually came to be known as Frederick the Great. Bach remained in the new king's service as court harpsichordist and accompanist. This must not have been an altogether satisfactory position since the king, who ruled musical life at the court with an iron hand and military discipline, was conservative in his musical taste and preferred the compositions of his flute teacher Johann Joachim Quantz (1697–1773), of whom Burney wrote that "his taste is that of forty years ago." The king took an active part in the hiring of musicians; he determined the repertory and tolerated no liberties with the written music, no improvised embellishments, under threat of corporal punishment! This rather sti-

---

[9]*Musikalisches Kunstmagazin*, 1 (1782), 196f. The fugue in question is No. 12 in *The Well-Tempered Clavier*, Part II.

fling musical atmosphere, combined with Bach's lack of recognition as a composer, eventually caused him to seek employment elsewhere. In 1767, he went to Hamburg to succeed Telemann as cantor (musical director) of several of that city's churches, enjoying the absence of court formalities in the free city and composing many sacred and secular works.

Most important for the development of musical Classicism were Bach's many keyboard compositions, beginning with the "Prussian" sonatas of 1742, followed two years later by the "Württemberg" sonatas and many other collections. Perhaps of equal significance is his *Versuch über die wahre Art das Clavier zu spielen* (Essay on the true art of playing keyboard instruments; parts I and II published in 1753 and 1762), a book which goes far beyond what we today would expect in a "piano method" in that it includes chapters on many aspects of musicianship not directly related to keyboard technique. C. P. E. Bach's *Versuch*, along with similar treatises by Quantz on flute playing and by Mozart's father Leopold on the violin, are among our best sources of information about musical practices of the mid-eighteenth century.

Many of the concepts in the *Versuch* are typical of the "Age of Feeling." Music, as an art of the emotions, must above all appeal to the heart; if it is to do this, the performer himself must feel what he plays, must be emotionally involved. Mere finger dexterity is not enough: "One must play from the soul, not like a trained animal." C. P. E. Bach, Quantz, and other composers of the Berlin school subscribed to the concept that extreme affections generally should be avoided, and that the composer's main concern was the representation of subtle shades of emotion. In line with this view, many fluctuations of mood occur in music that is *empfindsam* in nature. Bach discusses the free fantasy as a type of music specially suited to the expression of many changes of affection through frequent changes in dynamics and tempo and through such harmonic devices as startling modulations. The effect of a fantasia should be that of improvisation, a skill for which the author was greatly admired. Reichardt, who met Bach in 1774, was most impressed by the composer's playing of his own free fantasias: "For hours he would immerse and lose himself in his ideas, in a sea of modulations." Burney's description of Emanuel Bach's manner of playing has often been repeated: Seated at the keyboard he "grew so animated and possessed, that he not only played but looked like one inspired. His eyes were fixed, his underlip fell, and drops of effervescence distilled from his countenance."

A singing, expressive style was sought by composers of the *Empfindsamkeit*. Emanuel Bach stated that the human voice was the model for any kind of melodic writing, which should always stress simple beauty without excessive embellishment. His concern with vocal quality is also demonstrated by the inclusion of recitative-like sections in his sonatas and fantasias. Since a light, gentle tone was preferred, the clavichord was understandably a favored instrument of this age, its sound not only being delicate but admitting subtle dynamic shadings controlled by the player's touch. Other "gentle" instruments, including the viola da gamba, viola d'amore, and glass harmonica[10], were still in vogue but disappeared with the end of the age of *Empfindsamkeit*. Lightness of texture, as advocated in the *Versuch*, is typical of C. P. E. Bach's keyboard style.

Leopold Mozart (1719–87) voiced similar opinions in his *Gründliche Violinschule*. He makes fun of the player who adds "many foolish frills" to his part at the expense of expressive playing. A real test of musicianship, he notes, is the playing of a slow movement: "In an adagio many players betray their great ignorance, playing without order and expression."

The Baroque concept that *one* emotion should govern an entire movement still applies in general to Emanuel Bach's early sonatas; yet even in some of the "Prussian" sonatas he introduces several themes that are contrasting in character. At times Bach modifies or develops a motif immediately after its first statement, with frequent surprises including sudden key changes and dissonances resolved in an unexpected and abrupt manner.

More striking than the formal organization in these and subsequent sets of sonatas is their expressive nature. Compared with the *galant* music of the slightly earlier French clavecinists, Bach's sonatas and fantasias often maintain a far more serious tone; his melodic lines have an expressive, vocal quality; ornamentation often is an integral part of the line rather than an addition to it. These and other features of his style are most readily seen in the slow movements—adagios rather than the andantes later found in Mozart's sonatas. These adagios contain passages that impress us as great emotional outbursts, achieved by chromaticism, harmonic intensity including numerous enharmonic changes, augmented chords, and modulations to quite remote keys. This quality of Bach's style links him to the movement of "Storm and Stress," discussed below, and to the harmonic practices of Romanticism. A slow movement which is partly metrical, partly in a free, recitative style already occurs in the first "Prussian" Sonata (Example 2–1).

Similar and even more daring modulations may be found in Bach's free fantasias, a category of keyboard music that further stresses rhythmic freedom and variety by its absence of barlines. (Example in *HAM*, No. 296.)

Great vigor and emotional intensity also characterize some of C. P.

[10]Invented by Benjamin Franklin in 1761. Rotating glass cups whose moistened rims, when they are rubbed, produce a gentle, ethereal sound. Mozart wrote two pieces for this instrument (K.356[617a], K.617).

EXAMPLE 2–1. C. P. E. Bach, "Prussian" *Sonata No. 1*

E. Bach's concertos.[11] Both the general mood and specific style features of the Harpsichord Concerto in D Minor (1748) have led some historians to deem it a worthy predecessor of Beethoven's piano concertos. As often during this period, the accompaniment lacks wind instruments. There is little in this substantial concerto that is light and playful, much that is agitated and vigorous. Especially striking is the second movement, similar in mood to the slow movement of Beethoven's Fourth Piano Concerto (G major). A stern unison figure in the orchestra constantly alternates with a cantabile answer by the soloist (Example 2–2). The last movement reinforces this serious mood.

Another category of music in which the *empfindsamer Stil* is well defined is the solo song of the so-called "first Berlin school." The repertory represents a reaction to the elaborate style of Italian arias, according to which a number of composers—among them Karl Heinrich Graun (1704–59) and Friedrich Wilhelm Marpurg (1718–95), the editor of *Berlinische Oden und Lieder,* 1756)—favored simple, light songs closer to the French *ariette.* Melodies, they believed, must be easy to sing and ideally should require no accompaniment at all. Again the simple and unpretentious is preferred. Most of the songs are on a small scale, avoid serious moods, and have a very light keyboard accompaniment. C. P. E. Bach's songs furnish many examples. Most of them were printed on two staves only, voice part and bass, leaving the completion of the keyboard part to the accompanist. The *Singode,* from a collection published in 1765, shows by its melodic

---

[11]See Chapter 8 for a discussion of the pre-Classic concerto.

EXAMPLE 2–2. C. P. E. Bach, *Harpsichord Concerto in D Minor* (1748; Wq 23, Helm 427), Second Movement.

simplicity why the music of the *Empfindsamkeit* forms an important link between Baroque and Classic style (Example 2–3).

Popular acceptance of poetry and music are reflected in a 1780 newspaper review of C. P. E. Bach's songs:

> Whoever cherishes feelings of true edification *(wahre Erbauung)*, whoever knows the beneficial influence that such poetry and music exert on the human heart, must thank [the composer]. These songs are easy to sing and play provided the performer has one quality: *feeling*. Whoever lacks feeling should never touch any of Bach's works.[12]

Among the song writers of the second Berlin school the search for a simple style led to the reawakening of interest in folk song, and to the creation of songs in a folk-like style. The *Lieder im Volkston* (1782) of J. A. P. Schulz (1747–1800) may represent this late phase of the *Empfindsamkeit;* Schulz wished his songs to appear "artless," spontaneous and natural (See Chapter 10). A certain amount of patriotism, of incipient nationalism, is al-

[12]Quoted by Gudrun Busch, *C. P. E. Bach und seine Lieder* (Regensburg, 1957), p. 143.

EXAMPLE 2–3. C. P. E. Bach, *Singode*.

Angenehm und mässig

Ge - lieb - tes Feld,— dein auf - ge-klär-ter Him - mel,

der sanft und rein——— um stil - le Flu - ren fliesst,

ready mingled with this love for simple songs in the mother tongue, an attitude which eventually led to the more explicitly patriotic (and Romantic)
lyric poetry of the Wars of Liberation that ultimately led to Napoleon's
defeat.

      The displays of sentiment and the cultivation of tears and sighs dur-
ing this age can be related to what is best described as a late phase or an
outgrowth of the *Empfindsamkeit*—the period in German arts and letters
called *Sturm und Drang* ("Storm and Stress"). The name was taken from a
play by Friedrich Maximilian Klinger (1776), but the ideas associated with
the movement were formulated earlier. Its adherents were strong believers
in personal freedom, especially freedom for the artist, who, in order to develop his genius to the fullest, should not be chained by restrictions of law
or convention. Great emotional intensity and passionate, violent outbursts
characterize *Sturm und Drang* literature, both drama (Goethe, *Götz von
Berlichingen,* 1773; Schiller, *Die Räuber,* 1781) and prose (Goethe, *The
Sorrows of Young Werther,* 1774). Similar emotions distinguish music
stemming from this outlook. We find them in certain works of C. P. E.
Bach, already mentioned,[13] as well as in some symphonies and quartets of
the young Haydn. Here again it should be stressed that the terms "Rococo," *style galant, Empfindsamkeit,* and *Sturm und Drang* must be used
with caution and properly understood: They are not universally applicable
chronological labels; they do not refer to general "periods" in history but
are applied to developments in specific geographic areas and in certain categories of the arts.

      A fair amount of writing on music by the followers of *Sturm und
Drang* helps us to understand this movement. C. F. D. Schubart's *Ideen*

----

[13]Concerning C. P. E. Bach's symphonies see p. 48.

zu einer Aesthetik der Tonkunst (written about 1780 while the author was in prison and published in Vienna, 1806) includes chapters on musical genius and on musical expression. In the latter there are many references to the heart—to the *gefühlvolles Herz* which every performer must have—and to the importance of individual, personal expression. They show how closely related the *Sturm und Drang* aesthetic is to that of Emanuel Bach and the *Empfindsamkeit* in general.

Schubart, incidentally, was one of the first to see the significance of J. S. Bach's music, praising it in the typically effusive language of his age. Bach is "the German Orpheus . . . his spirit is so original, so gigantic, that it will take hundreds of years to comprehend him." Schubart singles out Bach's cantatas for daring modulations and novel melodic ideas that make it impossible not to recognize Bach as an *Originalgenie*—a term of which this age was quite fond.

By 1780, then, a new, more serious view of music had asserted itself. The spirit of Rococo, of *galanterie*, gave way to the spirit of Classicism. The late works of C. P. E. Bach belong to this period. Haydn freely acknowledged his indebtedness to him, a debt reflected not only in Haydn's works for the piano but in other categories as well. Many of Haydn's slow movements, particularly in the string quartets, contain modulations to distant keys and show qualities of pathos, reflectiveness, and seriousness that may well have grown out of his acquaintance with Emanuel Bach's music.

THE ITALIAN KEYBOARD SONATA

The early eighteenth century saw important changes in Italian keyboard music as well. The traditional Baroque keyboard forms had been dance movements, single or grouped in suites; sets of variations; free compositions including toccatas; individual fugues or groups of preludes and fugues. The Baroque sonata, as a major instrumental category consisting of several movements, had included harpsichord or organ for the realization of the basso continuo only, not as a solo instrument. The soloistic keyboard sonata now appeared, with Italy and Germany making important contributions. By the end of the eighteenth century it had acquired the important position it still holds today, so that its rise took place during the period when the piano gradually replaced the harpsichord as the principal keyboard instrument.

A prominent writer of keyboard sonatas was Domenico Scarlatti (1685–1757), son of Alessandro (who is chiefly remembered as a composer of operas, in spite of his many works in other categories). Domenico's works also include operas and sacred music, but today his name is likely to suggest keyboard works only, primarily sonatas, of which he wrote over

550. This number is imposing even when we realize that they are short, one-movement works, showing that even in the mid-eighteenth century the term "sonata" could be used in its literal sense: a piece to be played rather than sung, regardless of length or form.

Pianists have been fond of playing Scarlatti for some time. With the renewal of interest in the harpsichord the sonatas have become still more widely known and appreciated as music that is extremely well suited to the tonal characteristics of that instrument, aside from being distinguished by great charm, vitality, and variety. Variety applies to their form in particular: Only in a very general sense can we speak of a typical Scarlatti sonata. Most are in binary form, consisting of two parts, each of which is repeated. The first part begins in the tonic key and moves to the dominant or a related key; in the second part the harmonic motion is reversed. So far this suggests the overall plan of a Baroque suite movement. In a typical Baroque-era dance movement, however, both parts begin with the same melodic material, the difference being in the tonality. Many Scarlatti sonatas reveal a more complex structure. We are justified in calling this contemporary of Bach a Rococo composer by, above all, his use of varied melodic material—the breaking away from the continuous motion of a Baroque suite movement and the substitution of many smaller melodic phrases. When these fragments have a certain degree of self-sufficiency, when they are distinct from surrounding material, they can be regarded as themes. Quite often two or more themes, sometimes similar but often contrasting, occur within the first part of a Scarlatti sonata, suggesting the thematic dualism of Classic sonata form.

In considering the form of Scarlatti's keyboard sonatas, one should keep in mind that the composer in all likelihood intended many of them to be played in pairs, because they are consistently grouped that way in several sources. Yet the effect of the two-sonata or (in a few cases) three-sonata groups—the movements of each sometimes similar, sometimes contrasted—is unlike that of the more standardized multiple-movement sonatas of the Baroque or of the later Classic period.[14]

Opportunities for display of virtuosity are plentiful in Scarlatti's sonatas, particularly in his earlier works. Large skips, extended arpeggios, and an unusually wide range (five octaves in the late works) characterize his style, as well as frequent hand-crossing and close, overlapping playing by both hands. Repeated notes at a rapid tempo, brilliant passages in thirds and sixths, and trills in an inner voice are additional technical challenges testifying to the composer's virtuosity and originality; in the later eighteenth century these are less likely to occur in sonatas than in concertos.

The light, Rococo character of Scarlatti's melodies is also reflected in

[14]J. Sheveloff discusses this in "Domenico Scarlatti: Tercentenary Frustrations," *MQ*, 71 (1985), 430ff.

his preference for simple meters, especially 3/8 time. There is no consistent contrapuntal writing: The typical texture is light and free-voiced. The composer's readiness to experiment is shown in his harmonies as well, as in modulations (normally of short duration) to remote keys. Some key changes are abrupt and startling: In a sonata in C major (Longo 324; Kirkpatrick 460) the key of c♯ minor is reached by the fiftieth measure, while just before this B minor had been established.

Scarlatti's long stays on the Iberian peninsula are reflected in much of his music In the eighteenth century both Spain and Portugal produced a wealth of keyboard music, a repertory that in the past has been largely neglected by performers. The Portuguese Carlos de Seixas (1704–42) was court organist and harpsichordist in Lisbon during the 1720s, when Scarlatti also resided there. Seixas wrote keyboard sonatas (single or multiple movements) and a concerto for harpsichord and strings. (*SCE*, pp. 273ff.) Best known among Spanish composers of the generation that followed is Padre Antonio Soler (1729–83), choirmaster and organist at the monastery of El Escoriál where many of his keyboard sonatas are preserved. Characteristics of Spanish music, especially dance rhythms, lend a special flavor to his sonatas as they do in those of Scarlatti, with whom he studied. (*SCE*, pp. 279ff.)

Other Italian composers of keyboard sonatas, considerably less well known, are Giovanni Platti (1697–1763), Domenico Paradies (1710–95), Baldassare Galuppi (1706–85), and Giovanni Maria Rutini (1723–97).[15] In their sonatas melodies of an *opera buffa* nature are more in evidence than in Scarlatti's. Platti's six sonatas, Op. 1, published in Germany in 1742 with the subtitle "sur le goût italien," contain numerous examples. Characteristic are unison openings and short melodic fragments, suggesting the atmosphere of *La serva padrona* (Example 2–4).[16] Four movements are the

EXAMPLE 2–4. Platti, *Sonata in D Major*, Op. 1, No. 1, Fourth Movement.

norm in these works, in the order slow-fast-slow-fast, but both the melodic material and the formal arrangement of individual movements are quite different from the Baroque *sonata da chiesa* (which has the same external form). Light melody-and-accompaniment texture prevails, including bro-

[15]For discussions of Rutini's and Platti's sonatas, see *SCE*, pp. 202ff and 365ff respectively.

[16]See *HAM*, No. 284, from Platti's Op. 1, No. 2. Fausto Torrefranca, *Giovanni Benedetto Platti e la sonata moderna* (Milan, 1963), includes editions of the eighteen known keyboard sonatas by Platti. William Newman's review of Torrefranca's book (*MQ*, 50 [1964], 526ff), describes and evaluates it in detail.

ken-chord patterns for the left hand—the "Alberti bass," which now was becoming popular—along with harmonic simplicity and an absence of profound or intense moods. Rudimentary sonata form is suggested by the presence of several themes or groups of themes and by their harmonic treatment. There is no development to speak of, but the return to the opening material is organized along the lines of a recapitulation.

Keyboard sonatas by Galuppi and Rutini show the same Italianate style features. Most of them have either two or three movements. Two-part writing is predominant and features of sonata form are perceptible. Rutini's Sonata, Op. 3, No. 1 (published 1757), begins with a movement in a free, toccata-like style, with sweeping arpeggios and runs, followed by an allegro based on a rather extended but not yet very "classically" defined theme (Example 2–5). The movement is discursive, with little development. In

EXAMPLE 2–5. Rutini, *Sonata*, Op. 3, No. 1, Second Movement. Copyright 1965 by Edizioni De Santis, Rome. Printed by permission.

Allegro con spirito

the second section the original theme soon appears in the dominant key; it never returns in the tonic. The last movement is a simple and short menuetto without trio. Other sonatas of Op. 3 end with allegro movements very close in style to the concluding gigue of a Baroque suite (Example 2–6).[17]

EXAMPLE 2–6. Rutini, *Sonata*, Op. 3, No. 3, Last Movement. Copyright 1965 by Edizioni De Santis, Rome. Printed by permission.

Allegro

A sonata movement by Galuppi (from his Op. 3, No. 3) illustrates a disposition of thematic material frequently found in works of the 1770s and 1780s: The principal theme, dramatic and vigorous, is stated and repeated; the key of the dominant is clearly established; and there is a rest before the

[17]A similar movement from Rutini's Op. 6, No. 6, is found in *HAM*, No. 302.

continuation with a new theme, contrasting, cantabile, and with Alberti-bass accompaniment (Example 2–7).

EXAMPLE 2–7. Galuppi, *Sonata*, Op. 3. Copyright 1969 by Edizioni De Santis, Rome. Printed by permission.

These and other Italian composers whose music combines late Baroque and Rococo elements exerted some influence on the Classic writers of sonatas in Austria and Germany. We might remember that the music of John Christian Bach, whose style was largely formed in Italy, figured prominently in Mozart's musical background. Both Leopold and Wolfgang Mozart thought highly of Rutini's sonatas. Yet there still is disagreement on the extent of the Italian sonata writers' influence, particularly Platti, for whom a position of pioneering significance has been claimed by Torrefranca.[18]

BIBLIOGRAPHICAL NOTES

An excellent introduction to Rococo style in general, with many fine illustrations, is A. Schönberger and H. Soehner, *The Rococo Age* (New York, 1960). Many musical examples for the material discussed in this and subse-

[18]Fausto Torrefranca, *Le origini italiane del romanticismo musicale* . . . (Turin, 1930). See also *SCE*, pp. 365ff.

quent chapters are given in *HAM, Volume* 2: *Baroque, Rococo and Pre-Classic Music.*

Operatic developments during this period are discussed in Donald J. Grout's *Short History of Opera,* 2nd ed. (New York, 1965), with an extensive bibliography. Excerpts from satirical criticism of Italian opera are included in *SMH.* A modern edition of A. Scarlatti's operas, ed. D. J. Grout, is in progress (Cambridge MA: Harvard Univ. Press, 1975–   ). For a list of anthologies containing works by Rococo and Classic composers, see Grout's *A History of Western Music,* 3rd ed. (New York: Norton, 1980), pp. 787ff.

French music in the *galant* style is treated by W. Mellers in *François Couperin and the French Classical Tradition* (London, 1950).

The Collected Works for Solo Keyboard, by C. P. E. Bach, (6 vols., New York: Garland, 1985) is a valuable resource. Other editions, especially of the "Württemberg" and "Prussian" sonatas, are also available. The treatises by C. P. E. Bach and Leopold Mozart have been translated, the former by W. J. Mitchell (New York: Norton, 1949), the latter by E. Knocker (London, 1948).

R. Kirkpatrick's *Domenico Scarlatti,* rev. ed.; Princeton NJ: Princeton Univ. Press, 1968) is a thorough historical and stylistic study, much of it based on the author's intimate acquaintance, as a harpsichordist, with Scarlatti's keyboard music. Kirkpatrick has also edited two volumes of Scarlatti's sonatas (New York, 1943). W. S. Newman's studies of the sonata literature contain discussions of works by all the important and many of the lesser composers (*SBE, SCE*). Sonatas by Platti, Alberti, and Benda are included in Newman's edition of *Thirteen Keyboard Sonatas* (Chapel Hill, NC: University of North Carolina Press, 1947); other composers represented in this collection are Dittersdorf (1739–99), Joseph Wölfl (1773–1812), and Neefe (1748–98); there are introductory essays on each composer. Other modern editions of interest are L. Hoffmann-Erbrecht's *Platti: 12 Sonatas* (Leipzig, 1957); Hedda Illy's edition of keyboard sonatas by Galuppi (*Sonate per cembalo,* [Rome, 1969], includes a thematic catalog of Galuppi's sonatas and concertos); and six sonatas edited by Edith Woodcock (*Six Sonatas for Keyboard Instruments* [New York: Galaxy Music Corp., 1963]).

THREE
THE PRE-CLASSIC SYMPHONY

Orchestral music as such—music conceived with the sound of a specific and fairly large group of instruments in mind—was a development of the Baroque era. Its importance as a genre increased steadily, and some of the most significant developments of Classic music took place in the orchestral field. Indeed it has been claimed that the Classic period is primarily an era of instrumental music, a claim that might have startled Haydn, Mozart, and other composers of the time. It is obvious that opera continued to be of major importance in the musical life of the age. Quite typically, when J. F. Reichardt visited Berlin in 1774 he was anxious, first of all, to visit the opera house. He did the same when visiting Vienna in 1808–9. "The great Dr. Burney" would do the same in his sojourns in Italy.[1] Still, the significance of innovations found in the Classic symphony, concerto, chamber music, and sonata is beyond question. In a way, the increased importance

---

[1]Reichardt's impressions are related in his *Briefe eines aufmerksamen Reisenden . . .*, excerpts in Strunk, *SMH*, pp. 699ff.

of instrumental music is also reflected in opera of the Classic period: Slowly but surely the undisputed reign of the singer was broken and the orchestral "accompaniment" gained greater prominence in a development that, a hundred years later, was to culminate in the operas of Wagner and Richard Strauss. Characteristics of musical Classicism also appeared in sacred music, but that branch of music traditionally tended to be conservative and therefore showed innovations less clearly.

The main line of development in Classic music, then, took place in the instrumental field, and within that field the symphony was the medium that saw the greatest growth. We shall see all important changes of style reflected in it—changes in mood (from *galant* to serious), weight, length, and form. Later the main qualities of Romanticism are also clearly demonstrable in the symphony, in spite of the appearance of new types of orchestral music, and even in our own century the multiple-movement symphony remains one of the substantial categories cultivated by serious composers.

What accounts for the significance, for the favored position, of the symphony in the Classic period? We can only surmise that composers found in it, both as a whole and in its parts or movements, a framework for organizing their musical ideas which proved aesthetically pleasing. We should not think of musical "form" as a pre-existing concept to which a composer feels forced to adapt his expression; rather, symphonic form was created and recreated in so many works that composers must have found it a liberating rather than confining formal concept. The symphony in the Classic period became an increasingly complex structure showing, within generally observed conventions, remarkable variety and originality. This involved all elements of expression—melody, harmony, and tone color. Greater formal complexity, an abundance of musical "raw material" (motifs, themes), imaginative scoring for a larger orchestra—these and other style features offered challenges and satisfactions to the listener.

"SONATA FORM"

In general, the first movement of a Classical symphony embodies these qualities to a higher degree than the others: It often shows greater formal complexity and ingenuity. Again we have to guess about the reason; perhaps the composer felt that the listener's attention and sensitivity were greatest at the beginning of a symphony, especially since its length increased from the few minutes of a "curtain-raiser" *sinfonia* to almost half an hour for Haydn's mature symphonies.

The term "sonata form" has been applied to the organization of a typical first movement (and sometimes also the second and last) of instrumental works from the Classic period—a confusing term indeed since it refers to the form not of an entire sonata but of one movement. Furthermore, sonata form is found in movements from symphonies, concertos, and chamber music as well as in sonatas in our sense, i.e., works for one or two instruments. Due to its frequent occurrence in a first movement, which is usually an allegro, the terms "sonata-allegro form" and "first-movement form" are also encountered. Some characteristics of sonata form have been mentioned in the preceding chapter. Its main features are explained in virtually every textbook on musical form, history, or literature, as well as in most music dictionaries,[2] so that a brief summary will suffice at this point.

To understand the basic stylistic difference between a movement in sonata form and a typical Baroque instrumental movement we must consider the differences in melodic material. Examples 3–1, 3–2, and 3–3 show typical melodic material from Baroque, Rococo, and Classic instrumental works.

EXAMPLE 3–1. J. S. Bach, *French Suite No. 6*.

Example 3–1 shows the continuous line characteristic of Baroque style: a melody which may have a distinctive beginning, the pattern of which is then continued without major breaking points to the end of the section—in this kind of dance movement, to the double bar. Melodic fragmentation representative of Rococo and *Empfindsamkeit* is illustrated by Example 3–2. Some melodic fragments may be more striking, more clearly

EXAMPLE 3–2. C. P. E. Bach, *18 Probestücke in sechs Sonaten: Sonata No. 2*, beginning.

[2]For example, see the article "Sonata form" in *HD*.

EXAMPLE 3–3. Mozart, *String Quartet in D Minor*, K. 421, First Movement.

defined than others, and may recur at various points. Thus they impress themselves more strongly on the listener; they become "themes." Example 3–3 shows a typical theme from the later Classic period: It is more complex but completely self-contained; it represents a well-defined, rounded musical thought which, though long, is likely to be retained by the listener. A complete theme, moreover, is likely to contain one or more brief motifs of importance throughout the movement, e.g., in the case of the Mozart

theme just quoted. The concept of one or several clearly defined themes, coupled with certain principles of harmonic progression and contrast, is essential to sonata form. Such a theme will allow modifications of many kinds without losing its identity; it may be fragmented; its melodic outline or its harmonization may be varied; it may be played by different instruments or combinations of instruments. These and many other ways of giving variety to a theme, and hence to a movement as a whole, are referred to as "development"—another concept essential to sonata form. A Classic theme normally has this potential for growth or development: It is a "germ theme." The theme itself is important, but even more so is what the composer does with it. It has been frequently noted that it is the very simple theme or motif—concise, often based on the tonic triad—that lends itself best to thematic development in the Classic sense.[3]

Most movements in sonata form contain at least two clearly defined themes, or groups of themes, frequently of contrasting character and almost always in different keys. Thematic dualism of this kind we have noted in some keyboard sonatas of the Rococo; it became an essential structural element in Classic music, as opposed to the principle of one basic affection of Baroque music. To set off themes effectively from each other, a non-thematic transition or bridge section is interpolated, often ending in a decisive cadence and complete rest before the second theme or group of themes is heard. Whether or not the latter is contrasted by its melodic and rhythmic shape, it is likely to be presented in a different tonality, usually the dominant or the relative major. More non-thematic material may follow, bringing the first section or "exposition" to a close. In the section that follows (the exposition having been repeated), the composer develops the "germinal" possibilities of the thematic material as described above, modifying it in a variety of ways.

Thematic development may occur anywhere in the movement, but it is not normally emphasized until after the principal themes have been "exposed," that is, after the double bar. In the development section the composer usually works with *one* theme or part of a theme. For some time preference was given to the first theme; in works from the later Classic era other material (including fragments from transitional or closing sections) was frequently chosen instead. The great variety of procedures used in the development section drives home the point that sonata form is no rigid "mold" into which composers pour musical "content." Development through modulation became increasingly important; traveling through remote harmonic regions became one of the most effective ways to bring about the desired effect of the next section, the recapitulation. This is the sensation, on the part of a listener, of having arrived, of returning to familiar territory. Thematically and harmonically this means a return to the principal theme, in the tonic or main key of the movement. The recapitulation may not be a literal repeat of the exposition, but will restate its main thoughts in essentially the same manner. To achieve a feeling of finality it now stresses the tonic key, using it for material which in the exposition had been stated in a contrasting tonality (dominant or relative major, marked *R* in Table 3–1).

The melodic and harmonic aspects of sonata form and their relation to the earlier suite movement and *sinfonia* are shown in Table 3–1. The essentially binary nature of sonata form (as of the earlier types diagrammed)

[3]B. Churgin, "Francesco Galeazzi's Description (1796) of Sonata Form," *JAMS*, 21 (1968), 184ff.

Baroque Suite Movement

‖: T – R :‖: R – T :‖
(No clear-cut "theme") continuation | (No clear-cut "theme") continuation

Sinfonia, c. 1730

‖: T – R :‖: R – T :‖
1st theme | 2d theme or key area | 1st theme | (2d theme)

Later Sinfonia

‖: T – R :‖: R – T :‖
1st theme | (2d theme) | transition or brief devel. | 1st theme | (2d theme)

"Sonata Form"

‖: T – R :‖ R — V :‖ T – T – T ‖

1st theme | transition | 2d theme or group of themes, key area | closing section | repeat often indicated | modulating | 1st theme | transition | 2d theme or group of themes, | closing section

Exposition | Development | Recapitulation

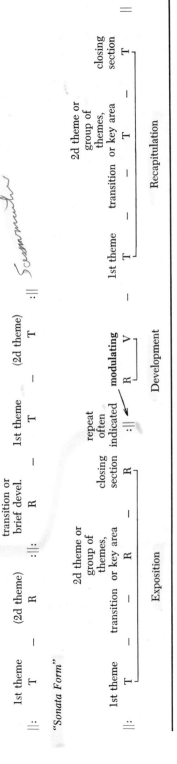

TABLE 3–1. Formal Designs, Early and Late Eighteenth-Century Instrumental Music

should be apparent, especially if we understand the basic key relationships—the harmonic layout of a movement—to be the chief characteristic, rather than the presence of several themes, contrasting or otherwise.[4] The tensions and resolutions found in such a movement, due in part to its harmonic structure, are not without dramatic qualities. It can be said that

> The sonata has an identifiable climax, a point of maximum tension to which the first part of the work leads. . . . It has a dynamic closure analogous to the dénouement of eighteenth-century drama, in which everything is resolved, all loose ends are tied up, and the work rounded off.[5]

As movements in sonata form increased in size, further modifications occurred, such as the addition of a slow introduction and a coda; these will occupy us in a later chapter.

In view of the frequency with which the sonata-form movement is encountered from the mid-eighteenth century on we would expect to find some description of it in the numerous theoretical writings of the time. Curiously enough no such account has been found. German writers shortly after 1750 (Quantz, C. P. E. Bach) refer to the sonata and to some aspects of its style but do not say anything about its form, a subject taken up apparently for the first time in a treatise on composition by Heinrich Christoph Koch.[6] More detailed accounts appear in works by Anton Reicha[7] and Czerny (about 1840) written almost a hundred years after the first works showing rudimentary sonata form were composed.[8]

The trouble with the term "sonata form," and with illustrative schemes and diagrams, is that they may be understood to imply a regularity of design which, in fact, did not exist in "sonata-form" movements of the age of Haydn and Mozart. Too often the textbook concept of sonata form, established in the nineteenth century, has been used too rigidly in describing the design of movements from the earlier age. This procedure is unfor-

---

[4]For more detailed discussions of this evolution, see Hans Engel, "Die Quellen des klassischen Stils," *International Musicological Society, Report of the Eighth Congress* (New York, 1961), 1: 289ff.; Jan La Rue, *Guidelines for Style Analysis* (New York, 1970), especially pp. 187ff.; and Rey M. Longyear, "Binary Variants of Early Classic Sonata Form," *Journal of Music Theory,* 13 (1969), 162ff.

[5]Charles Rosen, *Sonata Forms* (New York: Norton, 1980), p. 10.

[6]*Versuch einer Anleitung zur Composition* (3 vols, 1782–93). See also the article "Koch" in *Grove 6*, and Jane Stevens, "Theme, Harmony and Texture in Classic-Romantic Descriptions of Concerto First-Movement Forms," *JAMS,* 27 (1974), 25–60.

[7]*Traité de haute composition musicale* (Paris, 1824–26), discussed in Churgin, "Galeazzi's Description," pp. 187ff.

[8]William S. Newman, "The Recognition of Sonata Form by Theorists of the 18th and 19th Centuries," *Papers of the American Musicological Society 1941,* pp. 21 ff.; also Newman, "Carl Czerny's Op. 600 and the 'first' Description of 'sonata form,' " *JAMS,* 20 (1967), 513ff.

tunate because it tends to becloud and falsify the very compositional process it hopes to elucidate.[9]

THE CLASSIC ORCHESTRA

The makeup of the Baroque orchestra had been characterized by great diversity, by the existence within one instrument family (such as the double-reed instruments) of a variety of sizes and tunings far greater than those we are familiar with today. When we examine orchestral writing by Monteverdi or Bach, we are likely to encounter a number of instruments that have either become altogether obsolete or are at least no longer considered standard orchestral instruments. Among the former are the violino piccolo, viola d'amore, and the cornetto or zink; among the latter are the viola da gamba, lute, and recorder. Other instruments remained in the orchestra but underwent changes in construction and function. The trumpet belongs to this category. Very high and florid trumpet parts, in the so-called clarino register, disappear from orchestral writing after about 1750, for reasons that have only partly been explained. Apparently the skill of playing these parts, extremely difficult on the valveless Baroque trumpet, gradually disappeared together with the musicians' guilds in which trumpeters had enjoyed great professional esteem. On the other hand, florid and treacherous parts for the horn, then also a valveless instrument, are found occasionally in Classic orchestral literature, for instance, in Haydn's Symphonies 31 and 72.

A process of standardization characterizes the development of the orchestra in the mid-eighteenth century, affecting the kinds more than the numbers of instruments employed. Part of this process involved a shift in balance between wind and string instruments in favor of the latter. The delicate tone of the viols used in Renaissance and much Baroque instrumental music gave way to the fuller sound of violin, viola, and cello. Gentle wind instruments such as the recorder, limited also in dynamic variety, were no match for these and disappeared from the orchestra.

At the beginning of the Classic period the instruments of the violin family formed the nucleus of the orchestra, along with two oboes and French horns, to which a gradually increasing number of wind instruments was added. Trumpets and timpani appeared; frequently their parts were

[9]The reader who wishes to investigate this subject may also consult: *SCE*, 19ff.; Leonard Ratner, "Harmonic Aspects of Classic Form," *JAMS*, 2 (1949), 158ff.; *HD*, article "Sonata Form"; Jens Peter Larsen, "Sonatenform-Probleme," *Festschrift Friedrich Blume* (1963); and Larsen, "Some Observations on the Development and Characteristics of Vienna Classical Instrumental Music," *Studia musicologica,* 9 (1967).

not included in scores from the Classic period but (being restricted to a few notes) were quickly added when the occasion required. One or two flutes were not uncommon, but the use of both flutes and oboes was, since often one player doubled on both instruments. The clarinet began to appear gradually after 1750, but it took about a generation before it became a standard orchestral instrument, and it was still missing in the Salzburg orchestra of Mozart's time. The bassoon, prominent in the Baroque orchestra, continued to be used with regularity. That its function changed, however, is shown by the appearance of eighteenth-century scores. Until about 1780 the bassoon part (if at all written or printed) appeared below the string parts since this was where it belonged, functionally speaking, doubling the *basso* (cello and string bass) line. After this time its greater independence and melodic importance is symbolized by its appearance among the other woodwind instruments.

Trombones, interestingly enough, were not included in the normal Classic orchestra. Nicolai[10] reported that in northern Germany they had "gone out of fashion" while in Bavaria and Austria they were used a great deal and were generally played well; yet their chief use was in sacred music in which three trombones customarily doubled alto, tenor, and bass parts. This doubling was understood; therefore their parts were seldom written out in the score.

To this rather modest array of instruments (by twentieth-century standards) the harpsichord should be added for early Classic symphonies. Here again the written or printed scores of the time do not tell the whole story; we know from many contemporary descriptions that the composer-conductor officiated at the harpsichord through most of the eighteenth century, even though no separate part was included in the score. When Haydn journeyed to England in 1791, the custom still existed there, so that he was expected to play the harpsichord or fortepiano in performances of his most recent symphonies. A knowledge of this is important for the performance of early Classic symphonies today: The harmonic texture may appear thin and show gaps unless a keyboard player fills them in.[11]

As we shall see presently, composers entrusted more and more of the harmony to other instruments, notably the French horns and trumpets, thereby gradually rendering the harpsichord superfluous.

The number of performers on string instruments seems to have varied greatly depending largely on the financial resources of the supporting

[10]Friedrich Nicolai, *Beschreibung einer Reise durch Deutschland und die Schweiz. . . .* (Berlin, 1783–84), 4: 545.
[11]As late as 1829, Mendelssohn was expected to conduct a London performance of one of his symphonies from the piano. Neal Zaslaw's basic and well-documented study gives many details. "Toward the Revival of the Classical Orchestra," *Proceedings of the Royal Musical Association*, 103 (1976–77), 158–87.

prince. Statistics given by Carse[12] and Zaslaw are most informative and show, among other things, that the largest orchestras were found in the great opera houses, among them Naples, Milan, Turin, and Paris. An average string section for one of the lesser courts around 1760 might have consisted of six first and six second violins, two violas, three cellos, and one string bass. For a distinguished establishment such as the Dresden court the numbers may have been 8/8/4/4/2. Mozart, in 1781, describes a "most successful" performance of one of his symphonies in Vienna, with the participation of forty violins, ten violas, eight cellos, ten basses, six bassoons, and doubled winds—a sound which must have startled the audience as much as it apparently delighted the composer, since it was most unusual even for the later Classic period. In performances of major choral works large orchestras were not unusual. When Beethoven's *Christ on the Mount of Olives* was given in Vienna in 1817, an orchestra of seventy- to eighty-strong participated, with two players on each wind part, while the choir numbered about sixty voices.[13]

ITALY

The Italian concert *sinfonia,* based on operatic and other models, continued to be light and *galant* in style. Its function also remained close to that of the *sinfonia avanti l'opera:* It was often the opening work on a program, preparing the audience for more profound works that were to follow. Perhaps it was listened to with little more attention than was paid to operatic overtures by the traditionally noisy Italian audiences. Johann Georg Sulzer[14] still claimed that Italian opera *sinfonie* were mere tickling of the ears; that their sole purpose was to produce a "pleasant noise." Until the end of the century the term *sinfonia* could refer to operatic or concert pieces; only after the size of the composition had increased substantially did our term "overture" in its present-day meaning replace it.

The three-movement arrangement continued to be favored; around 1730–50 it can also be found in trio sonatas where the four-movement (slow-fast-slow-fast) sequence had been the rule. The symphony's middle movement, andante rather than adagio, was often in binary form. It was based on one theme, or sometimes included a complementary rather than

[12]Adam Carse, *The Orchestra in the 18th Century* (Cambridge, 1940), chap. 2. Churgin gives some statistics for Milan in the 1760s in *The Symphonies of G. B. Sammartini,* 1 (Cambridge MA, 1968), p. 11. See also Zaslaw, "Revival of the Classical Orchestra," pp. 170ff, "Personnel."

[13]Otto Biba, "Concert Life in Beethoven's Vienna," *Beethoven, Performers and Critics,* The International Beethoven Congress, Detroit, 1977 (Detroit, MI: Wayne State Univ. Press, 1980), pp. 88ff.

[14]*Allgemeine Theorie der schönen Künste* (Leipzig, 1775), 2, p. 726.

contrasting theme. A simple ternary form, with a return to the opening material, may also be found. For the third movement, similar two-part or three-part forms replace the dancelike final sections of the earlier *sinfonie*.[15] After 1750, rondos appear with increasing frequency, consisting of varied couplets and a refrain, while eventually the more extensive sonata-rondo emerges (to be discussed in connection with the symphonies of Haydn and Mozart). Mozart composed several three-movement symphonies while in Italy, conforming to the local tradition. Minuets exist for some of these; they were added later to bring the same works into line with what had become the normal four-movement symphony in Austria and Germany.

Other types of instrumental music besides the opera *sinfonia* contributed to the development of the Classic symphony. Terminology was not precise, and works entitled *concerto*, *concerto a quattro*, or *concerto ripieno* were often closer to the symphony than to the concerto—just as we shall find some early Haydn symphonies in which *concertante* writing is much in evidence.[16]

Italians whose symphonies belong to this early Classic period are Giuseppe Tartini (1692–1770) and G. B. Sammartini (1701–75), a Milanese composer and teacher of Gluck, who was highly esteemed at the time. Mozart met him in Milan, in 1770 and in 1771. Sammartini's symphonies, close to seventy in number, and his more than two hundred ensemble sonatas also exemplify the lack of clear differentiation, in designation and content, between the several genres. Some of his symphonies, in early editions, are labeled "sonatas" on the title page. Churgin has found that the compositions labeled *a* 3 intended for orchestra—that is, symphonies—are less imitative in texture than Sammartini's trio sonatas.[17]

Sammartini's symphonies begin to show the longer, cantabile melodic lines that we associate with Classicism. Some of his first movements have well-defined triadic main themes. There may be more than two distinct themes, presented in various keys, not merely tonic and dominant. Transition rather than development sections occur after the first part has been repeated. Often the bass line still has a basso continuo character.[18]

---

[15]It is an oversimplification to view the Classic symphony as having evolved exclusively from the Italian fast-slow-fast *sinfonia*, to which a minuet was then added (as a third movement). Indeed, in many examples of early Classic three-movement form the last movement is a minuet or Tempo di Menuetto, so that one might consider, with Larsen, the allegro or presto finale of later works to be the real addition. Larsen, "Some Observations," p. 136. Differences between opera *sinfonia* and concert *sinfonia* are discussed by J. La Rue, "Sinfonia", *Grove 6*. See also E. K. Wolf, *The Symphonies of Johann Stamitz* (Utrecht, 1981), pp. 79ff: "Structure of the Cycle."

[16]See also the essays by Wolf, Green, and Lazarevich mentioned in Bibliographical Notes. Concerning "symphonies" by Vivaldi and (of doubtful authenticity) Albinoni, see Marc Pincherle, *Antonio Vivaldi* (New York, Norton, 1957), pp. 169ff.

[17]*The Symphonies of G. B. Sammartini*, I: 5.

[18]As in the first movement printed in *HAM*, No. 283, an edition which in other ways is inaccurate.

Between statements of themes the violins engage in the sequential passage-work that was to remain typical for the late-eighteenth-century symphony. In the middle movement Sammartini may provide solo and accompaniment texture: a first violin solo with triplet figuration in the second violin and an inconspicuous, harmonic bass line, for instance. The last movement may be a minuet or other dance, as in so many opera *sinfonie*.[19]

GERMANY: BERLIN AND MANNHEIM

Composers of the Berlin school who were active as symphonists include Johann Gottlieb Graun (1703–71) and, to a lesser extent, his brother Carl Heinrich Graun (1704–59). The Italian orientation of the Prussian court musicians is shown in the preponderance of three-movement symphonies which, however, include much contrapuntal work in the German Baroque tradition. Among Emanuel Bach's works the symphony held a less important place than did the sonata or concerto. Though he, too, continued the three-movement form, there are obvious differences from the Italian models, including more concern with thematic development and modulation. The exaggerated dynamics of the *empfindsamer Stil* are also in evidence. The six symphonies for strings of 1773 exemplify his striking personal style with frequent, abrupt changes in dynamics, sudden pauses, and forceful passage-work interrupted by lyrical phrases (Example 3–4).

The movements may be connected, in some cases with surprising key changes (Example 3–5).

Contributing much to the flourishing of instrumental music in Germany was a group of composers of various national origins who held leading positions at the court of the Elector Palatine, whose main residence was at Mannheim. Music historians at the beginning of this century, chiefly Hugo Riemann, may have exaggerated the significance of the "Mannheim school" at the expense of certain Austrian composers who today are credited with a larger share in the development of the symphony. But certainly Mannheim was one of the main musical centers of Europe at this time; its musicians contributed substantially as composers as well as by establishing high standards of performance.

The city of Mannheim, located at the confluence of the Rhine and Neckar rivers, began its rise to political and cultural importance when in 1720 it became the capital of the Palatinate. Much of the fortified city had been destroyed in various military campaigns during the preceding century; now a period of relative stability began to be reflected in a vigorous

---

[19]The mixture of Baroque and Classic style elements in Sammartini's early works is also discussed by La Rue, *Guidelines*, pp. 122ff.

EXAMPLE 3–4. C. P. E. Bach, *Symphony in G Major*, Wq 182/1, measures 1–7. Copyright 1975 by Henry Litolff's Verlag/C. F. Peters, New York. Printed by permission.

building program. The new castle was large and impressive; modeled on Versailles, it reflected the cultural ambitions of the Elector. By 1742, the year of the marriage of Prince Karl Theodor, the opera house had been completed; its inauguration formed part of the elaborate wedding festivities. Johann Stamitz (1717–57), among the first generation of Mannheim

EXAMPLE 3–5. C. P. E. Bach, *Symphony in B♭ Major*, Wq 182/2, measures 37–
40. Copyright 1975 by Henry Litolff's Verlag/C. F. Peters, New York.
Printed by permission.

composers, had already entered the Elector's service and had made a name for himself as violinist and composer. The Mannheim musical establishment reached its greatest flowering during the following thirty to forty years. Music at the castle and at the summer residence in Schwetzingen was described in glowing terms by numerous visitors. One obtains the impression that court life was a never-ending succession of festivities in which performances by the court orchestra alternated with opera, drama, recitals by traveling virtuosos, gala balls, and hunting parties. Tremendous sums were spent on the arts and sciences during Karl Theodor's reign, but the resources of a German elector were not those of a French king, and when Dr. Burney visited Mannheim in the summer of 1772 he could not help but see behind the scenes:

> The expense and magnificence of the court of this little city are prodigious; the palace and offices extend over almost half the town; and one half of the inhabitants, who are in office, prey on the other, who seem to be in the utmost indigence. . . . His electoral highness's suite at Schwetzingen, during the summer, amounts to fifteen hundred persons, who are all lodged in this little village, at his expense.[20]

Other visitors were impressed by the size of the musical establishment, by the music performed, and, above all, by the quality of the performances. Burney comments on the orchestra: Not only was he impressed by its size but by its

> good discipline; indeed there are more solo players, and good composers in this, than perhaps any other orchestra in Europe; it is an army of generals, equally fit to plan a battle, as to fight it.

C. F. D. Schubart, in his *Essay on Musical Esthetics,* found somewhat more romantic words of praise: Listening to the orchestra,

> one believed oneself to be transported to a magic island of sound. . . . No orchestra in the world ever equalled the Mannheimers' execution. Its forte is like thunder; its crescendo like a mighty waterfall; its diminuendo a gentle river disappearing into the distance; its piano is a breath of spring. The wind instruments could not be used to better advantage; they lift and carry, they reënforce and give life to the storm of the violins.

Startling as the crescendo appeared to visitors, it was not a Mannheim invention; but, done carefully and uniformly by this large orchestra, such a gradual increase or decrease of volume, distributed over a long passage, had an electrifying effect on the audience. On at least one occasion it

[20]*The Present State of Music in Germany* . . ., 2nd ed. (London, 1775), I: 81–96.

made them literally rise out of their seats. As an effective orchestral device, the Mannheim crescendo was soon adopted by composers everywhere.[21]

Traditions of great discipline and precision in performing and rehearsing, including the use of uniform bowings, were established by Johann Stamitz, the first leader of the Mannheim orchestra. He was assisted and followed by other Bohemians or Austrians: Anton Filtz (1726–60; in Mannheim from 1754), Franz X. Richter (1709–89; in Mannheim from 1747 to 1769), Christian Cannabich (1731–98), who followed Stamitz as leader of the orchestra; Ignatz Holzbauer (1711–83; Kapellmeister after 1753). Carlo Toëschi (1724–88) was one of the few prominent Italian musicians in the Elector's service, which he entered in 1752.

As a violinist Stamitz probably established the Mannheim custom of leading the orchestra from the concertmaster's chair, while in many other places the maestro at the harpsichord continued to be in charge. But when Mozart attended a Paris rehearsal of one of his symphonies he found the playing terrible and threatened to "take away [the concertmaster's] violin and conduct myself."[22] The traditions established by Stamitz were continued under Cannabich, who systematically trained the string players and who is said to have controlled the orchestra "with a mere nod of his head and a twitch of his elbow," an achievement all the more impressive in view of the orchestra's size. In 1756, it included twenty violins, four violas, four cellos, and two basses; its wind section included four horns. It was thus among the largest in Europe, on a par with orchestras in Naples, Milan, and Paris.[23]

More important than the size of this orchestra is the way composers wrote for it. French orchestras during the late Baroque era often displayed large wind sections; these were still required in works by Gossec around 1760.[24] Stamitz, who spent a successful season in Paris directing La Pouplinière's orchestra, may have transplanted some of this emphasis on winds to Mannheim. Mozart visited Mannheim in 1777. Coming from Munich, which boasted a fine orchestra, he was nevertheless highly impressed by the performances he heard at the Mannheim court chapel. "That way one

---

[21]Eugene K. Wolf's researches have established that some of the stylistic innovations generally credited to Mannheim composers can be found, some years earlier, in works by Jommelli (who was active in Stuttgart after 1754), Galuppi, and other Italian composers. "On the Origins of the Mannheim Symphonic Style," *Studies in Musicology in Honor of Otto E. Albrecht* (Kassel, 1980), pp. 197ff. Wolf's *The Symphonies of Johann Stamitz* (Utrecht, 1981) is a basic, detailed study that includes a thematic catalog.

[22]Letter to his father, June 18, 1778.

[23]Zaslaw, "Revival of the Classical Orchestra," pp. 160ff, gives detailed information on orchestra placement and directing in opera, church music, and symphony.

[24]The role of French composers in the development of the Classic symphony has been investigated by Barry S. Brook, *La symphonie française dans la seconde moitié du xviiie siècle*, 3 volumes, (Paris, 1962), including scores of complete symphonies by Gossec (1756), Simon Le Duc *L'aîné* (1777), and Henri-Joseph Riegl (1785).

can really make music!" (Letter of November 4, 1777.) Having heard the Mannheim clarinets he regretted that these were not available at home, in provincial Salzburg.

Stamitz had earned considerable success in Paris during the 1754–55 season. His orchestra trios Op. 1 were then published there. Among the Paris musicians to come under his influence was the young François Gossec (1734–1829), some of whose symphonies were written soon thereafter. To some French musicians symphonic music became virtually synonymous with German music—an attitude reflected in the output of French publishers. Bayard, for instance, brought out around 1755 a series of symphonies under the collective title *La Melodia Germanica*. Many Frenchmen then spoke of the importance and superiority of a German school, and some German musicians began to move into leading positions all over Europe, as in Paris during the time of Gluck and Grimm.[25]

Several Stamitz symphonies were included in Bayard's collection. They call for larger instrumental resources and generally come closer to our concept of the Classic symphony than do his orchestra trios. The *sinfonia a 8* in D, "La Melodia Germanica No. 1," will serve as an example. A 8, Stamitz's standard scoring, refers to strings, two horns, and two oboes which may have been doubled by clarinets. The opening presto of this four-movement symphony must have served well to show off the precision attack of the entire string section, the *premier coup d'archet* to which Mozart refers as a convention or mannerism of the Paris and Mannheim orchestras and to which he conformed, perhaps tongue-in-cheek, when writing for Le Gros in Paris. After a forte-piano contrast we have a good example of the carefully written out Mannheim crescendo: Stamitz writes "pianiss." in measure 9, "cresc. il fr." in measure 13, and "frmo" in measure 17. All of this takes place during a tremolo, first for all strings, then in the upper strings with a running bass passage in eighth notes, leading to a cadence in the dominant. After a rest the second theme follows (Example 3–6), clearly defined and contrasted, though incorporating a rhythmic figure from the first theme. In the graceful, singing nature of this and many other Mannheim lyrical themes we see the strongest influence of Italian music on the incipient German symphony.

EXAMPLE 3–6. Stamitz, *Symphony in D Major*, "La Melodia Germanica No. 1."

[25]The German Baron Friedrich Melchior von Grimm (1723–1807) had become an important figure in the literary and musical controversies of that city. Leopold Mozart urged his son to cultivate the influential Baron (letter of April 6, 1778).

Some imitation occurs in the next section, which serves as a bridge
to another theme in the dominant, stated by the oboes with repeated-note
accompaniment in the violins. Such light texture continues to be favored
for the second theme or group of themes long after Stamitz's day. Tremolo
in the violins with passage-work in viola and bass occurs in several places
(transition sections), with rhythmic and harmonic support from the winds.
As to the formal organization of the movement, one notes the absence of a
double bar as dividing point, nor is there a recapitulation. Instead of a return to the opening theme another crescendo-tremolo passage leads to the
second theme, slightly modified through modulation (but not developed)
before it is finally restated in the tonic key, which prevails for the remain-
der of the movement. The opening theme never returns in its entirety.

The andante that follows brings a typically *galant* melody in the first
violin, with short phrases and many dynamic changes. Scored for strings
only, it is in simple binary form. The trio section of the minuet is characterized by solo writing for oboes and horns. Many Baroque orchestral works
contained movements for three instruments, such as the *alternativo* dance
movements in Bach's orchestral suites. The term "trio" originally referred
to these and was retained by later composers for the section following the
minuet proper, even when more than three instruments participated.
While in this Stamitz symphony the minuet has two strains of equal length
(eight measures each) the trio's second strain is sixteen measures long, an
extension that is common in symphonic minuets of Haydn and Mozart. The
last movement, prestissimo, again shows the wind instruments to good advantage, especially in the second half where the paired horns echo the
oboes over a light string accompaniment.

Characteristics of the Mannheim style not met with in this symphony include the famous "rocket" beginning, a theme composed of rising
triadic figures, of which Stamitz's symphony Op. 3, No. 1 supplies an example (Example 3–7). Another device or mannerism would be the *Mann-
heimer Walze*, a "steamroller" effect achieved by ostinato repetition of a
phrase with the gradual addition of instruments, as in the opening of
Stamitz's *Sinfonia a 11*, Op. 3, No. 2. For this, too, Italian precedents
exist.

EXAMPLE 3–7. Stamitz, *Synphony*, Op. 3, No. 1.

Most of the style features discussed so far can be found in the works
of Stamitz's Mannheim colleagues, though they may lack his fire and imagination. Anton Filtz, though less known today than Stamitz, had an excel-

lent reputation in the eighteenth century. Schubart refers to him as the best writer of symphonies who ever lived. *Galant* melodies are conspicuous in his symphonies, bringing them stylistically close to those of John Christian Bach and the young Mozart. Richter's symphonies are in three movements; occasionally a minuet serves as last movement as it also does in some symphonies by Austrian contemporaries. Yet cantabile themes and orchestral texture represent the Mannheim style.

Later composers in Mannheim, including Karl Stamitz (1746–1801), Anton Stamitz (1753–1820), and Carl Cannabich (1771–1805), no longer played a part in the formation of Classic style.

The great age of the Mannheim orchestra and opera lasted into the 1780s. When Karl Theodor became Elector of Bavaria in 1777, the residence was soon moved to Munich. Consequently Mannheim was depleted of most of its musical establishment, leaving the continued cultivation of music largely to the initiative of the city's amateur musicians.

AUSTRIA

Works by certain Austrian composers around 1750 show that they shaped the Classic symphony to a larger degree than had been assumed when Riemann "discovered" the Mannheim school. Symphonies by Mathias Georg Monn (1717–50) and Georg Christoph Wagenseil (1715–77) include the minuet as the third of four movements—a minuet which frequently displays rustic rather than courtly character.[26] Monn's symphony in D of 1740 may be the earliest example; in this work the minuet is not followed by a trio. A passage of melodic importance is given to the French horns in the second strain, as found in the trio sections of many later symphonic minuets.[27] All movements of Monn's symphony are in the same key, in the manner of the Baroque suite, the second movement being an "aria." In the outer movements Monn's works show contrapuntal and fugal writing, which reminds us that his was the Vienna in which Fux had reigned not many years earlier. Inner voices frequently show rhythmic and melodic life of their own, leading to an emancipation of the bass line as well, so that a basso continuo part was not always considered essential by the composer. Contrasting themes, or more than two themes, are not unusual; on the other hand, there are movements in which the distinction between thematic and non-thematic material cannot be made—a situation that also ex-

---

[26]Symphonies by Leopold Hoffman (ca. 1730–93), composed in the 1760s, likewise have four movements. J. La Rue, "Three Notes of Non-Authenticity," *Haydn-Studien* 2 (1969), pp. 69–70.
[27]The minuet of this symphony is printed in *Die musikalische Klassik*, ed. Kurt Stephenson (Cologne, n.d.) p. 33; the last movement in *HAM*, No. 295.

ists in some Mannheim symphonies—due to the great number of melodic fragments, presented seemingly at random, without prominent treatment being given to any one of them.

As might be expected in symphonies from this period, development sections tend to be very modest. Harmonically, many early Classic symphonies may appear primitive or unimaginative to us, but this simplicity must be understood as a reaction, once more, to what appeared to this generation as the overly involved and affective harmonic language of some late-Baroque music. It was not long before harmonic inventiveness was to characterize symphonic and other works from the mature Classic period.

INTERNATIONAL ASPECTS OF CLASSIC STYLE

In tracing the emergence of Classic style we have been concerned with activities at many European musical centers, and we have referred to various "schools," among others the Berlin, Mannheim, and early Viennese schools. Such terms are convenient but apply only in a very general sense. Eighteenth-century musicians frequently changed their places of activity, so that Bohemian and Austrian composers were among those shaping the Mannheim style; Italians were much in evidence in Vienna; German composers and performers made an impression on the Paris musical scene. Such internationalism was not new at this time: We have only to think back to the Renaissance period when the polyphony of Franco-Flemish musicians was understood and admired everywhere. Before the days of national states, political borders were frequently adjusted so that the nationality, language, and cultural heritage of the ruler were not necessarily those of his subjects. These and many other factors, among them the international character of the Roman Catholic Church and frequent intermarriage among the princely families of Europe, tended to give an international flavor to musical life before and during the Classic era.

The age also displayed an awareness of various national styles, a subject much discussed around the mid-eighteenth century. We have mentioned the many "comparisons" of French and Italian music. German musician-writers, well aware of the foreign elements in their own music, did not hesitate to enter the literary melée. Thus Quantz recommended that German composers make use of the best qualities found in all kinds of non-German music; in doing so they would arrive at a style with international appeal—the *vermischte Geschmack* which he considered typically German![28] Other writers shared the view that German music had borrowed

---

[28]Quantz, *Versuch*, 3rd ed., (1789); he discusses the subject for about 30 pages.

freely from other countries; in the opinion of Scheibe, around 1745, German composers had achieved distinction only by virtue of industry, regularity of execution, and profundity in the field of harmony. A combination of the precision and brilliance of the French manner with the ingratiating *(schmeichelhaft)* style of Italian vocal music is recommended for German performers in C. P. E. Bach's *Versuch.* While a few German writers, with some smugness, proclaimed the superiority of German music, Austrians seem to have been more receptive, in a less self-conscious manner, to musical influences from abroad because of geographical and political reasons. Quite possibly this may be why Austria and southern Germany rather than the north assumed positions of prominence and leadership in the later eighteenth century. This prominence is clearer to us in retrospect than it was to a contemporary such as Reichardt, to whom both Emanuel Bach and Haydn were proof that "We Germans [that is, German-speaking composers, including Austrians] have a style of our own, and our instrumental music is the most interesting to be found anywhere" (1782).[29] A decade earlier Gluck had already expressed hope that *his* music would appeal equally to all nations, saying that his goal was to "do away with the ridiculous national differences in music." Internationalism became typical in the age of Haydn and Mozart (though both at times voiced patriotic sentiments, especially when away from home); its ingredients also were present to a high degree in the music of John Christian Bach (1735–82).

This youngest son of the Leipzig cantor was largely overlooked by the nineteenth century, even more so than his brother Emanuel. The Romantics, led by Mendelssohn, had rediscovered J. S. Bach, especially the seriousness of the Passions and the contrapuntal mastery of the *Art of Fugue.* Next to this weight and magnificence the elegant style of John Christian suffered in comparison, but during the 1760s and 1770s when people mentioned the name Bach, they often meant him.

The boy was a mere fifteen years old when his father died; he had received his early musical instruction from him. Emanuel Bach in Berlin undertook John Christian's further education, but after four years the young musician yielded to the strong attraction of Italy and Italian music. For a while he studied with Padre Martini, but the "learned style" seems not to have held any lasting satisfaction for him. Instead he immersed himself in the vigorous operatic life he encountered in Milan, Rome, Naples, and elsewhere. His own attempts at opera in the reigning style were crowned with immediate success. His Italianization seemed complete when, about 1760, he embraced Catholicism. These years of study and employment in Italy, decisive in John Christian's career, fully justify his nickname of the "Milan Bach." His move to England in 1762 resulted in the

---

[29]*Musikalisches Kunstmagazin,* 1 (1782), 205.

additional label "London Bach," little justified by the style of his music, which continued to display strong Italian characteristics. He soon established himself at court, became music master to the Queen (who had been a German princess), and dedicated to her his six keyboard sonatas published as Op. 1. His own playing was much admired; no doubt he had developed technique and taste under his brother's supervision in Berlin. He had the additional talent of writing within the abilities of his aristocratic pupils. All of this must have contributed to his success in London society, both as composer and as performer.

To listen to one of Christian Bach's keyboard sonatas, concertos, or symphonies is to realize that here is a composer who stands at the doorstep of Classicism, for in his graceful melodies—small in design, elegant, and at times tinged with melancholy—we detect the language, above all, of the young Mozart. Good reasons exist for this: when the Mozart family reached London in 1764, John Christian already was one of the leading local musicians. He heard the eight-year-old Wolfgang play; he instructed him and grew very fond of him, an affection that was genuinely returned. Wolfgang's lasting high opinion of the "London Bach" is evident from his letters; equally significant is his concern with Bach's music, including the keyboard sonatas Op. 5, published shortly after the Mozarts left London, and among the first to be published as written *"pour le clavecin ou le Piano Forte."* Mozart arranged several of these as piano concertos (K. 107) and often performed them in public. A study of these sonatas is rewarding: Melodies are cantabile, elegant, ingratiating—their style is reflected in countless Mozart melodies. Op. 5, No. 2, one of the sonatas arranged by Mozart, is representative. Its opening does indeed suggest the orchestral introduction of a concerto, with repeated chords in both hands and, very soon, a bass melody under chord figuration in the right hand (Example 3–8).

EXAMPLE 3–8. J. C. Bach, *Sonata*, Op. 5, No. 2.

The second theme has all the characteristics of Mozart's melodic style (Example 3–9).

However, what Bach does with it in the course of the movement might not have satisfied Mozart ten or fifteen years later. "He succeeded better when he was tender or amorous than when he tried to be lofty and tragic"; so Schubart characterized John Christian Bach's writing. Leopold

EXAMPLE 3–9. J. C. Bach, *Sonata*, Op. 5, No. 2.

Mozart, anxious for his son to write music with popular appeal, urged Wolfgang to consider John Christian Bach as a model. *"What is slight can still be great,* if it is written in a natural, flowing and easy style—and at the same time bears the marks of sound composition."[30]

Mozart studied many of Bach's works long after their first London meeting. Some twelve years later he sent for the score of Bach's opera *Lucio Silla* and studied it with care. Fondness for the arias was coupled with admiration for his orchestral works. Bach's first symphonies date from about 1759, reminding us that he was a contemporary rather than a precursor of Haydn. They are mostly in three movements, some of them having originally served as operatic overtures. That many of his symphonies were printed at the time reflects Bach's success in England and on the continent. Enough of them are again available today to make us realize how much this Italianized German, who lived in England and whose works were printed in Holland and France, gave to the Austrian Mozart.

BIBLIOGRAPHICAL NOTES

Special studies, in English, of pre-Classic symphonies are rare. A. Carse's *18th-Century Symphonies* (London, 1951) includes brief analyses of works by many early Classic composers. C. S. Terry's *John Christian Bach* (London: Oxford Univ. Press, 1929; rev. ed. 1967) is still a basic source. The articles on Sammartini in *Grove 6* and *MGG* are recommended, along with B. Churgin's edition of the symphonies: *The Symphonies of G. B. Sammartini,* volume I (Cambridge MA: Harvard Univ. Press, 1968). A thematic catalogue of Sammartini's orchestral and vocal works, edited by Churgin and N. Jenkins (Cambridge MA: Harvard Univ. Press, 1976) includes biographical information and a chapter on his style. A wealth of new material is now available in the sixty-volume series *The Symphony 1720–1840* (New York: Garland, 1986). It includes the scores of 550 works by 244 composers from many European countries. The music is reproduced from eighteenth-century manuscripts or

---

[30]Letter of August 13, 1778. *The Letters of Mozart and His Family,* trans. E. Anderson (London, 1938), p. 889.

prints, or freshly edited. Series A, Volume I *(Antecedents of the Symphony)*, is relevant to this chapter, with the important introductory essays "The Ripieno Concerto" (E. K. Wolf) and "The Eighteenth-Century Overture" (D. Green and G. Lazarevich).

A complete edition of J. C. Bach's works is in progress (New York: Garland, 1984–). Symphonies by C. P. E. Bach can be studied in modern editions, including his Symphony in E Minor (1756), in K. Geiringer, ed., *Music of the Bach Family* (Cambridge, MA: Harvard Univ. Press, 1955); four symphonies written 1775–76 in *Das Erbe deutscher Musik*, series I, volume 18, ed. Rudolf Steglich (Wiesbaden, 1966); and six symphonies for strings (1773), ed. Traugott Fedke (Frankfurt, 1975). *Mannheim Symphonists* is a collection of twenty-four orchestral works edited by H. Riemann (repr. New York: Broude, 1956). Movements from symphonies by Monn, Wagenseil, and Stamitz are included in *Die musikalische Klassik*, ed. K. Stephenson (Cologne, ca. 1953; also published in English).

FOUR

THE BACKGROUND
OF THE CLASSIC PERIOD

The political developments which led to the French Revolution af- [handwritten: 1789] fected many aspects of European civilization. Its causes need not be investigated here, but it is important to remember that the age of Haydn and Mozart was an age of upheavals not restricted to France but felt, in varying degrees, in all of Europe, directly and indirectly influencing the musical life of the Classic era. The *ancien régime* still provided the setting for most of the period: Mozart had but two years to live when the French monarchy was overthrown; and when the first French republic was proclaimed, Haydn, close to sixty years old, had already earned his first triumphs in London. Yet the revolution had cast its shadows ahead; its ideas permeated the intellectual life of the late eighteenth century. Political absolutism was approaching its end, but it lasted longer in some places than in others. The violent events of the French Revolution affected that country as a whole. Germany, on the other hand, was not to emerge as a national state for some time and continued to consist of a great number of independent, autonomous principalities, some large (Prussia, Saxony, Bavaria) but many small to the point of being miniature states. Absolutism, modified and enlightened to varying degrees, continued to be the system of government there, but even before the turn of the century many princes, mindful of the events in France, had curtailed the lavishness of court life and instituted legal and other reforms which tended to give the middle class a larger voice in public affairs. After the Revolution, cultural life in France continued to be concentrated in Paris to a degree for which there was no German parallel. The flourishing of Germany's musical life may in part be explained by the continued existence of its many autonomous kingdoms, duchies, electorates, and lesser principalities, each with its own capital, court orchestra, theater, opera, and other manifestations of cultural ambitions and pretensions.

Among German princes the personality of Frederick the Great (reigned 1740–86) dominated much of the eighteenth century. We have noted earlier how he imposed his taste on the musical life of Berlin. Soon after his accession he embarked on a successful campaign to wrest Silesia from Austria (War of Austrian Succession); later, in the Seven Years War (1756–63), he encountered greater resistance, suffered serious setbacks, but eventually emerged victorious. The financial burden of that campaign, and the strain and worries it brought to the king, caused a decline of musical activity at the Prussian court, where, for example, no operas were given from 1756 to 1764. Other centers were also affected: the residence of the King of Saxony was moved from Dresden to Warsaw, resulting in Hasse's departure for Italy. Frederick's nephew, Frederick William II, who succeeded him as king (1786–97), lacked the military and administrative skills of the "Old Fritz," but he shared the musical enthusiasm which the latter had displayed in his younger years. As an accomplished cello player he inspired both Haydn and Mozart to write some distinguished works of chamber music for him.

Neither Frederick William II nor his son and successor was able to cope with the turbulent times. Prussia was greatly reduced in power by Napoleon, who defeated her thoroughly at the Battle of Jena (1806), and French troops were stationed in Berlin.

AUSTRIA

Looking at the little space Austria now occupies on the map of Europe, one might wonder how so small a country could have risen to such cultural significance in the eighteenth century. That the boundaries of the

Hapsburg Empire then were quite different might be demonstrated by the typical opening clause of a decree issued by the Emperor in 1783:

> We, Joseph II, by the grace of God, elected Roman Emperor . . . King of Germany, Jerusalem, Hungary, Bohemia, Dalmatia, Croatia, Slavonia, Galicia, and Lodomeria, Archduke of Austria, etc. etc. etc. . . .

Some of these imposing titles at this time amounted to mere window dressing, referring to conditions as far back as the Crusades, but to Hungary, Bohemia, and the other provinces mentioned one could have added Lombardy, Venetia, and Tuscany as territories which during the eighteenth century had been within the empire, along with further "et ceteras."

Austria, then, was a large empire with people of many ethnic and linguistic backgrounds. The talents of generations of Hapsburg rulers for enlarging their realm through advantageous alliances had become proverbial: "Let others wage war; thou, happy Austria, marry!"

When Charles VI died in 1740, the male Hapsburg line became extinct and Maria Theresa became empress. Austria was neither politically nor economically sound at the time, and the loss of Silesia soon aggravated these conditions. With the help of able advisers Maria Theresa achieved greater consolidation of the empire by tying the provinces closer to the heartland and by establishing a more centralized government in Vienna. Though a devout Catholic she desired a reduction of the secular powers of the church, at the same time enforcing decrees against Jews and Protestants. Her son, who had been co-regent during the last fifteen years of her life, tried to carry out consistently many reforms initiated by her, including the abolition of serfdom and various legal reforms. At his insistence German became the official language throughout the empire.

A true representative of enlightened absolutism, Joseph undertook further measures against the Church, attempting to remove the Austrian clergy from Rome's jurisdiction, an issue on which he clashed repeatedly with the Pope. He dissolved many monasteries, either turning them into schools or having their assets confiscated by the state. Typically, he believed that the chief purpose of religion was the betterment of humanity, a purpose to be achieved by instruction of the people, in the classroom and from the pulpit, and by improving literacy and doing away with superstitions and prejudices. Unlike Maria Theresa he believed in religious tolerance and, to an extent, in freedom of the press. Nevertheless his was still an absolute reign. Full and prompt compliance with the sovereign's wishes was enforced. Censorship was never entirely abolished, and other curbs on individual liberty continued to exist.

Joseph's reign was short (1780–90); there had not been time for many of the drastic reforms to take root. His successor, Leopold II, much

Vienna, Schönbrunn Castle: the theater, Austrian National Library.

intimidated by the opposition and frightened by the events in France (Marie Antoinette was his sister), revoked much of what Joseph had decreed. During the following years the Napoleonic Wars engulfed Austria. Napoleon entered Vienna in 1805 and again in 1809, staying at Schönbrunn Castle. After his overthrow the victorious allies gathered in Vienna to redraw the map of Europe (Congress of Vienna, 1814–15)—an occasion of great splendor enhanced by many festive musical occasions.

SALZBURG

The political power of the Catholic Church in the eighteenth century also manifested itself in numerous church states such as Salzburg, the city of Mozart's birth, which had been a small state within the empire for a thousand years, located between powerful Austria and Bavaria. The archbishop of Salzburg was both spiritual and political ruler of the province, though as a prince of church, his position was not hereditary. As the head of state, the Salzburg archbishop lived on a large, elaborate scale, attested to still by the *Residenz* and other palaces in and near the city. Close ties linked the church state, Salzburg, to Rome; indeed, the city has been

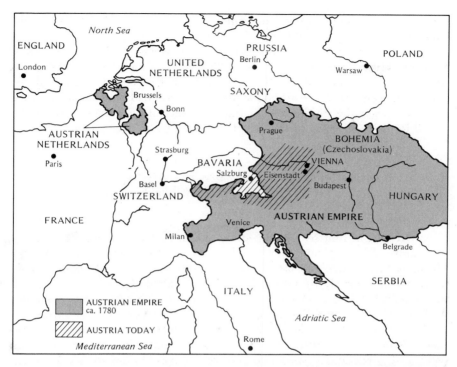

Boundaries of the Austrian Empire, ca. 1780, comparing the extent of the Empire with modern Austria. Adapted from *Listen,* third edition, by Joseph Kerman (New York: Worth, 1980), p. 262.

called "the German Rome." To many visitors, then and now, the panorama of Salzburg, its location, architecture, color, and atmosphere, have suggested something of Italy.

Under the rule of Archbishop Sigismund Graf von Schrattenbach (1753–71), Salzburg had gone through a period of economic decline. The musical life at court, in which the Archbishop displayed much interest, seems to have flourished just the same. Sigismund's successor, Hieronymus Graf von Colloredo-Waldsee (1732–1812), was an ardent believer in the ideas of the Enlightenment; tradition has it that busts of Rousseau and Voltaire were displayed in his study. No wonder that reform measures were soon forthcoming. They included the abolition of certain holidays to increase agricultural and other forms of productivity, a reduction in the number and duration of religious services including processions, and a general emphasis in religious matters on instruction and good works. Inevitably Colloredo encountered much opposition from clergy and laymen alike. In many ways his position was similar to that of Joseph II: What he had tried to eliminate as unenlightened and superstitious frequently had been deeply rooted and cherished traditions.

At the turn of the century, the war between revolutionary France and the European coalition, of which Austria was a member, brough occupation, looting, and other hardships to Salzburg. French troops entered the city on December 10, 1800, hours after Colloredo had fled—an action that only increased the dislike felt for him by many of his subjects. He abdicated formally in 1803. Salzburg had ceased to be an ecclesiastical state.

INTELLECTUAL BACKGROUND: POLITICAL PHILOSOPHY

A bust of Rousseau in the study of a prince of the church—the picture appears incongruous today as it did to many contemporaries. It does show, however, that the ideas of the philosophers of the Enlightenment were taken seriously by intelligent people in all walks of life. The belief that man is born free, voiced by Rousseau (*Social Contract*, 1762), Voltaire, and others, was eagerly taken up in many quarters. If man was born free, he had the right to freedom of inquiry, the right to use his mind uninhibited by authoritarian restrictions. Skepticism about religious authority and hostility toward dogma were natural consequences of this conviction. Much eighteenth-century thought concerned itself with moral philosophy rather than with theology, or one might say that the moral rather than doctrinal and ritual aspects of religion were stressed. Moral responsibility was seen to apply to both rulers and ruled; moral law was to regulate the relation of man to fellow man, to humanity. Humanitarian ideals came to be reflected increasingly in art of the late eighteenth and early nineteenth centuries, including opera. When, in Beethoven's opera *Fidelio* (see Chapter 13) the Minister of Justice tells the assembled people that he abhors tyranny, that he is like a brother to his subjects, he voices beliefs fervently held by many in the audience and by the composer.

Concern for humanity led to increased interest in and respect for other cultures and religions; tolerance in religious matters became an important characteristic of the age. Operas such as Mozart's *Entführung* and *Magic Flute* supply examples in which a Turkish pasha and an Egyptian high priest are represented as wise and moral human beings rather than as cruel or otherwise contemptible infidels.

Like many revolutionary concepts the newly proclaimed belief in *liberté, égalité, fraternité* had its effect on dramatic and other literature. Louis XV had objected to Beaumarchais' comedy *Le mariage de Figaro* because of its revolutionary implications. Only after some clever maneuvering did the author succeed in having the play performed. In Vienna similar obstacles were encountered by Mozart's opera based on the same play: The idea of a barber and other commoners outwitting an aristocrat appeared too revolutionary even to "the revolutionary Emperor," Joseph II. The excision of many lines that might have appeared politically dangerous, and the appeal of the music, which Mozart played for the Emperor, finally overcame Joseph's reservations. *Egalité* is not implied when, in *Don Giovanni,* the licentious nobleman invites the country girl Zerlina to accompany him to his castle—"there we shall be married" is not to be taken literally—but the ideas of equality are in evidence in other operas of the age where an aristocrat might cast aside class prejudices and marry a commoner.

The virtues of tolerance and brotherly love, the belief in the dignity of the individual regardless of birth—these and other concepts of the Enlightenment were essential to the creeds of the fraternal organizations that developed during the eighteenth century, particularly the Freemasons, an order that attracted many leading figures in politics, philosophy, and the arts. The first Masonic lodge had been established in London in 1717; aided by the anticlerical atmosphere of the age the order soon spread all over Europe. It counted among its members heads of state (Frederick the Great) and other aristocrats; poets and philosophers (Goethe, Lessing) as well as musicians, among whom Mozart, because of his wholehearted involvement, became the outstanding representative. Masonic ideas permeated much of Mozart's writing, not only those compositions which were written for specific Masonic occasions (such as his *Masonic Funeral Music,* K. 477, occasioned by the deaths of two of Mozart's lodge brothers, one a German duke, the other an Esterházy prince), but particularly his last opera, *The Magic Flute,* in which characters representing wisdom, reason, and tolerance are contrasted with those who represent superstition and hatred.

THE CLASSIC REVIVAL (NEOCLASSICISM) IN THE FINE ARTS

The greatest flourishing of neoclassicism took place after Haydn's and Mozart's time; yet the revival of interest in the civilization of antiquity had begun earlier in the eighteenth century. Enthusiasm for the study of Greek and Roman civilization was kindled by archeological discoveries, notably those made at Pompeii and Herculaneum, where excavations were begun in 1748. Some familiarity with the art of antiquity and awareness of the qualities which made it "classic" (discussed in our introductory chapter) were brought to a large public by Giovanni Battista Piranesi's (1720–78) collections of engravings *(Le antichità Romane; Vedute di Roma)* and by the enthusiasm of Johann Joachim Winckelmann (1717–68), who in his *History of Ancient Art* (1764) praised the Greek concept of beauty, describing its essential quality as "noble simplicity and silent grandeur." Winckelmann had esteemed Greek art more highly than Roman art, and popular taste followed him until the end of the century when, during the revolutionary period, the characteristics of republican Rome seemed more appropriate, causing Roman subjects and motifs to be favored in the visual arts and in literature, including music drama.

Jacques Louis David (1748–1825), one of the best known neoclassic painters, still evoked a Rococo atmosphere in his earlier works, which earned the praise of Fragonard. Having won the Prix de Rome in 1776, David was inspired by the sights of Pompeii and by other monuments of ancient Rome. From this period on—some years before the Revolution, of which he became an ardent supporter—his paintings evoke the spirit of classic antiquity. Canvases such as his *Death of Socrates* (1787) and *Brutus* (1789) were given enthusiastic reception as eloquent portrayals of morality and patriotism, expressing with force the mood of an age that was witnessing the overthrow of another tyranny.

Historians and philosophers extolled the civic virtues, the morality, the devotion to duty which they had encountered in their study of republican Rome. When these qualities were related to the arts, the resulting views amounted to a rejection of Rococo art as light and frivolous entertainment for the few. In line with classic philosophy art was believed to serve a moral, ethical purpose: the betterment of humanity.

The stern, serious mood of French neoclassicism pervades much of the music from the revolutionary period. (See Chapter 13.) Its heroic aspects were to find full expression in the music of Beethoven and his contemporaries.

SOCIAL CHANGES AFFECTING MUSIC— MUSICAL PATRONAGE

Changes in the structure of eighteenth-century society lent the middle classes increasing importance in political, economic, and cultural matters. The last-mentioned was largely dependent on the other two, for without the greater amount of material well-being and leisure time, previously enjoyed only by the ruling class, the common man would not have developed the skills, experience, and discrimination that now enabled him to participate actively in the artistic life.

In the field of music this participation meant, among other things, that the well-to-do citizen became a sponsor, a patron of music who would commission composers to write and hire performers to sing and play for him. An important difference between court and middle-class sponsorship of music lies in the fact that the former had a regular, continuing basis whereas bankers or merchants more likely commissioned single works and employed musicians on a casual basis. As the old social order dissolved, shifts in the musical economy inevitably occurred. At many smaller courts, for instance, opera companies were discontinued for economic reasons, and instrumental music, somewhat less expensive, was emphasized instead. Patronage by wealthy individuals did not generally provide the modest but secure livelihood of the old social order. In a sense the public at large now became the most important patron of music through the institution of the public concert with paid admission. There were important consequences for the professional musician: The public concert meant that performances now reached a far greater audience than ever before. Allowing some exceptions for sacred music and opera, attendance at court-sponsored musical events had been largely restricted to members of the aristocracy—to the sovereign, his family and *entourage*, and to invited guests. As public concerts became widely established the number of musically informed listeners grew—a development which, in turn, was related to the greater participation in music-making by the non-professional.

CONNOISSEUR AND AMATEUR

The economic changes of the times brought music-making within the reach of a large segment of society. Leisure time and money for the purchase of instruments (especially the expensive keyboard instruments which became so popular) and for their study were now more widely available. Much music was written for the amateur; publications and dedications frequently contain references to him in their titles. Boccherini[1] dedicated his first quartet to "veri dilettanti e conoscitori [connoisseurs] di musica," and many German publications, among them keyboard collections by Emanuel Bach, addressed themselves to the *Kenner und Liebhaber* (the connoisseur and amateur). Music specifically intended for the amateur was published in serial form as well, such as S. A. Steiner's *Journal für Quartetten-Liebhaber*. The editor, in announcing the journal, gave his reasons:

[1]See Chapter 7.

Vienna: Mehlgrube. Mozart gave public concerts here. A restaurant was on the ground
floor; the hall, also popular for balls, on the second floor.[3] Austrian National Library.

"Not every lover of music is well served by grand quartets that are difficult
to play."[2]

    In the twentieth century, the terms "amateur" and "dilettante" have
acquired a largely derogatory meaning, implying lack of musical ability or
taste. While some eighteenth-century music-making undoubtedly was "am-
ateurish" in that sense, the terms themselves did not imply this but were
used in their literal meaning. An "amateur" was simply a "lover" of music
whose training and ability may or may not have equaled that of a professional. Subtle, though not consistent, distinctions were made by the musicians themselves. In general, the terms "amateur" and "dilettante" (related
to our word "delight") implied interest primarily in performance itself—
playing and singing—whereas a connoisseur's interest extended to knowledge beyond this, to the meaning and structure—to the "why" of a composition.

    That the cultivated amateur became an important member of musi-
cal society appears from Mozart's letter to his father (May 18, 1782) describing the *Dilettanten Concerte* which had become quite successful in Vienna. The orchestra consisted almost exclusively of dilettantes, "very good

    [2]E. Hilmar, *Franz Schubert in seiner Zeit* (Vienna: Böhlau, 1985), p. 34.
    [3]For a detailed account of concert spaces in Vienna, see O. Biba, "Grundzüge des
Konzertwesens in Wien zu Mozarts Zeit," *Mozart-Jahrbuch* (1978–79), pp. 132ff.

ones at that," and proved useful to Mozart in making himself known to the Viennese, both as composer and as performer. The situation was the same in Beethoven's day. According to an early nineteenth-century account,

> one saw in the chorus and orchestra counts next to tradesmen, high officials next to civil servants, Doctors of Philosophy next to students, and in the soprano and alto sections aristocratic ladies next to middle-class women—all took their place with the sole ambition of contributing to the success of the whole.[4]

The amateur required not only music on various levels of difficulty, but also instruction. Three of the most important eighteenth-century instruction books or methods were written by Quantz (1752), Emanuel Bach (1753), and Leopold Mozart (1756) for flute, keyboard instruments, and violin respectively. Their success (shown by several editions and translations) is indicative of the need that such works filled for an ever-growing musical public. Other methods followed, often equally broad in scope, among them Türk's popular *Klavierschule*, first published in 1789.

CHANGING SOCIAL STATUS OF THE MUSICIAN

That the composer was slowly rising in general esteem has already been mentioned in connection with the ideas of the Enlightenment. The change manifested itself in a variety of ways. Music-making in aristocratic households may have been quite democratic, especially when the ruler or lord of the manor played an instrument while other parts were taken by valets, gardeners, or other help who might have been hired with a view to the musical contributions they might be able to make.[5] In situations of this kind, informal as they may have been, no leveling of social differences was implied. The professional musician in the employ of a prince, however, gradually achieved greater recognition; he came to be regarded as an artist rather than a servant and, on a human level, may have been on terms amounting to friendship and approaching equality with his employer. Haydn's relation to the Esterházy family is perhaps the most famous example of the emancipation of the artist. The contract drawn up when he first entered their service left no doubt about his being a servant, specifying the

[4]Ibid., p. 87.
[5]Class distinctions were not always rigidly observed during this age. Mozart's letter of November 25, 1781 is a hilarious account of what happened at a court ball at Schönbrunn Castle, in honor of Grand Duke Paul. Through a mistake many tickets for the ball had fallen into the hands of "hairdressers and chamber maids" who appeared at the ball, showing great curiosity and little deference to the Emperor and his guests.

uniform he was to wear and the hours he was to appear in the Prince's antechamber to receive orders. All music he composed was to become the Prince's property, and he was to compose such music as the Prince might order. In communications from this time he is referred to summarily in the third person singular, which was used then to address socially inferior persons: "*Er, der Haydn.*" By the 1780s, however, Haydn had acquired considerable fame, and times had changed. He now had greater freedom in the use of his compositions and, while still nominally employed, was free to travel. When Prince Nicholas died in 1790, Haydn was left a substantial annual pension and was paid an increased salary by the Prince's successor. His duties, in return, apparently consisted of little more than to call himself "Kapellmeister of Prince Esterházy."

Haydn had accepted his earlier inferior position, though with some grumbling; Mozart had resented his own servitude in Salzburg and fought continuously until the inevitable break with the Archbishop occurred. Finding himself without an employer, he left Salzburg for Vienna and tried to make a go of it as an independent artist by giving lessons, performing in public, and composing. Times, however, were not yet ripe for such independence. In spite of his great industry and productivity Mozart's financial circumstances worsened steadily until his untimely death. Only in the nineteenth century did artists achieve independence from an employer; some undoubtedly wished for the relative security of the earlier system.

Independence meant for the composer that there was no longer an immediate consumer for his works. Haydn often composed under great pressure from an impatient Prince with a tremendous musical appetite; Mozart's music also was usually written with a specific performance (and performer) in mind. His "Linz" Symphony, K. 425, was written "at breakneck speed," for a performance only four days away, when he noticed that he had no other symphony with him that was suitable for the occasion.

It would be a mistake to assume that music that is written to order cannot be inspired or sincere. Most music before the nineteenth century, and a good deal since then, has been composed this way. The close relation between the eighteenth-century composer and his audience did mean that music, while sincere and at times intensely personal in expression, was largely separated from the personal life, from the external conditions of the artist. His music lacked the subjectivism of the Romantic era. His were not autobiographical compositions, and expression more often was on a "classic," universal level. The pathetic circumstances of Mozart's last years did not result in music that was predominantly gloomy: Some works are introspective, resigned, and serious in mood, but others are vigorous, exuberant, and sparkling. The Romantic composer, less frequently obliged to compose a work of specified type, length, and instrumentation, or to deliver it by a certain day, tended to look for inspiration—in nature, poetry, philosophy—and to wait for the divine spark, to create music out of an inner need.

MUSICAL LIFE IN THE CLASSIC ERA

The extent, never equaled before, to which amateurs brought serious music-making into the home is among the most significant contributions to the musical life of the Classic era. One thinks of *Hausmusik*—music in and for the home—primarily as chamber music, but Classic symphonies, requiring relatively few instruments, were also heard in aristocratic and middle-class homes. In his well-known painting, *The Symphony*, Moritz von Schwindt recreated such a setting and included his friend Schubert among the singers and players represented. Some of Mozart's and Haydn's symphonies had their first performances in the home of a Viennese music lover. However, it was chamber music of various kinds, with or without keyboard instruments or voices, which formed the backbone of music-making in the Classic period. The family string quartet remained an essential part of European middle-class culture through the nineteenth century, even though much of the repertory written after Haydn addresses itself primarily to the professional player.

Music-making in the family circle continued to be a cherished activity among the aristocracy as well. In the Hapsburg family it was based on a long tradition of musical interest, going back at least to the early seventeenth century. A hundred years later Empress Maria Theresa took a warm interest in her children's musical training. Princes and princesses, including the four-year-old Marie Antoinette, appeared in palace concerts performing concertos and arias or taking part in the family orchestra. Both Joseph II and Francis II (reigned 1792–1835) were accomplished performers, the latter maintaining a string quartet in which he played first violin.

As an institution the imperial court chapel varied in size and quality according to political and economic conditions. Some decline had taken place during the difficult years Maria Theresa had to face. By 1770, the court chapel still had not recovered its former excellence, so that during the Classic period it was not the place where the most important musical developments took place. Haydn had no connection with the court; Mozart, late in life, tried in vain to obtain a substantial position; Beethoven's friendship with Archduke Rudolph was but a loose tie to the imperial court.

The continued importance of the church in the musical life of the age was not restricted to sacred music. In monasteries in Austria and southern Germany many kinds of secular music, including symphonic and chamber music, were cultivated as well. As in earlier days many monasteries

Moritz von Schwind, *The Symphony*. The painting shows the artist himself (turning pages for the pianist), Schubert (in chorus, left), the writer Grillparzer, and the pianist Maximiliana Brentano, to whom Beethoven had dedicated his Piano Sonata, Op. 109. Also included are Schubert's friends Lachner (conducting), Vogl (singing), and Schober. The painting, an homage to Beethoven (whose laurel-crowned bust is in the center), represents a performance of the Fantasy for Piano, Chorus, and Orchestra, Op. 80. Munich, Neue Pinakothek.

were famous for their libraries, including collections of music. Some of the most valuable source material for a study of eighteenth-century symphonic music is preserved in the libraries of monasteries where these works were avidly performed, often within a few months of their composition.

Public concerts were not unknown before the eighteenth century. Many cities, especially the wealthy free cities and university towns, maintained a *collegium musicum* in which students and professional musicians took part. These originally closed groups appeared at civic or church functions presenting what amounted to public concerts, though admission fees may not have been charged. During the eighteenth century, public concerts were organized, often on a continuing basis, in many cities. Among these were the Bach-Abel concerts (London, from 1764); the *Concerts spirituels* (Paris, 1725) and the *Concerts des amateurs* (1769); the *Grosses Konzert* (Frankfurt, 1740); the *Liebhaber Konzert* (Berlin, 1770); and concerts by the *Tonkünstler Sozietät* (Vienna, 1771). Some concerts by the *Sozietät* included many performers. According to a review in the *Wiener Zei-*

tung, Haydn used an orchestra of over one hundred and eighty performers for a concert in 1793 which included some of his works written for England.[6]

Aside from regular concerts, subscription concerts were organized by individual musicians, including Mozart and Beethoven in Vienna. Mozart had planned a series of quartet concerts during the 1790–91 season;[7] such chamber music series gradually established themselves early in the nineteenth century. During this age public concerts took place in theaters or in larger rooms normally serving other purposes. (See illustration p. 70.) The first concert hall in the modern sense of the word opened in Vienna in 1831.[8]

Traveling virtuosos appeared in such numbers toward the end of the eighteenth century that they often played to nearly empty houses.[9] Nicolai's vivid description of musical life in Vienna includes some criticism of audiences who played cards and took refreshments during concerts.[10] He and other travelers comment on the many serenades that took place during the summer months in the city's major squares and, privately, in the enclosed courtyards of many houses. Serenades, involving vocal and instrumental groups of all sizes, were especially popular on the evenings before important feast days; they would draw large crowds which followed the musicians from one place to another.

Solo recitals, so common after the mid-nineteenth century, were unusual. Sonatas (for piano, violin, cello, for instance) would be heard in the home or in some other intimate setting. In a public recital an artist was more likely to present concertos, operatic excerpts, and other works with orchestral accompaniment. The exception is stressed in a concert announcement for April 3, 1781: After a symphony "by Chevalier Wolfgang Amadi Mozart the Chevalier will be heard, all by himself, playing on a Piano Forte." (See illustration on page 76.)

Solo instruments heard increasingly often in the late eighteenth century were the guitar (see below, p. 247), string bass, and harp, its pedal mechanism having been greatly improved by Sébastien Erard (1752–1831).

[6]C. F. Pohl, *Denkschrift aus Anlass des 100-jährigen Bestehens der Tonkünstler-Sozietät* . . . (Vienna, 1871), pp. 43ff. Not only did orchestras during the Classic period vary greatly in size, but the figures given in accounts of the time are at times misleading. See Neal Zaslaw, "Improvised Ornamentation in Eighteenth-Century Orchestras," *JAMS,* 39 (1986), 573ff.

[7]See his letter to Konstanze, October 8, 1790.

[8]O. Biba, "Concert Life in Beethoven's Vienna," *Beethoven, Performers and Critics* (Detroit, 1980) p. 77. See also the same author's "Grundzüge des Konzertwesens . . .," 132–48.

[9]Eberhard Preussner, *Die bürgerliche Musikkultur,* 2nd ed. (Kassel, 1950), p. 46.

[10]Friedrich Nicolai, *Beschreibung einer Reise durch Deutschland und die Schweiz, im Jahre 1781* . . . (Berlin, 1783–84), IV: 552.

[11]Domenico Dragonetti (1763–1846) was a composer-performer well known in London and Vienna.

Nachricht.

Morgen Dienstag den 3ten April 1781. wird
in dem k. k. priv. Schauspielhause nächst dem Kärntnerthore
Zum Vortheile
der errichteten Tonkünstlergesellschaft
gehalten werden

Eine große musikalische Akademie,

in welcher den Anfang machet

Eine Sinphonie, von der Komposition des Herrn Ritters Wolfgang
Amadi Mozart, in wirklichen Diensten Sr. Hochfürstlichen Gnaden des
Erzbischofs von Salzburg.

Dann wird sich Herr Ritter Mozart ganz allein auf einem Piano
Forte hören lassen.

Es war selber bereits als ein Knabe von sieben Jahren hier, und hat
sich schon damals theils in Absicht auf die Komposition, als auch in
Ansehung der Kunst überhaupt, und der besonderen Fertigkeit, und
Delikatesse im Schlagen den allgemeinen Beyfall des Publikums erworben.

Darauf folgt zum zweytenmal das Haupttanz Drama,
von Friederich Wilhelm Zacharià, genannt:

Die Pilgrime auf Golgatha.

Ganz neu in Musik gesezt, von Hrn. Georg Albrechtsberger,
Kaiserl. Königl. Hofmusikus.

Wobey die Hauptstimmen singen werden, als:

Die Rolle des ersten Pilgrims.	Mlle. Cavalieri.
Die Rolle des Engels.	Mlle. Teyber.
Die Rolle des zweyten Pilgrims.	Hr. Adamberger.
Die Rolle des Einsiedlers.	Hr. Fischer.

Chor der Pilgrime.

Die Einlaßpreise sind folgende:

		fl	kr
Erster Parterre		1	25
Zweyter Parterre und vierter Stock		—	24
Dritter Stock		—	40
Fünfter —		—	10
Logen ersten und zweyten Stock		4	14
dritten —		3	—
Gesperrter Siz		1	42

Die Bücher vom musikalischen Drama sind beym Logenmeister für 10 kr. zu haben.

Der Anfang ist um halb 7 Uhr.

Concert announcement for "A Grand Musical Academy," April 3, 1781. According to Deutsch, this was Mozart's first public performance in Vienna, given with the Salzburg archbishop's reluctant permission, and in the presence of the emperor. Austrian National Library.

In view of all this flourishing musical activity we can well understand Mozart's enthusiasm as reflected in a letter from Vienna (April 4, 1781): "This is a magnificent place; for my profession the best in the world."

Concert programs from this age impress us by their length: Audiences for whom a concert may have been more of an event than it is today must have had substantial musical appetites and endurance, considering that halls were inadequately, if at all, heated. A benefit program that Beethoven gave on April 2, 1800 included a Mozart symphony, a Beethoven piano concerto performed by the composer, his First Symphony, and several other works. Another benefit concert in 1808 lasted four hours. The concert during which the "Eroica" Symphony was first performed ("A Grand Musical Academy, with Augmented Orchestra") must have lasted at least that long.

Mozart, in a letter to his father (March 29, 1783), describes one of his academies, also of substantial length. On this program the individual movements of symphonies were separated from each other by the performance of other pieces, a procedure that would appear improper to most

Announcement of concert at which Beethoven's "Eroica" Symphony ("A grand new symphony in D-sharp") was first performed. Austrian National Library.

conductors and audiences today. In general, the eighteenth century was less bothered by considerations of stylistic unity and propriety. Some operas were written by composer-apprentice teams, with the latter providing the recitatives; for others several composers contributed an act each. Great flexibility was observed in performing orchestral works; instruments not specified by the composer may have been added for outdoor performance.

Great amounts of new music were constantly needed for the vigorous musical activity of the era. We cannot but marvel at the list of works that Haydn "remembered to have written from his 18th to 73rd year" (recorded in the so-called *Haydn-Verzeichnis* made by Johann Elssler in 1805): it includes over 100 symphonies, 118 baryton trios, 83 quartets, 48 sonatas and trios for the piano, 14 Masses, and many other works. Though the figures may not be entirely accurate, the output is impressive in most categories of music. The number of substantial works written decreases as the size of the individual work increases. Haydn's symphonies exemplify the trend: from 1760–70 he wrote approximately 40 symphonies, followed by approximately 30 between 1770 and 1780 and 21 between 1780 and 1790.

It is important to remember that much of this activity was carried on by composers who today are little known or forgotten, but whose music enjoyed widespread popularity in the late eighteenth and early nineteenth centuries. The neglect of some of this music—music by Clementi, Hässler, Hoffmeister, Kozeluch, Pleyel, Vanhal, and Wölfl, to mention but a random few—is unfortunate and undeserved. (Some, to be sure, is justly forgotten!) In recent years a small selection has again become available in modern editions.

The social and political upheavals of the Napoleonic era (see below, pp. 233ff) found ample reflection in music. Examples are the "battle pieces," not unknown in Renaissance and Baroque music but now revived with a view to commercial success. Beethoven's "Battle" Symphony (*Wellington's Victory;* see below, p. 226) is an orchestral example; programmatic piano compositions were popular also. Vanhal contributed several, such as "The Great Naval Battle of Abukir (August 1–3, 1798), Dedicated to the Hero, Sir Horatio Nelson."[12] Such pieces, far from subtle, were intended to cash in on the headlines of the day; other compositions resulted from more profound thoughts about the events of the time.

Much of the tremendous musical output of the age never reached print, since it was commissioned for specific occasions. Nor did publication always mean printing: Houses such as Breitkopf in Leipzig sold music in manuscript copies, even distributing catalogues of music available from them in that form. Many copyists made a living by selling manuscript cop-

---

[12]Haydn's *Nelson Mass* was written during July and August 1798. Nelson visited Eisenstadt two years later.

Title page for Vanhal's "Characteristic Sonata for Clavier or Piano Forte" entitled "The Great Naval Battle at Abukir." Austrian National Library.

ies, authorized or otherwise. Burney complains that he was "plagued" by Viennese copyists: "They began to regard me as a greedy and indiscriminate purchaser of whatever trash they should offer."[13] Nevertheless, the amount of instrumental music that was engraved (in parts only, seldom in scores) reflects the ever-growing group of consumers. Now publication began to be of economic importance for the composer, who no longer had regular employment, while in earlier times it had mostly been a matter of prestige, the cost usually having been assumed by the patron to whom the work was dedicated. Publication, as well as the public concert, made success dependent on the taste of a larger public. Concern with mass appeal, therefore, became an increasingly important aspect of late eighteenth-century and nineteenth-century music.

"Unethical" is the adjective often used to describe Beethoven's dealings with his publishers, notably his repeated offering of one and the same work to several publishers. Our judgment of Beethoven and others in this regard will be somewhat more lenient if we remember some of the peculiar and complicated conventions of the time with regard to author's rights. Before the Classic period safeguards were slow to evolve, and what little pro-

[13]Burney, *The Present State . . . Germany . . .*, I: 263.

tection there was differed from one country to another.[14] For the composer this meant a lack of material benefit from his works as soon as they were out of his physical control, duplicated through manuscript copies or publication. A newly engraved work might be offered on a subscription basis first; after that it might be published and sold at a somewhat lower price. Thus it was to the composer's disadvantage to have a printed edition appear before all possible subscribers had been solicited. As soon as publication had taken place, the composer felt free to offer the same work to other publishers, especially abroad. If he did not do so, others might, for their own profit. These "pirated" editions were plentiful, and composers who had achieved some success necessarily developed business acumen and often considerable shrewdness for their own protection. Mozart's opera *Die Entführung* had been an immediate success. To benefit from this, the composer soon prepared various arrangements and a vocal score, but a pirated edition of the latter appeared in print before Mozart was able to finish his own.[15]

Laws for the protection of authors had been enacted in England and France before the beginning of the nineteenth century.[16] In Germany a copyright law was not universally accepted until 1856.

BIBLIOGRAPHICAL NOTES

Much background material on the Classic period is provided in Henry Raynor, *A Social History of Music* (London, 1972). Other recommended sources include *NOHM*, VIII, Introduction and Chapter 1 ("General Musical Conditions"); *SMH*, Chapter XVI ("The European Scene"); the diaries and other writings of Charles Burney, in addition to the excerpts in *SMH*; Carol McClintock, *Readings in the History of Music in Performance* (Bloomington, 1979), Part IV, and "Vienna, 1800," an account taken from a musical journal of that year, as translated in P. Weiss and R. Taruskin, eds., *Music in the Western World* (New York: Schirmer Books, 1984), pp. 321ff.

Further information on music printing, publishing, conducting, and the composition of orchestras is contained in Adam Carse's *The Orchestra in the Eighteenth Century* (Cambridge, 1940) and in the study by Zaslaw cited above. The treatises by C. P. E. Bach and Leopold Mozart, mentioned repeatedly in the text, are good sources of information about musical prac-

[14]This complex subject is discussed in some detail in "*Urheberrecht*," *MGG*. See also J. Sachs, "Hummel and the Pirates: the Struggle for Musical Copyright," *MQ*, 54 (1973), 31ff.

[15]Blume, "Mozart," *MGG*.

[16]See the public notices published by Beethoven in 1803 and Weber in 1826, quoted by Preussner, *Die bürgerliche Musikkultur*, pp. 186ff.

tices of the era; Türk's *Klavierschule* has been translated into English (Lincoln, NB: University of Nebraska Press, 1982).

Details on the beginnings of public concerts are given in the articles "Konzertwesen" in *MGG* and "Concert (ii)" in *Grove 6*. The articles on major cities ("London," "Paris," "Vienna," etc.) in *Grove 6* augment the picture. Two important works in German should be mentioned for the general cultural and musical background respectively: Richard Benz, *Die Zeit der deutschen Klassik* (Stuttgart, 1953); Eberhard Preussner, *Die bürgerliche Musikkultur,* 2nd ed. (Kassel, Bärenreiter, 1950). The second chapter of H. C. R. Landon, *Essays on the Viennese Classical Style* (London, 1970), also describes the musical life of the period.

FIVE

HAYDN AND MOZART

JOSEPH HAYDN (1732-1809)

In the short autobiographical sketch that he was asked to write in 1776 for inclusion in *Das gelehrte Oesterreich* Haydn gave this account of his career:

I was born *anno* 1732 the last of March in the hamlet of Rohrau in Lower Austria, near Bruck on the Leytha River. My father was a wheelwright by profession . . . and had a natural love for music. Without being able to read music he played the harp, and when I was a boy of five I was able to repeat all of his short and simple songs. This caused my father to send me to Hainburg in the care of the school director, a relative, so that I might learn there the rudiments of music and other elementary general subjects. The almighty God (to whom alone be thanks for His bountiful grace) gave me enough musical talent so that in my sixth year I was able to sing along with the choir during Mass and to play some on the violin and piano. When I was seven years old the [Imperial] Kapellmeister von Reutter [Georg Reutter, jr., 1708–72] came through Hainburg. He happened to hear my small but pleasing voice and accepted me at once for the *Kapellhaus* [in Vienna]. Aside from being instructed in academic subjects I learned from excellent teachers how to sing and had instruction in piano and violin. Until I reached the age of eighteen[1] I sang there, with much applause, soprano parts, both at St. Stephen's Cathedral and at court. When my voice finally changed I barely managed to stay alive by giving music lessons to children for about eight years. In this way many talented people are ruined: They have to earn a miserable living and have no time to study. I had this experience myself, and I would never have reached this moderate degree of success if I had not continued to compose diligently during the nights as well. I wrote a great deal, but I lacked the solid grounding until I had the good fortune to be taught the fundamentals of composition by the famous Mr. Porpora [Niccolò Porpora, 1686–1766] who lived in Vienna during this time. Through the recommendation of Mr. von Fürnberg (who showed me special kindness) I eventually was given a position as music director to Count Morzin, and following this as Kapellmeister to His Highness Prince Esterházy; there it is my desire to live and to die.

Haydn's musical career thus began in a very simple setting—promising but far from spectacular. He was no child prodigy; later in life he continued to be modest about his performing abilities: "I was no sorcerer [*Hexenmeister*] on any instrument, but I knew the possibilities and effects of each." To be accepted for the *Kapellhaus* no doubt was considered a stroke of good fortune for a lad from the country, amounting to a free primary and secondary education, along with room and board. But the choir boys did not receive musical training beyond what was considered immediately useful. Inasmuch as no instruction in the rudiments of composition was available to him, the boy tried to study the subject himself from a copy of Fux's *Gradus ad Parnassum*. Some of his youthful attempts attracted the attention of the busy Reutter, then at the height of his career. Years later Haydn recalled how Reutter "laughed at these immature creations, at parts which no voice or instrument could execute, and he reprimanded me for writing in sixteen voices before I had mastered two-part counterpoint."

Haydn spoke with feeling about the hardships following his dismissal from the court chapel, a period of poverty and struggle. On the recommendation of a bookseller he bought Emanuel Bach's *Versuch*. Dies and Griesinger, Haydn's early biographers, agree on the influence Emanuel Bach exerted on Haydn, not only through his treatise but also through the "Prussian" sonatas, which Haydn discovered in the 1750s. "I could not tear myself away from my pianoforte until I had played them. Whoever knows me well must realize that I owe a great deal to Emanuel Bach."

Vienna afforded many (if poorly paid) opportunities for a talented young musician. On Sunday mornings at eight Haydn played the violin at

---

[1]Seventeen, according to Griesinger. See also A. van Hoboken, *Discrepancies in Haydn Biographies* (Washington, DC: 1962).

An early edition (1781) of Haydn's songs, showing typical Classic design. Museum Salzburg.

one church, two hours later the organ at a private princely chapel, and at eleven sang at the cathedral.

His appointment in 1759 as music director to Count Morzin gave Haydn for the first time what promised to be a relatively secure existence. Unlike some noblemen whose musical interests waned in the summer, Count Morzin enjoyed music-making at his country residence, Lukavec, in Bohemia. Haydn wrote at least one symphony for the Count. Allegedly the work pleased Prince Paul Anton Esterházy, and when, due to financial difficulties, Morzin was forced to disband his orchestra, Haydn, who had recently married, entered Prince Paul's services as Vice-Kapellmeister, moving to Eisenstadt in 1761.

The Prince, who played both violin and cello, was anxious to modernize his musical establishment. Gregor Joseph Werner (1695–1766; Kapellmeister from 1728) had distinguished himself as a composer in the Baroque tradition of the "strict" style. In spite of Werner's occasional hostility, Haydn regarded him with esteem and respect. A fairly clear separation of their responsibilities, spelled out in Haydn's contract, avoided more serious conflict: Werner remained in charge of sacred music; in all other musical matters Haydn was in command. The contract, ratified on

May 1, 1761, is a detailed document; from it we learn much about the manifold tasks of an eighteenth-century Kapellmeister with regard to both musical and administrative matters.[2]

Prince Paul died within a year of this agreement. His successor was Nicholas I (reigned 1762–90) who came to be called "The Magnificent" because of his ambitions to emulate court life in Vienna and Versailles. Early in his reign he built an extensive and lavish summer castle, Esterháza, on Neusiedl Lake (today Esterháza is in Hungary while Eisenstadt remains in Austria); the shallow lake and surrounding swampy terrain formed an ideal hunting preserve. An opera house, palace, and formal gardens provided the setting for all kinds of music-making, so that Haydn's talents were put to good use during the summer months as well. The beauty of Esterháza and the magnificence of its entertainments became widely known and attracted many distinguished visitors. (Sadly neglected and vandalized at the end of World War II, it is now being restored.) The Empress stayed at Esterháza in 1773; she was particularly impressed by Haydn's opera *L'infedeltà de-*

Vienna: Michaelsplatz and (right) the old Burgtheater. Mozart's *Entführung, Figaro,* and *Cosi fan Tutte* were first given here. Colored engraving by Postl. Vienna, Austrian National Library.

[2]Quoted in full in Geiringer, *Haydn: A Creative Life in Music,* 3rd ed. (Berkeley, CA: University of California Press, 1982), pp. 43 ff.

PROSPECT NACH DEM GARTEN UND WALD GEGEN SÜDEN.

PROSPECT DER FÜRSTLICHEN   RESIDENZ ESZTERHAZ VON DEN
        HAUPT THOR   GEGEN NORDEN.

Two views of Esterháza Castle, ca. 1784. Austrian National Library.

lusa, causing her to remark—greatest compliment of all—that if she wanted
to hear good opera, she would go to Esterháza.

In this environment Haydn could barely keep up with the demand
for new compositions of all kinds. The manuscript of a horn concerto dated
1762 carries the remark "written in my sleep"; we can assume that the pro-

An opera performance, about 1775. According to tradition, the painting represents a performance at Esterháza of Haydn's opera *L'incontro improvviso*, with the composer at the harpsichord.[3]

verbial midnight oil was burned for many other works as well. The Prince, pleased with a new composition, might give orders to pay Haydn a bonus, at the same time requesting "six more pieces like the ones just sent"—to be delivered, of course, at once. He was an enthusiastic player of the baryton (a string instrument related to the viola da gamba, with sympathetic strings plucked by the left thumb) and constantly demanded new music for his instrument. Haydn provided his employer with well over one hundred fifty baryton compositions.[4]

In spite of visits by distinguished artists, traveling virtuosos, and theater troupes, Haydn felt artistically isolated; while admittedly this forced him "to become original," he often wished for greater opportunities to travel. Nicholas valued the services of his Kapellmeister (since 1766) so highly that he rarely granted him even a few days' leave to go to Vienna, to say nothing of the journey to Italy which Haydn, quite active as a composer of operas, was most anxious to undertake. There was some consolation in the fact that under the Prince's patronage—the musicians were

[3]The accuracy of this attribution has been doubted; see Laszlo Somfai, *Joseph Haydn: sein Leben in zeitgenössischen Bildern* (Kassel: Bärenreiter, 1966).
[4]See Oliver Strunk, "Haydn's Divertimenti for Baryton, Viola and Bass," *MQ*, 18 (1932), 216–51.

paid better than those in Vienna—music-making of high quality was possible, with ample opportunity for Haydn to experiment in his compositions and to put the experiments to the test by having them performed at once by competent musicians.

The relative seclusion and many responsibilities did not prevent Haydn from making a name for himself in faraway places. The *Wiener Diarium* of 1766 refers to him as "the darling of our nation"; ten years later he is commissioned to write an opera for the reopening of the *Hof-und Nationaltheater* in Vienna—a mark of distinction even though, due to various intrigues, the work was not performed there. By 1780, his music had found

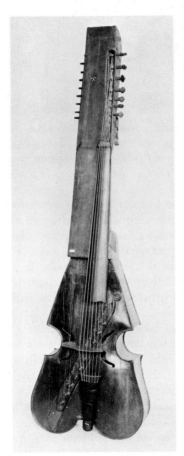

Baryton, Austria, 1779. The favorite instrument of Prince Esterházy, for which Haydn wrote many compositions. The Metropolitan Museum of Art, The Crosby Brown Collection of Musical Instruments, 1889.

recognition in Spain, France, England, and other distant countries, resulting in numerous commissions, such as the "Seven Last Words" for the cathedral in Cadiz (1785), the six "Paris" symphonies of 1784, and the concertos requested by King Ferdinand IV of Naples (1786). The 1780s also marked the beginning of Haydn's friendship with Mozart and his joining the order of Freemasons.[5] Repeated invitations were extended to Haydn to go to England; they were declined by the composer, who apparently was reluctant to resign altogether from his position and who knew that an extended leave was not likely to be granted.

Events took a new turn with the death of Nicholas in 1790. His successor, Prince Anton, displayed very little interest in music and dismissed virtually all the court musicians. Haydn was retained as Kapellmeister but, for the first time in his life, was given freedom to leave the Esterházy domains. Now he gladly accepted the invitation of the violinist and concert manager, Salomon, to go to London. He was almost fifty-nine years old, and the long journey to a country in which an unfamiliar language was spoken must have seemed like an extraordinary adventure to Haydn, as it did to some of his friends (including Mozart) who tried to dissuade him. But England's active concert life and the attractive financial arrangements proposed by Salomon prevailed over all scruples: On New Year's Day, 1791, Haydn set foot on English soil.

His stay proved extremely successful. A very appreciative public displayed great interest in him as a person and composer; members of the royal family and many influential citizens showered him with invitations and honors, culminating in a doctor's degree conferred at Oxford in July, 1791. After years of comparative restriction and servitude Haydn could write to his friend Marianne von Genzinger, "How sweet is the taste of liberty!" He was flattered by the many displays of esteem and amazed by the financial success then possible only in England. Music-making on the scale he encountered there, especially the size and quality of the orchestras, impressed and inspired him and affected the style of his own works, particularly the symphonies. Handel commemorations had been held in Westminster Abbey for some years, with massed performances of excerpts or entire oratorios. Haydn attended several of these and was profoundly moved. These experiences were still vividly before him when some years later he wrote his own large oratorios, *The Creation* and *The Seasons*.

Haydn left London in the summer of 1792. On his way home he stopped in Bonn and met the young Beethoven, who was soon to study with him in Vienna. After the excitement and satisfactions of London,

---

[5]Jacques Chailley describes the many ways in which Masonic ideas are reflected in Haydn's music in "Joseph Haydn and the Freemasons," *Studies in Eighteenth-Century Music: a Tribute to Karl Geiringer on his Seventieth Birthday* (New York: Da Capo, 1970), pp. 117 ff. Mozart's own, more active involvement in Freemasonry is well documented.

Haydn felt let down on his return to the Austrian capital: Few people seemed to take notice. The sudden death of Marianne von Genzinger contributed to his low spirits. When, in the summer of 1793, Salomon broached the subject of a second trip to England, Haydn's acceptance seems to have depended only on the consent of Prince Anton; once this was obtained, preparations were made and Haydn started out in January, 1794. His last six symphonies were written for this new series of Salomon concerts, which again brought artistic and financial success to the composer. One marvels at the energy and the diversified interests of the sixty-two-year-old Haydn, who not only conducted his symphonies from the keyboard, composed much other music, concerned himself with the soloists, orchestra members, and other musicians, but also had an open eye for life around him, for the history and sights of England. (On his travels as well as in London he committed his impressions to notebooks and diaries.) During his second stay in London, his relations to the royal house became even closer. Haydn was pleased but nevertheless declined invitations to remain in England, for reasons not altogether known. The death of Prince Anton and the accession of the musically more ambitious Prince Nicholas II, who had asked Haydn to return, provided an official reason; there may have been others of a personal nature. Haydn's relation to his new employer was none too cordial; fortunately, he could delegate some of his former duties to other court musicians, saving his own strength for composing.

The Prince's interest in sacred music resulted in a series of six Masses written between 1796 and 1802, for the name day of Princess Maria Hermenegild. They were substantial works, but few other compositions were required of Haydn, who could now devote himself to the realization of another plan close to his heart since the London journeys: an oratorio about the story of creation. A poetic text, based on Milton's *Paradise Lost*, was translated for Haydn by Baron Gottfried van Swieten (1734-1803), the diplomat and musical amateur in whose house Mozart had received important musical impressions. Work on *The Creation* took up all of 1797. Haydn approached the gigantic task with reverence. "Daily I asked God on my knees to give me strength for my work." Feeling that old age was upon him, he summoned his physical, spiritual, and musical resources to make this work a crowning achievement of his long career, a work by which he would want to be remembered by posterity. His ambition was fully realized: In spite of some quite critical reviews, the work achieved immediate and lasting popularity. It reflects Haydn's prestige that several Viennese noblemen paid him a substantial fee for the score, underwrote all costs of the performance, then returned the score to him (so he could offer it to a publisher) along with the receipts from the performance—all this to insure that *The Creation* would be brought out in Vienna rather than London.

Greatly pleased by his success, Haydn, in spite of worsening health,

Heute Dienstag den 19ten März 1799.

wird in dem K. K. Hoftheater nächst der Burg

aufgeführt:

Die Schöpfung.

Ein Oratorium

in Musik gesetzt

von Herrn Joseph Haydn, Doktor der Tonkunst, und hochfürstlich-Esterházyschen Kapellmeister.

Nichts kann für Haydn schmeichelhafter seyn, als der Beyfall des Publikums. Den zu verdienen hat er sich stäts eifrigst bestrebt, und ihn bereits oft, und mehr, als er es sich versprechen durfte, zu erwerben das Glück gehabt. Nun hoffet er zwar für das hier angekündigte Werk diejenige Gesinnung, die er zu seinem innigen Troste und Danke bis jetzt erfahren hat, ebenfalls zu finden; doch wünscht er noch, daß auf den Fall, wo zur Aeußerung des Beyfalls sich etwann die Gelegenheit ergäbe, ihm gestattet seyn möge, denselben wohl als ein höchstschätzbares Merkmahl der Zufriedenheit, nicht aber als einen Befehl zur Wiederhohlung irgend eines Stückes anzusehen, weil sonst die genaue Verbindung der einzelnen Theile, aus deren ununterbrochenen Folge die Wirkung des Ganzen entspringen soll, nothwendig zerstöret, und dadurch das Vergnügen, dessen Erwartung ein vielleicht zu günstiger Ruf bey dem Publikum erwecket hat, merklich vermindert werden müßte.

Der Anfang ist um 7 Uhr.

Die Eintrittspreise sind wie gewöhnlich.

Die Worte werden bey der Kassa gratis ausgegeben.

Announcement of first public performance of Haydn's *Creation*, March 19, 1799. The audience is asked to refrain from insisting on encores since these "of necessity destroy the effect of the whole." Austrian National Library.

agreed to van Swieten's plan of collaboration on another oratorio, based on James Thomson's poem *The Seasons*. Again van Swieten provided the libretto, along with numerous unsolicited instructions for the composer. Haydn was not happy with the text; later he blamed the infirmities of his last years on the great efforts its composition had required. Nevertheless, *The Seasons*, first performed under Haydn's direction in 1801, was another great success. A reviewer could justly say that the master's "inexhaustible genius . . . is admired from Lisbon to St. Petersburg and Moscow." In 1804, Haydn was made an honorary citizen of Vienna where many benefit performances of both oratorios had provided substantial sums for charitable purposes.

Few works followed *The Seasons*. Aware of his declining powers, Haydn devoted much time to putting his affairs in order. The "catalogue of all compositions which I remember offhand to have written from my 18th to 73rd year" was compiled in 1805 by Johann Elssler, the copyist and servant who had accompanied him to England in 1794. Many visitors from abroad called on the famous man who, on days when he was feeling well, enjoyed conversing and reminiscing.

Haydn's last public appearance was occasioned by a performance of *The Creation* by a group of amateurs at the University, on March 27, 1808. "To the sound of trumpets and drums, and accompanied by many of Vienna's lovers of the arts, Haydn was carried . . . to a place in front of the orchestra. . . . All who could get close to him expressed their veneration, their concern for his feeble state and their joy that he could be present on this happy day. . . . Fearing that too extended an emotional strain might endanger his health, the aged man asked to be carried out at the end of Part I. Tears were in his eyes when he took leave, and he stretched out his hand in blessing toward the orchestra." A painting of this memorable event, which Beethoven attended, was presented to Haydn by Princess Esterházy. A few months before his death, Haydn showed this painting to Reichardt.[6]

Haydn died on March 31, 1809, soon after the city had been shelled and occupied by French troops. A few days before, a French army officer had come to call on him, expressing his profound admiration and singing for him an aria from *The Creation*. At the memorial service on June 15 Mozart's *Requiem* was performed, in the presence of many French officials and generals.

In spite of great successes and the many honors bestowed on him, great modesty and sincerity were Haydn's outstanding traits. His admiration and affection for Mozart, his younger colleague, speak in an often-quoted remark addressed to Leopold Mozart in 1785: "I tell you before God and in all honesty: Your son is the greatest composer I know, in person or by reputation. He has taste and composes with great knowledge." The simplicity of Haydn's background, coupled with an equally simple, sincere religious faith, may account for these traits. He practiced his religion by showing generosity to relatives and others, by being charitable in his judgment, and by displaying an eagerness to help and encourage young composers. His kindness to the musicians under him and his fatherly concern for their well-being were expressions of the same modesty. According to Dies the appellation "Papa Haydn" was used, affectionately, by Mozart and other friends and pupils. A later age unfortunately misapplied it to his music, creating the image of Haydn as a jovial composer of old-fashioned pieces.

He was philosophical about his inferior social position during most of his life: Self-control and lack of artistic "temper" distinguished his personality from that of Beethoven—a difference which may partly explain why no real friendship developed between the two.

---

[6]The occasion is described in Reichardt's letter of November 30, 1808, translated in *SMH*, pp. 730 ff. See also H. C. R. Landon, *Haydn:* Bloomington, IN: Indiana Univ. Press, 1976–80, 358 ff. *Haydn: Chronicle and Works V.*

Performance of Haydn's *The Creation*, March 27, 1808. This was the composer's last public appearance. Painting by Wigand. Austrian National Library.

Out of Haydn's love for the beauties of our world grew the gaiety and affirmative spirit apparent throughout all his creative periods. . . . Even in his advanced age this gaiety did not entirely desert him. Nurtured by his noble humanity and a victorious optimism maintained through all the vicissitudes of a long and arduous life, this radiant joyfulness again and again manifested itself, and Haydn considered it his mission to let his fellow beings share in his unique gift.[7]

If substance, restraint, and balance are important characteristics of Classic style, it is not difficult to see why they should be so well represented in the music of a composer whose personality contained these qualities to such a marked degree.

WOLFGANG AMADEUS MOZART (1756–91)

From his beginnings as a child prodigy to his last years, Mozart's life, so lacking in spectacular successes or international recognition, moved

[7]Geiringer, *Haydn,* p. 369.

along paths entirely different from that of Haydn. Mozart's father Leopold
was not only a professional musician but a well-educated, conscientious,
and industrious citizen of the world. He left his native Augsburg in 1737,
ostensibly to study theology at the Benedictine University in Salzburg, but
soon after his arrival turned away from this and other academic subjects
and devoted himself to music. After entering the Archbishop's service in
1743, he slowly rose through the ranks and attained the position of Vice-
Kapellmeister in 1763. Aside from composing and playing the violin he put
to good use his talents as a teacher; in fact, Leopold's most significant
achievements lay in that field. His *Violinschule*, a thorough and popular instruction book, was published in the year Wolfgang was born. Leopold's
talents as a teacher were applied with love and devotion to Wolfgang and
his sister, Maria Anna, whose unique musical abilities began to show themselves at a most tender age. Some biographers have represented Leopold
as a cruel and mercenary exploiter of his prodigy children, but the un-
selfishness with which he gave up the furthering of his own career speaks
against this. Leopold took complete charge of their education, musical and
otherwise, both at home and while traveling. Not to have reached the position of Kapellmeister must have hurt his pride, but it was no secret to him
that the many absences from his place of employment were in part to
blame for the Archbishop's coolness to father and son. Even after Wolfgang
had grown up and gone his own way, Leopold's zeal as a teacher and advi-
sor never stopped; however, well intended and sensible as they were, his
recommendations often produced a reaction opposite to that intended.

Leopold's German background—documented, for instance, by compositions in the instruction books he prepared for his children—was at vari-
ance with the Archbishop's preference for Italian music, yet it served as a
balancing and broadening element both in the Salzburg musical life in general and in the musical development of young Wolfgang.

Much information about Mozart's early life, some perhaps anec-
dotal, is contained in a famous letter by Andreas Schachtner, a musician-
friend of the Mozart family. It was written soon after Mozart's death and
contains reminiscences for use in the *Nekrolog* for the year 1791, published
by Schlichtegroll in 1793. Schachtner describes the little boy's precocity:
Neither games nor toys meant anything to him when he became engrossed
in music. Most activities had to be accompanied by music to satisfy him,
such as carrying toys from one room to another. He did whatever was to
be done wholeheartedly. "When he learned arithmetic the table, chairs,
walls, even the floor would be covered with chalk figures." He relates a
wonderful story—he "swears it is true"—about the four-year-old Wolfgang
writing a "concerto," and he recalls the unusually acute sense of pitch
which only two years later enabled the six-year-old to point out minute differences in the tuning of two violins that had been played on different days.

Wolfgang never attended schools of any kind. His nonmusical education may not have been extensive, though it included Latin and modern languages (Italian, French, and some English), which were of practical value on his journeys. A lifelong interest in opera led him to read dramatic literature; he was forever looking for suitable subjects and librettos. Salzburg had a flourishing theatrical life with a great variety of spoken and musical drama, including sacred plays written for and staged by students. From his childhood days, Mozart absorbed dramatic literature not only as a reader or spectator but as a participant and composer as well.

Mozart's many journeys represent milestones in his life. The first of these took the six-year-old boy and his eleven-year-old sister to the Elector's court in Munich; later in the same year a more extensive trip was organized, with the imperial court in Vienna as the main objective. The children's precocious talents charmed everyone including the Empress. Leopold wrote that Wolfgang "climbed on the Empress' lap and hugged and kissed her thoroughly." Less than half a year elapsed before the family set out again, this time on a journey of over three years' duration. At Paris and Versailles and at many courts along the way the children harvested successes and compliments. Yet Leopold accomplished more than a mere exhibition of the children's talents. To hear much music and to meet many musicians was an important part of Wolfgang's education; he was developing critical faculties, a keen interest in people, and a phenomenal memory. Musical impressions that he received were reflected sooner or later in his own compositions, which now began to appear in surprising numbers. His first violin sonatas, K. 6–9,[8] were published in Paris during 1764. In April of that year, the Mozarts reached London. The children appeared before the King and Queen; Wolfgang's ability to read music at sight impressed the King profoundly. The London Bach's warm interest in the boy has already been described, as well as its reflection in Mozart's music. (See pp. 58)

After this long absence from home—and, for Leopold, from his duties—less than a year was spent in Salzburg; hardly a sufficient "breather," it would seem, for the children, whose health left something to be desired. Musically Wolfgang had matured: The boy now had to be taken seriously as a composer. He was asked to contribute one act to the oratorio *Die Schuldigkeit des ersten Gebotes*, K. 35, the other acts being written by two prominent Salzburg colleagues: Michael Haydn (1737–1806) and Cajetan Adlgasser (1729–77). On another trip to Vienna (September 1767 to January 1769) Wolfgang was asked to write an opera (*La finta semplice*, K. 51) for the Emperor. This invitation was an honor, but the work was not performed. As a performer Mozart this time did not create the same sensa-

[8]Abbreviations refer to Köchel's thematic catalog of Mozart's works, using the old numbering. See above, "Abbreviations."

tion—the novelty had somehow worn off and the child prodigy now was all of twelve years old!

In November 1769, Wolfgang was appointed Salzburg Court Concertmaster, an honorary appointment involving no pay. Just before this he had composed for the ordination of a family friend a Mass, K. 66, one of a long list of sacred works written for specific occasions in Salzburg.

The following month Leopold and Wolfgang set out for the first of three journeys to Italy that were to have a profound influence on the young composer. He performed in aristrocratic circles and in public, but more and more his talents as a composer attracted the hoped-for attention. Lessons with Padre Martini of Bologna, the widely venerated master of the *stile antico*, led to Mozart's acceptance into the *Accademia filarmonica* of that city, though a point was stretched in his passing the required written examination. In Rome during Holy Week they heard Allegri's famous nine-part *Miserere* on which Wolfgang, according to Leopold's proud report, prepared a score from memory. Jommelli and others befriended the boy in Naples. Had he not accepted a contract to write an opera for Milan, there would have been many other such opportunities. The work in question, *Mitridate*, received much acclaim. The success of the voyage led to a second trip to Italy in August of the next year; a third trip lasted from October 1772 to March 1773. The number of compositions from these restless years is astounding. Included are many symphonies and sacred works for the Salzburg Court.

After another attempt to repeat earlier successes in Vienna (July to September 1773), Mozart for the first time spent more than an entire year at home. At the same time both he and his father realized more and more how limited a future Salzburg had to offer. That no attractive court position ever materialized, before or after the Italian trips, is one of the tragedies of Mozart's career. Difficulties with their employer, the Archbishop, increased—understandably so in view of Mozart's repeated requests for leave. In August 1777, he asked for his dismissal, which was readily granted. He was now free to try his luck elsewhere.

He believed strongly that travel was necessary—for himself, for any artist—to keep up with his field. "Without travel one is a poor creature." And so he promptly set off on another trip of over a year's duration. This time the father had to remain at home. Wolfgang, accompanied by his mother, stopped in Munich and Mannheim. The latter stay was prolonged due to the attraction of the fifteen-year-old Aloysia Weber, daughter of one of the Mannheim musicians. Again the correspondence between father and son is revealing: Wolfgang gave all kinds of reasons for staying in Mannheim except the most compelling one. Mannheim's musical life and Wolfgang's hope for a position there both contributed to the delay. The father, even by letter, tried to take charge and eventually succeeded in having

Wolfgang move on. "Off to Paris! *Aut Caesar aut nihil!*" (letter of February 12, 1778).

Paris, where Mozart arrived in March, brought few musical satisfactions. His disappointments were intensified by grief over his mother's death, and his loneliness in Paris provided the right psychological moment for Leopold to have Wolfgang consider a return to the Salzburg Court. "If I could have you here I surely would live many more years." Wolfgang continued to hope for engagements and composed whatever seemed marketable: violin sonatas, keyboard sonatas, his concerto for flute and harp, and some sets of keyboard variations. He gave lessons, succeeded in having some works performed at the *Concerts spirituels*, and made the acquaintance of publishers—but none of this was enough for a secure existence.

Reluctantly he started the voyage home, again stopping in Mannheim. An appointment as Court organist awaited him in Salzburg, but it was to be of short duration. A commission to write an opera (*Idomeneo*, 1781) for Munich raised his spirits somewhat, but he increasingly resented the Archbishop's autocratic treatment. He had already confessed to his father that "I would be so pleased if he [the Archbishop] wrote to me saying that he no longer needed me." The break came later in 1781; with Count Arco's famous foot kick, Mozart was dismissed from Colloredo's service.

In the meantime, the Weber family moved to Vienna and Aloysia

Vienna: St. Peter's church and square. Mozart lived here (house on the right) after leaving the employ of the Salzburg archbishop. Austrian National Library.

married the actor, Joseph Lange. After his dismissal, Mozart remained in
Vienna; strangely enough he took quarters with Aloysia's mother and
daughters, in spite of his father's strong disapproval. Teaching and composing at first kept Mozart busy and happy. *Die Entführung* attained immediate and lasting success. Soon after its first performance in 1782 Mozart married Konstanze Weber, a step for which his father never forgave him. The
young couple visited Salzburg the following year; Konstanze sang the soprano solo part in the *C Minor Mass* when the incomplete work was first
heard at St. Peter's.

　　Mozart, who earlier had distinguished himself as a violinist, now was
eager to make a name for himself in Vienna by appearing as a pianist, in
concerts given by himself and by others. Many of his piano concertos were
written during the 1780s, usually with a specific occasion in mind. When
his father came for a visit in 1785, things were still going tolerably well.
The Emperor, who thought highly of Mozart, attended several of his academies but did little else for him. Eventually there was an appointment as
Court composer, but there were next to no orders for compositions. As
"Court and Chamber Musician" his chief assignment was to provide dance
music (minuets, *Deutsche*, *Ländler*, contradances) for masked balls in the
Redoutensäle. When a salary was added to the title, it was a meager one,
and Mozart's last years, in spite of some notable successes *(Figaro*, 1786),
were beset by financial worries, aggravated by Konstanze's many sicknesses
and confinements.

　　In 1787, Mozart visited Prague where both *Die Entführung* and *Figaro* had been well received; the composer was already well known and
liked when he arrived in the Bohemian capital. He added to these successes by conducting *Figaro* and other works including the Symphony in
D, K. 504, and he signed a contract for a new opera to be produced in
Prague. Da Ponte again supplied the libretto as he had done for *Figaro* (see
below, p. 200). *Don Giovanni*, the result of their collaboration, turned out
to everyone's satisfaction, yet even the most complimentary reviews referred to an aspect of his music that was mentioned with increasing frequency from then on: the difficulty of execution. Many of Mozart's late
works lacked general acceptance because of musical and technical problems
with which performers and audiences, accustomed to the lighter fare of
Dittersdorf, Vanhal, and other fashionable composers, could not cope.

　　After *Don Giovanni*, Mozart's optimism about the future, which had
often worried his father, disappeared and reversed itself. There were many
setbacks. His lack of success at Court may have been partly responsible for
the fact that he now was less in demand as a performer. One of his academies in 1790 had to be cancelled for lack of subscribers. His last three symphonies, after his death and ever since among his most popular works,

Redout-Ankündigung.

Vermög Allerhöchster Begünstigung wird die Gesellschaft bildender Künstler in Wien, zum Vortheile ihres Wittweninstituts, den 24. November in den kaiserl. königl. Redouten-Sälen den zweyten maskirten Ball geben.

Voll Dankgefühles für den über ihre Erwartung gütigen Zuspruch vom verflossenen Jahre, gründet sie auch dieß Mahl ihre Hoffnung auf die Großmuth eines gefühlvollen hohen Adels und verehrungswürdigsten Publicums, welche wohlthätige Absichten so gern unterstützen.

Die Musik zu den Menuetten und deutschen Tänzen für den größern Saal ist eine ganz neue Bearbeitung von der Meisterhand des so beliebten k. k. Hofkammer-Kapellmeisters und Hofcompositors, Herrn Leopold Koželuch. Im kleinern Saale werden die Tänze von den berühmten Lieblings-Kapellmeistern Joseph Hayden, und Herrn Wolfgang Mozart gegeben werden.

Eintrittspreise, Beleuchtung, Masken, Erfrischungen, Zu- und Abfuhre, und alles Übrige ist nach dem Fuße der gewöhnlichen Redouten.

Wien den 16. November 1793.

Announcement of a masked ball in the two Redouten-Säle, November 24, 1793. "In the smaller hall, dances by the famous, favorite Kapellmeister, Joseph Hayden and Herr Wolfgang Mozart will be played."

were written in 1788 for a concert which did not materialize; quite possibly he never heard them performed.

In 1789, another journey took him to Dresden, Leipzig (where he played on Bach's organ at the St. Thomas Church), and Berlin. Of the six quartets he had planned to dedicate to the King of Prussia only three were written; in general the trip brought few material results. Once more a request for an opera, this time coming from the Emperor himself, gave him temporary encouragement: *Così fan tutte*, although written under most difficult and depressing circumstances, nevertheless turned out to be a delightful comedy with many downright farcical touches. It had been played five times when Joseph II died (February 1790); only after the official period of mourning did a few further performances take place.

Leopold II was crowned German Emperor in Frankfurt. No one had asked the Court composer Mozart to contribute to the occasion, but in an almost desperate attempt to gain official and public recognition, Mozart journeyed to Frankfurt at his own expense and arranged a concert at which he performed two piano concertos "of his own composition" (K. 459 and K. 537) as well as "a new great symphony" and other works.[9] The financial success, Mozart had to admit, was meager, and he left on the following day.

Work on *The Magic Flute* occupied much of Mozart's time in the first half of 1791, in collaboration with his friend and fellow Mason, Schikaneder. It was interrupted in July by the appearance of a mysterious messenger from an unidentified patron: Mozart, for a considerable fee, was to compose a Requiem Mass. The mystery, though not solved during the few remaining months of Mozart's life, upon examination loses much of its romantic flavor. Attempts by amateur composers to shine with someone else's work were not unheard of in the days before copyright protection. Mozart, in poor health and greatly depressed, was shaken by the experience and obsessed by the idea that this was to be his own Mass for the Dead.[10]

A further interruption came in the form of a last-minute request from Prague to write an opera for the coronation of Leopold II as King of Bohemia. Metastasio's often-composed libretto *La Clemenza di Tito* was given to Mozart, who had little more than two weeks to write the music. To accomplish this feat he enlisted the help of his pupil, Süssmayer, who wrote the recitatives. Both of them worked feverishly, even during their three-day journey to Prague. Success was only moderate. The Empress allegedly referred to *Tito* as *"una porcheria tedesca."*

All accounts agree that Mozart's health had deteriorated visibly and rapidly. The incredible haste with which work on *Tito* and *The Magic Flute* had to proceed make this plausible. The latter was performed in Vienna on September 30, less than a month after *Tito*. Death came on December 5; to the end Mozart felt compelled to continue to work on the *Requiem*, which he did not finish.

No easy generalizations will do for a description of Mozart's personality. It is as complex as the music in which it is reflected—music that is light and dark, exuberant and melancholic, humorous and profound. To Stendhal, a melancholy quality was at the heart of Mozart's music; other Romantics heard in it only lightness and serenity and tended to think of the man in the same way. Many listeners today may, with Stendhal, be aware of the melancholic quality, especially in certain late works, but would not consider it Mozart's most conspicuous trait. His life, far more than Haydn's, has received subjective interpretations by generations of bi-

---

[9]The announcement of this concert, October 15, 1790, is reproduced in *Grove 6*, XII: 715.

[10]Understandably, the story has fascinated writers ever since. A thorough account of what is known and unknown about the creation and completion of the *Requiem* is given by Friedrich Blume, "Requiem but no Peace," *MQ*, 47 (1961), 147 ff.

ographers. So much has been invented, covered up, excused, distorted, and dramatized that it is good to have the composer's own letters as valuable primary sources of information. To many who worship Mozart's music the very human traits revealed in his correspondence have seemed disturbing, especially the letters to his cousin, Maria Anna Thekla, almost all of which contain coarse jokes, puns, and obscenities. In a similar mood, perhaps as a pastime, Mozart wrote canons with texts that were soon suppressed since they did not fit the nineteenth century's picture of Mozart. Banter and lighthearted sociability were a necessary antidote and release to an artist with Mozart's sensitivity and powers for intense and concentrated work. The picture painted in Schlichtegroll's *Nekrolog* became widely known and accepted, establishing the notion that Mozart had reached artistic manhood very early but that "in all other ways he always remained a child." Today this picture has received far wider dissemination through the play and motion picture *Amadeus*.

That Mozart was sincerely religious need not be questioned, in spite of the fact that both he and his father were often critical and skeptical about institutionalized Catholicism. His wholehearted involvement in Freemasonry need not be interpreted as disbelief, since many Masons in eighteenth-century Austria considered themselves Christians and Catholics, even though state and church authorities viewed Masonic and other secret societies with understandable suspicion.

Mozart's vivid interest in people and his ability to evaluate and to describe them are amply demonstrated in his correspondence. Considering the wide range of his travels he gave surprisingly few descriptions of scenic or architectural beauties, but he was forever concerned with new acquaintances, musical or otherwise, whose personalities and talents he evaluated with candor, often quite critically. No wonder that a composer so interested in human beings should have had a lifelong interest in opera.

Some of these observations about Haydn's and Mozart's lives and personalities invite comparisons. Haydn's interest in the people he met, especially on the journeys that came so late in his life, did not overshadow his concern with the material world around him. In general, Haydn displayed greater ability to cope with practical requirements. His wisdom and success in economic matters stand in contrast to Wolfgang's constant difficulties. Mozart's stronger dissatisfaction with the reigning social order may account for his participation, more active than Haydn's, in Freemasonry, with its emphasis on brotherhood. Unlike Mozart, Haydn had a distinct affinity for nature, revealed in several of his works, but he lacked the powers of dramatic characterization of his younger colleague. Temperamentally they were much different; again this helps us to understand some of the differences of their careers. Haydn in general managed his gradual rise to success by making the right moves at the right time, by avoiding head-on

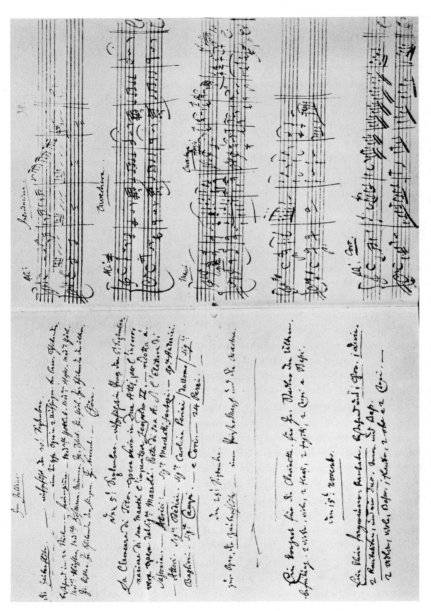

Mozart, "Catalog of all my works," autograph manuscript. Mozart began this thematic catalogue in 1784; the pages reproduced are the last two, of 1791, with entries for *The Magic Flute, La Clemenza di Tito,* the Clarinet Concerto, and the *Masonic Cantata,* K. 623. Austrian National Library.

clashes. Mozart, due to his temperament and a variety of circumstances, could not and did not want to avoid the clash at the Salzburg Court. He felt in general superior to his colleagues there, and he thus resented all the more being treated as a "lackey."

BIBLIOGRAPHICAL NOTES

Only a few important studies can be listed here. To obtain an idea of the extensive literature on Haydn and Mozart, the reader should consult the bibliographies at the end of their entries in *Grove 6*. For them and for other major composers, *Grove 6* also provides detailed and reliable lists of compositions. The early biographies of Haydn by Dies and Griesinger, based on personal acquaintance, have been translated and provided with an introduction and notes by V. Gotwals, in *Joseph Haydn, Eighteenth-Century Gentleman and Genius* (Madison, WI: University of Wisconsin Press, 1963). A basic study, including discussion of the composer's works, is K. Geiringer's *Haydn: A Creative Life in Music,* 3rd ed. (Berkeley, CA 1982). The American scholar H. C. Robbins Landon has devoted his life to Haydn studies and has edited much of his music; his major books are *The Symphonies of Joseph Haydn* (London: Universal Edition, 1955, with supplement, 1961), *The Collected Correspondence and London Notebooks of Joseph Haydn* (London: Barrie & Rockliff, 1959), and *Haydn: Chronicle and Works*, 5 volumes (Bloomington, IN: University of Indiana Press, 1976-80). The article "Haydn" in *MGG* by J. P. Larsen and Landon is recommended. F. Blume's article "Klassik" in *MGG* has been incorporated in translation, in his *Classic and Romantic Music* (New York: Norton, 1970). A. van Hoboken's *Joseph Haydn: Thematisch-bibliographisches Werkverzeichnis* (Mainz, 1957–78), like the Köchel *Chronologisch-thematisches Verzeichnis* cited below, is far more than a mere list of works; it also contains a wealth of information on virtually every composition, including the existence and location of autograph manuscripts and citation of early editions. After several incomplete earlier attempts, a complete edition of Haydn's works, to consist of about 60 volumes, is being issued by the Haydn Institut of Cologne (1958–   ).

Valuable publications on Mozart in English include A. Einstein's *Mozart: His Character, His Work* (New York: Oxford, 1945) and *The Letters of Mozart and His Family*, ed. E. Anderson (London: Macmillan, 1938, rev. ed. 1966). Köchel's thematic catalog of Mozart's works has been revised several times, most recently in 1964 (6th ed.). Important biographies include that by O. Jahn, rev. H. Abert, *W. A. Mozart*, 7th ed. (Leipzig, 1955). Essays on various aspects of Mozart's life and works are contained in *The Creative World of Mozart*, ed. P. H. Lang (New York: Norton, 1963). F. Blume's article "Mozart" in *MGG* is outstanding and incorporates much recent research. Blume also contributed a chapter, "Mozart's Style and Influence," to *MC*.

The new complete edition of the works (Kassel, 1955–   ) includes Mozart's letters and volumes of pictorial and documentary material. The latter (ed. O. E. Deutsch) has been published in English as *Mozart, A Documentary Biography*, trans. E. Blom (Stanford, CA: Stanford University Press, 1966).

Some studies of individual categories of works by both composers are listed in the bibliographical notes of the chapters following. Many articles containing the results of recent Haydn and Mozart research are found in *The Haydn Yearbook* (1962–   ), *Haydn-Studien* (1965–   ), and *Mozart-Jahrbuch* (1950–   ).

part two

The Main
Musical Categories
of the Classic Period

SIX
THE CLASSIC SYMPHONY

HAYDN

In an earlier chapter, investigations of the origins of the Classic symphony led us to various countries and types of music, including the three-movement *sinfonia* of the London Bach, the earliest four-movement works by the Viennese Monn and Wagenseil, and the flourishing orchestral practices in Mannheim, Paris, and Italy. As knowledge of the pre-Classic and early Classic symphony has increased, the traditional view of Haydn as "father of the symphony" has had to be revised—a revision which in no way detracts from his stature as a symphonist.[1] Through most of his long and full life Haydn gave new dimensions to the symphony; his imagination and

---

[1]The phrase was already in use before Haydn's death: "Haydn, genius of the quartet and father of the symphony . . .," in "Übersicht des gegenwärtigen Zustandes der Tonkunst in Wien," *Vaterländische Blätter für den österreichischen Kaiserstaat* (May 31, 1808), pp. 49–55.

inventiveness, his constant desire to experiment, and his amazing productivity affected the development of the symphony more than the contribution of any other composer.

To give within these pages an account of all of Haydn's symphonies would be patently impossible; instead, we shall attempt to describe the main style features of his early, middle, and late symphonies, with specific references to a few important works.

Haydn's earliest symphonies, beginning with No. 1 of 1759,[2] show the variety in number and type of movements that we have encountered elsewhere during this period. There are three-movement *sinfonie* as well as works with added minuet, which was regularly included by Haydn after 1765. Slow introductions occur in some instances (Nos. 6, 7, 15); in subsequent works they are discarded, to return in No. 50 of 1773. Occasionally (Nos. 21, 22) we find an adagio that amounts to a complete opening movement rather than a mere introduction. But experimentation extended beyond the number and sequence of movements. With works being written for the requirements of the day—for local, immediate performance—Haydn took the capabilities of his players into consideration, giving prominent and difficult parts to those who were able to do justice to them. Several early works include *concertante* writing, at times to such an extent that they remind us of the Baroque concerto grosso. The lack of any rigid distinction in the early works between chamber music and orchestral music is also reflected in this practice: As Haydn developed a characteristic quartet style, soloistic passages became rare in his symphonies.

Experimentation further affected musical texture. Haydn's symphonies from the 1760s and 1770s contain many movements in a largely or completely contrapuntal manner (finale of No. 44), including the use of canon (in some of the minuets) and fugue (finales of Nos. 3, 13, and 40). Other minuets are rustic in character, as they often were in works by Monn and other Austrian contemporaries. This folk character appears in some later symphonies as well. Haydn never regarded the minuet as a fixed, conventional form but found new ingenious approaches to it. "I wish someone would try to compose a really new minuet," he once remarked in conversation; characteristically he did not wait for someone else to do so. Continuing the Baroque tradition, Haydn accords greater importance to the winds in the trio section, as in No. 22 with solos for English and French horns.

Names or titles have been given to many Haydn symphonies, but they seldom originated with the composer, reflecting instead the popularity of the works so named. Among those with authentic titles are Nos. 6, 7, and 8, written soon after Haydn had entered the service of the Esterházy family and entitled *Le Matin*, *Le Midi*, and *Le Soir*. The Prince himself

[2]Our numbering is that of the Breitkopf and Härtel edition, ed. E. Mandyczewski (1908–   ), which is also used in Hoboken's thematic catalogue.

may have suggested the idea of a series of symphonies on the times of the day, but we lack precise information about this or about the extent to which Haydn intended each work to be programmatic. *Le Midi* has no obvious program, but in the finale of *Le Soir* a stylized thunderstorm breaks loose. The title "La Tempesta" for this movement probably goes back to Haydn. All three symphonies contain extensive solo writing. Programmatic symphonies were written by others, among them Haydn's friend, the Viennese-born Karl Dittersdorf (1739–99; program symphonies based on Ovid's *Metamorphoses*, published in 1785).

Another early symphony demonstrating Haydn's constant experimentation is No. 26, "La Lamentatione." In several of its movements Haydn uses an ancient Gregorian Passion melody—a lamentation chant sung during Holy Week. The melody is stated as a *cantus firmus* by oboe I and violin II with much embroidery by the first violin. Such use of an ecclesiastical melody shows that Haydn must have thought of the symphony as being no longer purely social, entertainment music. *Cantus firmus* writing returns in at least one other symphony (No. 60, ca. 1775) but in general the experiment does not seem to have satisfied the composer. "La Lamentatione" ends with a minuet which in general character comes close to the later symphonic scherzo.

Great variety of form and instrumentation characterizes other works from this early period. They are far from primitive; their freshness and ingenuity may surprise the modern listener who knows only the more majestic Haydn of the London symphonies. No. 31 belongs here—the hunting symphony entitled *With the Horn Signal*, the score of which includes four horn parts of great difficulty. Instrumental color is amply supplied in the last movement, a set of variations. In a surprise ending Haydn brings back the opening bars of the first movement, showing that the idea of a cyclic symphony, so important in the nineteenth century, was not without earlier precedent.

The early 1770s were a period of crisis in Haydn's artistic development, though not, as far as is known, in his personal life. His symphonic writing shows a "storm and stress" quality in that a great number of movements are in minor and express intense, dark, and stormy moods. To this group belong No. 44 in E minor, the "Mourning" Symphony, and No. 49 "La Passione" of 1768, in F minor. The title of the latter is appropriate for the entire work but particularly so for the second movement with its leaps, syncopations, and generally restless mood.[3] The most famous example, however, is No. 45 in F♯ minor, the "Farewell" Symphony. The circumstances of its composition have often been told: To impress on the Prince that his musicians, after a long summer at Esterháza, were more than anx-

[3]The title may also derive from performances of this symphony during Passion or Holy Week.

ious to return to their families at Eisenstadt, Haydn provided the last movement with a coda, adagio, in which the parts end gradually, one by one. In the performance each player was directed to put away his instrument as soon as he had finished his part, to blow out the candle on his music stand and to leave, so that at the end only two solitary violinists were left. Despite this humorous ending, the "Farewell" Symphony is a stormy and serious work, supplying good examples of the qualities under discussion here. The same qualities (including agitated moods, abrupt dynamic changes, use of canon and other contrapuntal devices) figure in Haydn's string quartets of the same period. Barry Brook has pointed out that these *Sturm und Drang* qualities also characterize some works by French and Italian composers: "*Sturm und Drang* is part of a continuous thread of early Romantic thought that leads directly, through Beethoven, into the nineteenth century."[4]

No predictable layout (along the lines of sonata form) is found in the symphonies from this period, and great variety exists in the treatment of the second theme, when Haydn introduces one. In the "Farewell" Symphony the new theme does not appear until the development section, and then in the unexpected key of D major; it does not appear in the recapitulation. Haydn is fond of the "false reprise": After some development the main theme may return, only to be discarded before the real recapitulation begins. The element of surprise, harmonic and other, is an important feature of Haydn's "storm and stress" period;[5] humorous effects in these and later works are often the results of unexpected harmonic turns. Key relationships between movements may be distant—a reaction, perhaps, to the self-conscious simplicity of the *galant* style.

The results of years of experimentation appear in the symphonies from around 1780. Most noticeable is the change in the nature of themes in the opening movements: They seldom consist of the earlier triadic or scale figures. Instead, they have become more concise, simple, and pliable, thus lending themselves to the Classic technique of "working out," of development. Symphony No. 73, "La Chasse" of 1781, is among the first to reveal this technique, which was then being perfected in both symphony and quartet. The rhythm ♪ ♫ | ♩ emphasized toward the end of the slow introduction, becomes the basic ingredient of the allegro theme and permeates the movement from beginning to end. Orchestral color is displayed more vividly and frequently—not, as before, by isolating an individual instrument but by creating a full orchestral texture in which thematic material is entrusted to all participants including the woodwinds. Some finales

[4]B. Brook, "Sturm und Drang and the Romantic Period in Music," *Studies in Romanticism*, IX (1970), 269ff.
[5]See the examples given by Landon, *The Symphonies of Haydn*, pp. 326ff.

now show a mixture of sonata and rondo ingredients: What in a simple rondo (for example ABACABA) would be the C section now may be a development of A while the return of both the A and B portions may give the effect of a recapitulation to the last part of the movement.

The "Paris" Symphonies, Nos. 82 through 87 (1784–86), contain further examples of the new style features. Included in this group are several which acquired nicknames testifying to their popularity: "L'Ours" ("The Bear," No. 82, the name referring to the drone basses in the dancelike last movement); "La Poule" ("The Hen," No. 83, with "cackling" by the oboe in the first movement); "La Reine" ("The Queen," No. 85, with variations on a French melody that may have been a favorite of Queen Marie Antoinette). Aside from the innovations mentioned, the works contain more chromaticism (e.g., the first movement of Symphony 82, transition from first to second theme), perhaps as a result of Haydn's growing familiarity with Mozart's style. Experimentation with formal arrangements continues, but now it is the kind of experimentation that reveals mastery—a kind of playfulness rather than a tentative groping for acceptable solutions.

Symphonies Nos. 90, 91, and 92 were written in 1788. Of these No. 92, the "Oxford" Symphony, has become especially popular; the title derives from its performance in Oxford on the occasion of Haydn's doctorate in 1791. It may well be discussed together with Haydn's last twelve symphonies, written for and during the two London visits. Haydn's orchestra in these late works is large; great care is bestowed on the wind section as well as on the strings. The cello parts now frequently have melodic significance and are independent from the basses. Even timpani parts at times are given prominence. Solos are occasionally provided—a violin solo for Salomon, even a harpsichord solo for Haydn himself—but these are not on the *concertante* level of his early works. While in the slow movements of early Classic symphonies the woodwind instruments often were altogether silent, their participation now may be particularly eloquent (e.g., No. 104/II, measures 114ff). Entire phrases or sections of a movement may display expressive writing for winds only, forming an effective color contrast to the preceding sonorities.

We know that Haydn was anxious, particularly in the London symphonies, to create works on a grand, impressive scale, with brilliant and surprising effects, suited to the English taste and to London's concert life with its large orchestras and large audiences. The famous fortissimo chord that gave the "Surprise" Symphony its name represents such an effect. Haydn denied that its purpose had been to awaken someone in the audience, as countless later writers would have it. Special instrumentation helps to achieve the desired brilliance: In No. 100 a bugle call, prominent wind section, and special percussion (triangle, cymbals, bass drum) produce the famous stirring "military" effect.

An appropriately majestic mood is set by the slow introductions to the first movements of almost all the late symphonies. Other features distinguish these introductions from those occasionally found in earlier works: They are longer and musically more substantial. Often they are thematically related to the main, fast part of the movement, not necessarily its beginning, as in the "Oxford" Symphony (Example 6–1) and several of the

EXAMPLE 6–1. Haydn, *Symphony No. 92,* "Oxford," First Movement.

London symphonies (Nos. 98 and 103). In No. 103 the slow introduction returns shortly before the end of the first movement. Often the first movement, which by now is quite long, is further unified by similar first and second themes (Example 6–2). Many first movements provide contrast pri-

EXAMPLE 6–2. Haydn, *Symphony No. 101,* "Clock," First Movement, first and second themes.

marily through tonality and instrumentation of a recurring theme, though a new theme may appear in a place other than the expected one. In the "Oxford" Symphony, for instance, the key of the dominant is established in the accustomed manner, preparing the listener for a second theme. Instead, the first theme returns; only at the very end of the exposition does a new idea occur—a closing theme which then figures prominently in the development, ingeniously combined with the principal theme.

As Haydn's technique of thematic development was being perfected it tended to permeate the entire movement, not only the development section. Some development frequently occurs before the end of the exposition is reached. The coda often is extensive, amounting to a second development rather than a mere concluding passage emphasizing the home key. Developing thematic material often involves contrapuntal texture, with a theme or fragment of a theme being treated imitatively. Counterpoint in the late symphonies tends to be sectional rather than continuous: a certain motif in the course of a movement acquires importance and is then handled in the manner of a fugato, or as a canonic passage (No. 102/I), but sooner or later the full, chordal sound of the entire orchestra will assert itself again.

By giving greater substance and length to the other movements as well as the first, Haydn kept the balance of the symphony as a whole. Great formal variety exists in the slow movements, which may be sonata form, ternary form with a middle section in minor, or a set of simple or double variations. Some combine elements of several of the above. Extensive codas may also occur in slow movements, as in No. 100.

Variety is also encountered in the minuets, where it extends to their character, tempo, and form. That little remains of the courtly dance is apparent from the tempo indications allegro or allegro molto. Nor do all the minuets have a folk-like, popular flavor; many give the impression of being abstract, symphonic music which merely preserves rhythmic and formal features of the earlier type.[6] The traditional minuet form also may be modified; The repetition of a section may contain changes in orchestration and dynamics. Haydn's last symphony contains a minuet in D followed by a trio in B♭—an unusual key relation for him but one that was to appear frequently from this time on, especially in works by Beethoven. A smooth return to the minuet is effected by a ten-measure bridge passage following the trio.

Abrupt harmonic changes and pauses are plentiful in the finales of the London symphonies. As mentioned earlier, Haydn used them to achieve humorous effects. No. 100 supplies delightful examples of key changes so sudden that they seem accidental and unpremeditated, and grand pauses in unexpected places. Contemporaries were startled and impressed by the mastery shown in Haydn's finales. In one review published in 1802 the writer showed fine insight when he attributed humorous effects to the incongruity between the seemingly carefree themes and the serious and elaborate treatment to which Haydn subjected them. Whether humorous or not, the finales of the works inevitably provide a happy and vigorous conclusion to these compositions, which are among the best examples of Classic style, representing many levels of experience and expressiveness.

MOZART

The different personalities and careers of Haydn and Mozart, and the different pace at which they developed, are manifested in their symphonic writing. Haydn's first symphonies were composed when he was twenty-seven; the category continued to occupy him to the age of sixty-

[6]Similar transformations can be found in nineteenth-century dance types, especially the waltz, polonaise, and mazurka.

three. All of Mozart's symphonies were written between his ninth and thirty-second years—an artistic development of astounding proportions for such a short span of time, especially when one considers the youthful age at which he penned his earliest works. For these the *sinfonia* of the kind he had heard in Italy and London served as model. Young Mozart wrote both operatic *sinfonie*—without breaks between the sections—and independent works, mostly consisting of three short movements (K. 16 and K. 19; 1764–65). The mood is *galant*, unproblematic; minor keys are avoided; wind parts receive little attention. In symphonies written for the Italian journeys of 1769–70, dimensions and style have changed somewhat. Three-movement and four-movement works are found; in some, the minuet may have been added later. There still is no dividing line between symphonies for the theater and those for the "chamber"; the "theatrical" nature of K. 96 led Wyzewa to believe that it might have been intended to serve as overture to *Lucio Silla*, written for Milan at this time. Similarly, Mozart may have combined the presto movement K. 120 (111a) with the overture and No. 1 (dance music) of *Ascanio in Alba*, to form a three-movement symphony.[7]

A group of symphonies written after Mozart's return to Salzburg in 1771 (K. 73, 75, 110, and 114) shows a somewhat different style. Counterpoint is occasionally introduced, as in the second movement of K. 110, but the thematic material contains little to set it apart from that of *galant* composers of the time (Example 6–3). A more Mozartean flavor appears in K.

EXAMPLE 6–3. Mozart, *Symphony in C Major*, K. 73, First Movement.

133 of 1772, recognizable by the rhythmic drive of the opening movement, notably in the transition sections (Example 6–4a), and by the quality of the second and closing themes (Examples 6–4b and 6–4c). Mozart uses the familiar harmonic scheme of sonata form but begins the recapitulation with the original first transition, withholding the return of the opening theme until the coda.

Mozart's growth as a symphonist was rapid: Only a year later several symphonies were forthcoming which, though written by a seventeen-year-

[7]G. Alroggen in Preface, *NMA*, IV:11/ii (1985).

EXAMPLE 6–4. Mozart, *Symphony in D Major*, K. 133, First Movement.

old, can no longer be called "youthful works." Among the symphonies of 1773–74 those in G minor (K. 183) and A major (K. 201) are outstanding. The former, Mozart's first in the minor mode, has justly been compared to his famous later work in the same key, the "great" G Minor Symphony (K. 550). Though on a smaller scale, it rises to a seriousness of expression not encountered before. Agitated syncopations, dramatic chordal accents in the winds (which include four horns), and dynamic variety result in a first movement which, though brief, displays passion and intensity—qualities that have caused listeners and writers to look for explanations in Mozart's personal life. In mood this work is related to a Haydn symphony in the same key (No. 39, written before 1770) and for the same instruments, but the extent to which Mozart at this time was familiar with Haydn's works is uncertain. Comparisons with the later G Minor Symphony are also suggested by other movements of K. 183. The andante in E♭ major gives needed emotional relief. It does not approach the profundity of the corresponding movement in the later work (St. Foix speaks of the "banality" of the second subject); except for some chromaticism in the strings and brief passages of cantabile writing for the bassoons, a Rococo atmosphere prevails.

    Greater kinship exists between the minuets of K. 183 and K. 550. Both are in minor and the general mood is similar, but the earlier work lacks the boldness and drive found especially in the second strain of the minuet from the "great" G Minor Symphony. The finale, starting with a unison theme, piano, again establishes a stormy atmosphere, accentuated by jagged leaps in most parts. The development, while modest in scope, maintains the momentum generated by the first section. The coda by its brevity again demonstrates that Mozart's symphonies from this period,

while showing musical individuality and maturity, were still conceived on
the small scale of most contemporary works. The proportions of K. 201 are
similar except for the longer andante. What strikes us in this brightly colored work is the transparent part-writing and the ingenious contrapuntal
treatment of several themes (Example 6–5).

EXAMPLE 6–5. Mozart, *Symphony in A Major,* K. 201, First Movement.

In 1773, at about the time these symphonies were written, Dr. Burney referred to Vienna as "the capital of German music." Gluck, Dittersdorf, and Haydn are among those whom he considers chiefly responsible
for this prominence, along with Johann Baptist Vanhal (1739–1813), whose
symphonies Burney calls "masterworks of their kind."[8] He could not have
known that the symphonies Mozart was to write later, after settling in Vienna, would outshine by far the creations of Vanhal and other fashionable
contemporaries.

Mozart composed few symphonies between 1773–74 and 1782, a period that included the great journey to Mannheim and Paris. This is surprising, since Mozart's position at home might well have led him to write
some. He spent much time in Mannheim and was impressed by the orchestra; it would have been natural for him to demonstrate his abilities (he was
looking for a court position) by writing symphonies. But K. 297 of 1778 is

[8]Vanhal, or Wanhal, one of the "forgotten" composers referred to in Chapter 4, was
a Bohemian who settled in Vienna, where he became acquainted with both Haydn and Mozart. He was a very prolific and (especially in his younger years) successful composer. Modern
editions include symphonies, several concertos, and chamber music. Paul R. Bryan's disserta-
tion "The Symphonies of Johann Vanhal" (University of Michigan; Ann Arbor MI, 1957) includes a thematic index and transcriptions of six symphonies.

the only symphony that owes its existence to such considerations. Written in Paris, it reflects Mozart's acquaintance with the brilliant style in vogue both there and in Mannheim. Traditionally, French orchestras included a large wind section; no doubt Mozart was happy to score the "Paris" Symphony accordingly, including clarinets as well as flutes, oboes, bassoons, horns, and trumpets. To display these large forces to good advantage Mozart wrote a work which, though lacking a minuet, is longer and more brilliant than its predecessors. Eager to please Le Gros, the director of the *Concerts Spirituels* where his work was to be heard, he replaced the original andante, declared by Le Gros to be too long and to contain too much modulation. The French director apparently knew his public: The new version achieved success both locally and abroad, earning praise from Gluck when it was performed in Vienna several years later.

Returning to Salzburg, Mozart wrote several symphonies for the smaller orchestra at his disposal there. His opinion of the "slovenly Salzburg Court musicians" may have sunk to an even lower level after his reluctant return. These symphonies, though brilliant in places, offer considerably less challenge to the players, especially the wind section. In K. 338, again a three-movement symphony, the brightness of the outer movements is contrasted by the andante di molto for strings (two bassoons double the bass line) with divided violas.

Mozart's remaining symphonies, those most frequently performed today, were written after the break with the Salzburg Archbishop. The series begins with K. 385, composed in Vienna during the summer of 1782 but intended for a celebration in the family of a Salzburg friend, Sigmund Haffner. (The earlier "Haffner" Serenade, K. 250, had a similar purpose.) Mozart, in a letter to his father, calls the work "the new Haffner Symphony," but in its original version it has the dimensions of a serenade, opening with a march and including a second minuet. The shortened version was first heard at one of Mozart's academies in 1783. During the following year, one symphony was written—in extreme haste, as indicated before—for a concert in Linz (K. 425). Chronologically close to the "Linz" Symphony is K. 444, formerly attributed in its entirety to Mozart but almost wholly composed by Michael Haydn; Mozart's authorship extends merely to the slow introduction in the first movement.

No symphonies exist from the following years, which saw a staggering amount of writing in other categories, until K. 504, written in 1786, soon performed in Prague, and known, somewhat misleadingly, either as the "Prague" Symphony (it was not written there) or "Symphony without Minuet" (there are others). There remains the group of three symphonies (K. 543 in E-flat major; K. 550 in G minor; K. 551 in C major) written in the incredibly short span of six weeks during the summer of 1788. We do not know who is responsible for the title "Jupiter" for the C Major Symphony; it was used soon after the composer's death and may have been coined by Haydn's friend and manager, Salomon. The trilogy has been admired, rightly and universally, as the crowning achievement of Mozart's symphonic writing, and of the Classic symphony in general. The mood of the G Minor Symphony, especially, brought forth strong response from the early Romantics.

It has often been said that some stylistic traits of the "late" Mozart symphonies (he was twenty-six years old when he wrote the "Haffner" Symphony) appear in the symphonies Haydn wrote for and during the journeys to England. That the older composer's attention should have been attracted is understandable, for the Mozart symphonies beginning with K. 385 exhibit new and striking characteristics which were also to appear in works other than the symphonies. Mozart's melodies now contain a greater amount of chromaticism, which tends to make individual lines more expressive and is related to the generally bolder concept of harmony found in the late symphonies. Harmonic surprises, such as startling modulations or abrupt changes in key, are not as frequent as in Haydn's mature works, but Haydn hardly surpasses Mozart's writing int he last movement of the G Mi-

EXAMPLE 6–6. Mozart, *Symphony in G Minor*, K. 550, Finale.

nor Symphony, at the beginning of the development (Example 6–6). The passage, aside from its distinct rhythmic profile, is remarkable for traversing, in a few measures of unison writing, no less than six tonalities. In the ensuing development, due to the limitations of the (valveless) instruments of the time, the horns have to withdraw whenever distant keys are reached. Much of the chromaticism occurs in melodically prominent passages for the woodwind section, which in only a few instances includes clarinets. Mozart's masterful handling of this section of the orchestra impressed his contemporaries: Niemetschek (*Life of Mozart,* 1798) claimed that in this regard no one could rival his genius. The statement seems valid even today.

Concern with variety of tone color is not restricted to the winds. To create a certain mood the color of various registers and groupings is also considered, as in the opening of the G Minor Symphony with its divided

EXAMPLE 6–7. Mozart, *Symphony in G Minor*, K. 550, First Movement.

violas. To state the second theme of this movement both strings and wood-winds are enlisted (Example 6–7).

To search for and listen to the principal themes in Mozart's late symphonies is to realize how numerous and varied they have become. Each theme has a distinct personality; together they cover a greater range of thought, emotion, and structure. The famous opening theme of the G Minor Symphony is a particularly eloquent complete musical sentence, longer than most.

A slow introduction, rare in Mozart's symphonies, occurs for the first time in K. 425, and again in K. 504 and K. 543. Mozart's language here is profound, not merely dignified. Expressive melodic chromaticism appears soon after the unison opening of K. 504. This introduction also employs dramatic dynamic changes. The "dominant pedal," a typical harmonic device, lends an inconclusive, preparatory quality to the end of the slow introduction. For K. 543 Mozart composed an introduction remarkable for its seriousness and breadth, paralleled only by the work of Beethoven. It proves, if such proof should still be needed, that Mozart the symphonist goes "beyond invariable grace and charming elegance" (St. Foix).

The opening movement of K. 385 (the "Haffner") shows great boldness of thematic conception and development. The principal theme with its characteristic octave leaps is present throughout, overshadowing any subsidiary material that might be called thematic. Here the absence of a contrasting second theme reminds us of some Haydn symphonies. The extensive contrapuntal work is a reminder that Mozart's last symphonies were written at a time when he had developed a profound interest in the polyphony of Bach and Handel. All instruments may participate in a way that is thematically important, frequently even at the beginning of a movement, as in the opening of K. 543/I. Since so much thematic manipulation takes place in the exposition and coda, the brevity of the development proper (as in K. 425, 543, and 550) is understandable and satisfactory with regard to the balance of the movement as a whole. Elsewhere, as in the G Minor Symphony, the recapitulation is the scene of further development and the coda is correspondingly brief. Elements of sonata form exist in several second movements and finales, but Mozart provides so many modifications that standardized textbook concepts of form do not suffice for intelligent analysis. Development is often based on motifs that appear insignificant when first introduced: a small part of the first theme in the "Prague"; a portion of the closing theme in the "Jupiter."

In the slow movements of the last three symphonies the skillful and imaginative wind-writing is particularly striking, occasionally conveying Romantic effects. At other times we are impressed by harmonic progressions that must have sounded audacious to eighteenth-century audiences (Example 6–8). Unity is achieved in the long andante from the G Minor Sym-

EXAMPLE 6–8. Mozart, *Symphony in E♭ Major*, K. 543, Second Movement.

phony by a small fragment of thirty-second notes, a seemingly insignificant part of the first theme which eventually permeates the entire fabric.

The stormy minuet of K. 550 has already been mentioned. Lively part-writing distinguishes the late symphonic minuets, again including the winds ("Jupiter," second strain). The lilting, *Ländler* character of Viennese dance music appears in several of the trios, most beautifully in that of the E♭ Major Symphony where the second clarinet has accompaniment patterns in its distinctive low register while the strings provide an after-beat rhythm.

An excited but subdued beginning, piano and presto or allegro molto, is found in most of the finales. Light texture and mood may suggest, as in the "Prague" Symphony, the writing in one of Mozart's lively operatic finales. A few hushed opening measures lead to a sudden forte by the entire orchestra, completing or restating and expanding the opening theme. Again sonata form is preferred. There may be a considerable number of themes, in two contrasting tonalities; or, as in the E-flat Major Symphony, the movement may be monothematic. A masterly and extensive fugato distinguishes the finale of the G Minor Symphony, along with the extraordinary modulations already mentioned, but contrapuntal skill and imagination reach a high point in the famous finale of the "Jupiter" Symphony. The several thematic ideas are soon used, one by one, as subjects for imitative sections (e.g., measures 56, 64, and 94), in the manner of consecutive fugatos, before Mozart combines several of them and, in the extensive coda, introduces all of them in what amounts to a five-part fugato. The term "sonata form" applies to this remarkable finale in a very general sense only: Several developments using the contrapuntal devices of inversion and stretto have taken place before the first double bar is reached. The "recapitulation" represents in so many details a modification and intensification of the first part of the movement that the term hardly seems applicable. Nor is the movement a fugue if any meaning of form is attributed to that term (a meaning denied it by many). In writing the finale of what was to be his last symphony, Mozart demonstrated that he had assimilated—not merely understood or copied—the elements of contrapuntal writing which he had diligently studied in earlier and contemporary models. The result is a work *sui generis;* it stands above any models, it has no companion among Mozart's own works, and it could not have been written by anyone else.

BIBLIOGRAPHICAL NOTES

In addition to the general works listed at the end of the previous chapter, the following deal with Classic symphonies in particular: J. P. Larsen, "The Symphonies," in *MC;* G. de St. Foix, *The Symphonies in Mozart* (New York:

Knopf, 1949), descriptive rather than analytical; B. S. Brook, *La symphonie française dans la seconde moitié du xviiie siècle* (Paris, 1962). Landon's *The Symphonies of Joseph Haydn* has been cited earlier. Studies of eleven late Haydn symphonies and five late Mozart symphonies are included in D. F. Tovey's *Essays in Musical Analysis, I* (London, 1935). See also F. E. Kirby, "The Germanic Symphony in the 18th Century: Bridge to the Romantic Era," *Journal of Musicological Research,* 5 (1984), 51–83. A selection of symphonies by Dittersdorf and Michael Haydn appears in *DTO,* volumes 81 and 29 respectively. Recent performing editions of symphonies by these and other, less well known Classic composers (e.g., Hoffmeister and Kozeluch) are making this repertoire more readily available. The series *Diletto Musicale,* issued in Vienna since 1953, serves this purpose particularly well, as does the series *Recent Researches in the Music of the Classical Era* (Madison WI: A–R Editions) with symphonies by C. F. Abel and Vanhal. See also the bibliography for chap. 3, "The Pre-Classic Symphony."

SEVEN

THE CLASSIC SONATA

In Chapter 2 we looked at some of the changes that the sonata for one or more instruments underwent during the eighteenth century, noting in particular the emergence of the keyboard sonata. Works by John Christian and Emanuel Bach and by some of the Italian *galant* composers were widely known during Haydn's and Mozart's formative years; their style speaks to us from many early sonatas by the two Austrian composers.

With the disappearance of the Baroque sonata for one or two melody instruments and continuo, the importance of the keyboard sonata increased, while in ensemble sonatas the (written-out) keyboard part became the focus of attention. Keyboard sonatas were frequently published with optional violin, or violin and cello parts; from sonatas of this type a gradual development leads again to the later Classic violin sonata and to the new category of the piano trio.

Among Mozart's sonatas the works for violin and keyboard have an important place; Haydn's "violin sonatas," on the other hand, were not originally conceived as such but are, for the most part, arrangements of keyboard sonatas.[1] The importance of the latter in Haydn's work thus symbolizes the dominant place that the keyboard sonata was to retain in the later Classic and Romantic periods and, to some extent, in the present.

HAYDN'S KEYBOARD SONATAS

Among the many categories of Haydn's compositions only the keyboard sonatas[2] were published nearly completely during his lifetime, in the *Oeuvres complettes* issued 1800–06. The forty-nine sonatas cover a long span of the composer's life, from 1760 to 1794. As can be expected they show great variety of style and they vary as to the intended medium of performance: clavichord, harpsichord, and pianoforte. Only gradually did the piano, with its hammer action, replace the two other instruments,[3] so that titles of publications, aimed at the largest possible market, may specify another instrument than that intended by the composer. Thus the autograph of Haydn's Sonata No. 49[4] of 1790 is marked "per il Forte-piano"; the version published in 1792 is entitled "pour le clavecin ou Piano-Forte."[5]

In the earliest sonatas a mood of gay simplicity dominates; they are *galant* without being ornate or sophisticated. Like his Viennese contemporary Wagenseil, Haydn at this time uses the terms "divertimento" and "sonata" interchangeably. Three-movement form is preferred, with a minuet in the second or third place. All movements may be in the same key, justifying the term "partita" also used by Haydn. Melody and simple accompaniment is the normal texture, with many uses of Alberti basses. Certain movements from early sonatas show the strong impression which Emanuel Bach's music had made, among these the largo in G minor of Sonata No. 2, bringing an expressive melody in the right hand with elaborate rhythmic subdivisions, while the left hand maintains a steady eighth-note pulse. Sonatas No. 44–47 are also early works, in spite of their high number in the

---

[1]E.g., Sonatas Nos. 24–26 and 43 of the complete edition. Violin parts for some keyboard sonatas were provided by Dr. Burney.

[2]*SCE*, pp. 461ff., with a chronological chart.

[3]John Christian Bach publicly performed on the pianoforte as early as 1768.

[4]Numbers refer to the complete edition begun by Breitkopf and Härtel, Serie XVI, ed. Karl Päsler (1918). The results of more recent research into Haydn's keyboard sonatas, including newly discovered works and changes in chronology and authenticity, are discussed in H. C. R. Landon's *Essays on the Viennese Classical Style* (chap. 5), with numerous music examples. Christa Landon's edition of these sonatas (Vienna, 1962–66; 3 vols.) also presents a different chronological arrangement. See *Grove 6*, vol. 8, pp. 389f.

[5]E. Ripin discusses clavichord, harpsichord, and fortepiano, pointing out that in the late eighteenth century they were closer to each other in sound quality than is generally thought. See his "Haydn and the Keyboard Instruments of His Time," *Haydn Studies*, pp. 302ff.

complete edition. Among these No. 46, with an extensive modulatory middle movement, is outstanding. The sonatas from the 1770s still reflect indebtedness to Emanuel Bach, coming from a period in Haydn's development variously referred to as his years of "storm and stress" or "romantic crisis," the latter a somewhat misleading term for which no evidence can be found in Haydn's personal life. The C Minor Sonata, No. 20, with its constant dynamic changes and irregularly shaped melodic lines and cadenza, belongs here.

Serious and complex melodic writing extends to the minuets and trios—a seriousness not typical of Haydn's symphonic minuets from this period. Example 7–1 is from Sonata No. 28 (1776). The finale of No. 25,

EXAMPLE 7–1. Haydn, *Piano Sonata in E♭ Major*, No. 28, Second Movement.

marked *tempo di menuetto*, is in strict canon; in the following sonata Haydn writes a minuet and trio *al rovescio:* The second half of each is the retrograde version of its first half. Yet this sonata, and others from these years, have finales that are short and gay. In the six sonatas of 1774–76 (Nos. 27–32) there are still many movements of serious and dramatic character. The presto finale of No. 32 is intense and agitated and includes much contrapuntal writing. In No. 30 Haydn experiments with the sonata's overall design by connecting the first and second movements. The concluding third movement is a *tempo di menuetto* in variation form. Sonata No. 21 already displays the tendency, noted in many later Haydn movements in sonata form, to use similar rather than contrasting thematic material in the tonic and dominant areas (Example 7–2).

A formal feature found in some Haydn sonatas, especially the later ones, is the double variation. Two themes, often in different tonalities, are

EXAMPLE 7–2. Haydn, *Piano Sonata in C Major*, No. 21, First Movement.

First Theme

stated and then followed by pairs of variations according to the scheme AB-A¹B¹A²B², etc. Occasionally repetitions of the theme are inserted between variations. Such double-variation movements occur in Sonata No. 33/III (last movement) where the two themes are related, No. 34 (last movement), and Nos. 40/I and 48/I (first movements).

Haydn's last four sonatas are extensive, musically substantial, and technically challenging to the performer. No. 49 was written for Marianne von Genzinger; Haydn comments on the sonata in a letter of June 20, 1790, recommending the adagio as "rather difficult but full of feeling" and regretting that the recipient did not have one of Schantz's fortepianos on which to perform it.[6] He adds that he no longer writes for the harpsichord. In the first movement of this sonata special care is given to motivic work and harmonic variety as well as to timbres of the different registers of the instrument. The adagio contains increasingly complex elaborations on a cantabile theme.

The three remaining sonatas were written in 1794 for Theresa Jansen, an English pianist who must have possessed considerable facility, judging by these sonatas and other works Haydn dedicated to her. Aside from their pianistic requirements (rapid octave passages in one hand; other brilliant runs and cadenzas; long chains of syncopations) these sonatas show the greater breadth and dramatic vigor also associated with Haydn's mature symphonies. In many ways they form a link to the sonatas of Beethoven. No. 52 in E♭ major contains many harmonic surprises in the first movement; a middle movement in E major is an adagio with definitely Romantic undertones. No. 51 consists of an andante and finale only; its first movement has a subordinate theme which, with its extension in the second phrase, exemplifies the Romantic lyricism found in these sonatas (Example 7–3).

[6]Wenzel Schantz was a Viennese instrument maker whose pianos Haydn preferred. They had a lighter action than those of Mozart's favorite Viennese maker, Anton Walter.

EXAMPLE 7–3. Haydn, *Piano Sonata in D Major*, No. 51, First Movement.

MOZART'S KEYBOARD SONATAS

Sonatas for various instruments account for almost one-fourth of Mozart's instrumental works,[7] a larger proportion than in Haydn's. The importance is not one of numbers only: Mozart's sonatas have remained in the repertory of pianists and violinists to a substantially larger degree than those by Haydn. Mozart's excellence as a performer on both violin and piano may in part explain this more central position of the sonata (and, as we shall see later, the concerto) in his instrumental writing.

For what instrument did Mozart write his keyboard sonatas? Today it is generally believed that although clavichord, harpsichord, and piano (pianoforte, or fortepiano as it was sometimes called in the eighteenth century) were available to him, he favored the last-mentioned with its hammer action, which was then rapidly establishing itself.[8] Mozart repeatedly expressed his satisfaction with the tonal possibilities of the *Hammerklavier*. His detailed and enthusiastic description of the instruments made by Stein of Augsburg fills a good part of a letter to his father (October 17–18, 1777); their even tone and perfected mechanism supplied the tonal characteristics that appeared most desirable to Mozart for a realization of his concept of keyboard style. Two months later Mozart's mother writes from Mannheim that

> Wolfgang is greatly esteemed everywhere—but then he plays differently from the way he did in Salzburg. Here there are pianofortes everywhere, and he plays them incomparably well. One has never heard anything like it.[9]

[7]*SCE*, p. 481.

[8]German terminology during this period of transition is at times confusing. Zelter, in a letter to Goethe, recalls Friedemann Bach's admirable playing on "Flügeln, Fortepianos und Clavieren," meaning, most likely, harpsichord, fortepiano, and clavichord, though the term "Clavier" could refer to any keyboard instrument, including the organ. P. Rummenhöller, *Die musikalische Vorklassik* (Kassel, Bärenreiter, 1983), p. 84.

[9]Letter of December 28, 1777.

A typical piano from this period had a considerably lighter action than a modern instrument. Thinner strings produced a lighter, "silvery" tone, especially in the upper register. The generally smaller volume of sound was in part due to the wooden frame; only the later cast-iron frame could support the larger tension of a greater number of strings, many of them heavier.

Although the tone of an eighteenth-century piano was relatively small in volume, it did not lack variety. Dynamic shadings were controlled by the player's touch—hence the name "pianoforte" or "soft-loud" for the new instrument—and further variety was achieved by devices such as the damper control, operated by the player's knees before it acquired its present position as a pedal. Though we know that pianos with pedal keyboards existed in the late eighteenth century and continued to be made well into the nineteenth century, we are not certain to what extent they were used in Mozart's performances of his keyboard sonatas and concertos. Perhaps pedal tones served to extend the range of the instrument and to increase the volume by doubling important notes.[10]

An early edition (1784) of three Mozart sonatas (K. 330–32) "for the harpsichord or pianoforte." Museum Salzburg.

[10]Concerning the use of the pedal piano in K. 466, see Eva Badura-Skoda, "Mozart's Piano," *The American Music Teacher,* 12, No. 6 (July–August, 1963), 12f. The instrument illustrated there may be the kind to which Leopold Mozart refers in his letter of March 12, 1785.

The growing popularity of the pianoforte can be understood when we consider how well it could realize the expressive characteristics of the Mannheim style and the *Empfindsamkeit*. The "singing allegro" or the sustained melodic line of John Christian Bach and Mozart could be produced more successfully on the pianoforte than on the harpsichord, on which each note, being plucked, receives an incisive and explosive attack. That a singing, expressive quality was most important to Mozart is evident from many of his own remarks, often critical, about the playing of others such as Clementi, who may have possessed great technical facility but whose playing Mozart considered "mechanical."

Many models exist for Mozart's earliest keyboard sonata movements. Aside from Christian and Emanuel Bach there were other North German composers whose works Leopold Mozart had included in the instruction books for his children, arranged in the form of suites. Wolfgang's early sonatas, such as K. 6, were largely made up of individual movements written at various times and places, with improvements by his father. A set of these was published as *Oeuvre I* in 1764. As was customary at the time, a violin part was added. The London sketchbook of 1764–65 includes many sonata movements and also allemandes, gigues, and other short pieces. Three-movement sonatas are frequent, in the sequence allegro-andante (or adagio)-minuet I and II. Other sonatas (K. 12 and 15, written in London) follow the two-movement form found in John Christian Bach's sonatas.

Greater individuality speaks in the sonatas that Mozart wrote for his own use in 1774–75, K. 279–84. In the interim, the composer had traveled widely; there had been further exposure to Italian sonata writers and to works by Schobert in Paris (to be discussed below, in connection with the violin sonatas) and by others. Dennerlein speaks of these sonatas as the "beautiful product of a common European culture"[11]—acknowledging the international aspects of Classic style. Leopold Mozart considered these sonatas "most difficult," as did Wolfgang, who still performed them frequently on the 1777–78 tour. They already contain many features that are typical of his later sonatas as well. The three-movement design, allegro-andante-presto, is the norm. The first movements, unlike Haydn's, always contain several themes which are clearly defined and contrasted. Thematic material is distributed between both hands. Harmonic treatment in the development sections does not yet show the ingenuity of the later sonatas. Recapitulations are complete; when they are kept entirely in the tonic key, there is a lack of harmonic interest, which Mozart avoided in later works. In the middle movements three-part song form prevails; the last movement may bring sonata-allegro form or rondos of varying structure and complexity, often with the inclusion, typically French, of an episode in minor. In

[11]Hans Dennerlein, *Der unbekannte Mozart* (Leipzig, 1951), p. 32.

Pedal piano by Johann Andreas Stein, Augsburg, 1778, front view. The Metropolitan Museum of Art, The Crosby Brown Collection of Musical Instruments, 1889.

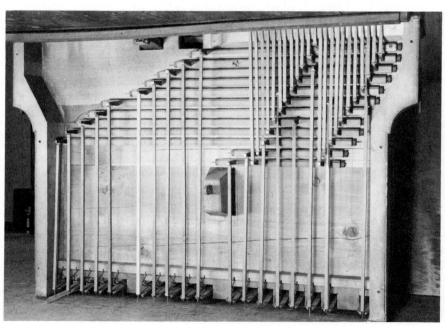

Pedal piano by Johann Andreas Stein, Augsburg, 1778, back view. The Metropolitan Museum of Art, The Crosby Brown Collection of Musical Instruments, 1889.

the andante amoroso of K. 281, crescendo and decrescendo signs are used for the first time in Mozart's sonatas. How far these works go beyond any models is demonstrated by many movements, among them the adagio in F minor of K. 280, very serious, resigned, and rather Romantic in mood (Example 7–4).

EXAMPLE 7–4. Mozart, *Piano Sonata in F Major*, K. 280, Second Movement.

More exuberant and less personal is K. 284, with a first movement of symphonic character (it could be orchestrated easily and effectively) followed by a *Rondeau en Polonaise*. Instead of closing with another rondo, Mozart provides a theme with twelve variations. Such variation movements enjoyed great popularity during both Mozart's and Beethoven's times. In this and other variations-movements Mozart preserves the harmonic framework of the theme as well as its dimensions. Each successive variation tends to be more florid; there is customarily a variation in minor as well as one in a slower tempo. The last variation, again allegro, changes to triple time.

Though Mozart commented on the difficulty of this set of sonatas, the following ones, written in 1777 and 1778, offer similar challenges. Mozart's own account of playing "a magnificent sonata in C . . . it made a lot of din and noise" may refer to K. 309, though possibly to the other C major sonata, K. 330, both probably dating from 1777. Again, there is an abundance of dynamic marks; these may have been in father Leopold's mind when he found something of "the mannered taste of the Mannheimers" in K. 309 (letter of December 11, 1777).

The mood of the A Minor Sonata, K. 310, has been the subject of much comment. It is more serious than its companions though kindred in spirit to the E Minor Violin Sonata. The opening theme establishes this mood of darkness and pessimism; it is then intensified by restless, *calando* afterbeats, by many temporary modulations and extensive chromaticism. Once more what Mozart has to say is far removed from the world of *galanterie*. Written in Paris close to the time of his mother's death, the work seems to reflect Mozart's frame of mind during those difficult months—yet its companion piece is the cheerful A Major Sonata, K. 331, a work of unusual form. Here a theme and variations movement provides the beginning. The lyrical rather than courtly or robust minuet and trio which stands in the middle makes the final "Turkish March" *(Alla Turca)* all the more effective. The writing of compositions with a (rather stylized) Turkish flavor was a fad in eighteenth-century Austria, related to a period, not long before, when Turkish armies, with their military (Janissary) bands, had advanced across Eastern Europe and actually laid siege to Vienna.[12] In addition, there was a more general interest, during the Age of Enlightenment, in Eastern civilizations—an interest that found expression in art, literature, and philosophy. (See pp. 206f.) The fad is reflected in several works by Mozart and other composers including Gluck and Michael Haydn. Static harmonies that do not change when the melody seems to require it, frequent alternating between major and minor, and the heavy, jangling bass chords suggestive of a Janissary band are the chief devices by which a "Turkish" effect was created.

Among Mozart's late sonatas K. 457 is outstanding. C minor has been called Mozart's "key of wild passion and despair" (Dennerlein); the term seems appropriate for this opening movement with its stern, unison beginning and jagged figures in the right hand (measures 14ff.). Unusual is the return to the main theme in E♭ major at the end of the exposition, in imitation between right and left hands, a procedure that is expanded in the coda. The movement ends pianissimo, as though all emotional and physical energy had been spent. The adagio middle movement is necessarily calmer but also serious and of great breadth. Figuration of increasing complexity appears, all of it important and expressive, with great dynamic variety including the crescendo leading to a sudden piano so typical of Beethoven. The final molto allegro proceeds with much drive and intensity, again suggesting a comparison with Beethoven's style. The year after the C Minor Sonata was completed (the autograph is dated 1784) Mozart wrote an extensive fantasy in the same key, K. 475, to serve as an introduction to the so-

[12]The *Jahrbuch der Tonkunst von Wien und Prag* (Vienna, 1796) describes the military music there, consisting of the "ordinary field music" (two oboes, horns, and bassoons) and the Turkish music. The latter, in addition, used two clarinets, trumpet, triangle, piccolo, large drum and small drum, and two cymbals. Both bands performed regularly in public.

Janissary band. The "Turkish music" in works by Mozart, Gluck, and other eighteenth-century composers was inspired by the sound of these bands. (From Arif Pascha, *Les anciens costumes de l'Empire Ottoman*, Paris, 1864). The New York Public Library.

nata. The emotional content of this remarkable, startling work reminds one of the bold fantasies of Emanuel Bach. Romantic composers of keyboard music drew inspiration from this kind of writing. The term "fantasy" suggests freedom and improvisatory character, but Mozart's work has an overall sectional structure of its own. Though intended to be coupled with the sonata, it is musically and formally self-sufficient.

As a result of his visit to Berlin in 1789, Mozart had planned to write six "easy" keyboard sonatas for Princess Friederike of Prussia. Of these only one, K. 576, materialized, and it is far from easy. Its first movement in rapid 6/8 time demands great fluency, all the more since some lively contrapuntal sections occur. In the exposition, after a transitional passage that cadences to the dominant, the first theme reappears in that key. A kind of development within the exposition then follows before the second theme, dolce, is introduced. All three movements of this sonata show a remarkably integrated texture; there are no *galant* melodies or Alberti basses. Unlike Haydn, Mozart usually placed the several movements of a sonata in closely related keys, but he made up for this by constant use of expressive chromaticism, as in the adagio of this sonata where the immediate repeat of the initial theme is already harmonically modified (Example 7–5). The andante of another late sonata (K. 533 of 1786, the last movement

EXAMPLE 7–5. Mozart, *Piano Sonata in D Major*, K. 576, Second Movement.

of which, K. 494, had been written two years earlier) contains instances of remarkable harmonic usage. The theme itself, though in B♭ major, introduces D♭ and E♮ in the second measure (Example 7–6). Consecutive seventh

EXAMPLE 7–6. Mozart, *Piano Sonata in F Major*, K. 533, Second Movement.

chords heighten the coloristic effect (Example 7–7). At the end of the first part, chromatic alterations result in constant fluctuation between major and

EXAMPLE 7–7. Mozart, *Piano Sonata in F Major*, K. 533, Second Movement.

minor (Example 7–8). A passage in the first part of this movement, which had originally been fairly simple harmonically (measures 14ff.), later is ex-

EXAMPLE 7–8. Mozart, *Piano Sonata in F Major*, K. 533, Second Movement.

panded and developed, resulting in remarkable clashes (Example 7–9). Einstein rightly points to the "grandeur of harmonic and polyphonic con-

EXAMPLE 7–9. Mozart, *Piano Sonata in F Major*, K. 533, Second Movement.

ception,"[13] to the profundity of feeling revealed in these and other movements from Mozart's late piano sonatas; they reveal an emotional depth comparable to that encountered in much of Beethoven.

Mozart's compositions for the piano include many works other than the solo sonatas. In addition to several sonatas for piano four-hands and for two pianos, there are numerous individual rondos, sets of variations, fantasies, fugues, and other pieces, a discussion of which would be beyond the scope of this study.

[13]*Mozart*, p. 248.

CLEMENTI AND OTHER CONTEMPORARIES

Of the keyboard composers of the Classic era, Muzio Clementi (1752–1832) comes closest in stature to Haydn, Mozart, and Beethoven.[14] Though this stature may not be generally acknowledged today, it was recognized during Clementi's lifetime. Thus Breitkopf and Härtel published a collection of his keyboard music as *Oeuvres Complettes* from 1803 on, on a subscription basis—something they had previously done only for Haydn and Mozart. During his long life, Clementi saw success not only as a composer, performer, and conductor but as a publisher and manufacturer of instruments as well. A resident of England from his early youth, he also traveled widely and was in contact with many leading musicians of the day. He was esteemed by Haydn, if rather harshly judged by Mozart. Many of his works were admired by Beethoven, whom he met in 1807. Beethoven recommended to his students Clementi's *Introduction to the Art of Playing on the Piano Forte*.[15] According to Schindler, Beethoven's early (and often unreliable) biographer, Beethoven owned nearly all of Clementi's sonatas and thought highly of his style of piano-playing—a cantabile manner, based on vocal models.[16]

Of particular interest in the context of Classicism are Clementi's early keyboard sonatas, especially those written during the 1780s. Their proximity in style to Beethoven's has often been noted, though they are played today far less often than the well-known Sonatinas Op. 36, the *Gradus ad Parnassum* (3 volumes, 1817, 1819, 1826), and a few of the later sonatas.

Op. 7, No. 3, first published in 1782, is a good example of Clementi's early style. Its substantial technical challenges include brilliant passages in octaves and the simultaneous use of very high and very low registers typical of Beethoven's piano writing. The last movement in particular, a stormy presto, foreshadows nineteenth-century pianism, with its runs in double octaves in contrary motion, abrupt and extreme changes in dynamics, and syncopated sforzatos.

The sonatas of Op. 12 (1784) likewise contain many characteristics of the mature Classic piano style, such as full, chordal writing, rhythmic vigor, dynamic contrasts, and great range (Example 7–10).

---

[14]Newman, *SCE*, pp. 738ff., discusses Clementi's sonatas and provides a chronological chart.

[15]London, 1801; published in German in Vienna, 1802 and 1807; facsimile reprint, New York, DaCapo Press, 1974.

[16]Anton Felix Schindler, *Beethoven as I Knew Him*, ed. Donald McArdle (Chapel Hill, NC: University of North Carolina Press, 1966), pp. 414ff.

EXAMPLE 7–10. Clementi, *Sonata*, Op. 12, No. 4, First Movement, development (the exposition had ended in B♭ major, piano).

Allegro

It is possible that the young Beethoven knew some of these early sonatas (for instance, Op. 13, No. 6, published in 1785). Leon Plantinga[17] points out general qualities in this sonata that remind one of Beethoven, including a theme that is very similar to one in the Finale of the "Eroica" Symphony. Another theme in the same symphony movement is anticipated in Clementi's sonata Op. 7, No. 3:[18] Op. 34, No. 2, of 1795 likewise displays elements of Beethoven's style: a great range of dynamics (including the indication < pp), much chromaticism and modulation, and generally full and vigorous keyboard writing.

EXAMPLE 7–11. Clementi, *Sonata*, Op. 7, No. 3, Beginning of First Movement.

The sonatas of Johann Nepomuk Hummel (1778–1837) display qualities that align him more closely with the pianism of nineteenth-century Romanticism.[19] Hummel was a pupil of Mozart and succeeded Haydn in the service of the Esterházy family. His career as a virtuoso pianist took him to

---

[17]*Clementi: His Life and Music* (London: Oxford University Press, 1977), p. 105.
[18]Alexander Ringer, "Clementi and the *Eroica*," *MQ*, 47 (1961), 454ff.
[19]See Longyear, *Nineteenth-Century Romanticism in Music*, 2nd ed., pp. 88ff.

England and Russia. Successful as a composer of brilliant piano sonatas and concertos, he also wrote chamber music and a fair amount of orchestrally accompanied sacred music. Some of these works, with graceful melodies and imaginative harmonic style, continue to be heard in Germany and Austria today.

Johann Wilhelm Hässler (1747–1822) was another prolific sonata composer of the Classic period. Over one hundred of his sonatas were published between 1776 and about 1815.[20] These include *galant* works such as the simple two-movement sonatas for flute (or violin) and piano from a collection entitled *Leichte Sonaten,* published in 1786–87 (modern edition in *Nagels Musik Archiv,* No. 11), and also the more ambitious *Deux sonates instructives* of the same period. The first of these two sonatas has an impressive grave introduction in E♭ minor leading into the main body of the movement, E♭ major, allegro. The second sonata, in C minor, has a very effective presto finale with ingenious use of the tightly organized thematic material and much modulation.

The music of Leopold Anton Koželuch (1747–1818) enjoyed great popularity in Vienna at the end of the eighteenth century. He excelled in many musical categories, including the keyboard sonata,[21] concerto, and chamber music. Joseph Wölfl (1773–1812), born in Salzburg but active in Paris, London, and Vienna, is another forgotten musician whose compositions (including sonatas, symphonies, and operas) were widely known during his time.[22] There are other contemporaries, like Emanuel Aloys Förster (1748–1823), who wrote music of originality and substance and were appreciated at the time; but now, in the absence of modern editions of their music, many are little more than names. Their former popularity confirms, at any rate, our general observations about the musical life of the Classic period (see above, p. 78).

FOUR-HAND PIANO MUSIC

Music-making in the home, as we have seen, came to play an increasingly important part in the musical life of the late eighteenth century. With the great popularity of the piano came the need for more, and more

---

[20]See Newman, *SCE,* pp. 579ff, which includes references to the few modern editions available.

[21]Newman (*SCE,* p. 557) considers Koželuch's sonatas "models of classic perfection in form, line, and fluency."

[22]A cello sonata of 1805, very close to Beethoven in style, is published in *Hortus Musicus,* No. 111.

varied, repertory, including chamber music for piano and other instruments (see Chapter 9). In addition, demand arose for piano music for two players. For practical reasons, this meant chiefly works to be played on one instrument—the piano music known since then as four-hand music. Composers since Mozart have accommodated this demand, not only with original compositions but with many arrangements. Given the versatility of the piano, it was put to many uses. Playing four-hand arrangements of symphonies, for instance, became a most satisfying way for music lovers to get to know that repertoire, before the phonograph provided a new way (easier, but not one necessarily providing greater insight and enjoyment).

While there is a great deal of Renaissance and Baroque ensemble music, both vocal and instrumental, we have little repertory for two keyboard players, on one instrument or two. (Harpsichord concertos with orchestral accompaniment do not belong to this category of *Hausmusik*.) The seventeenth-century virginalists provided but a few pieces; nor is there much four-hand repertory from the early eighteenth century. Among the earliest pieces are sonatas by John Christian Bach, some of which may go back to his years in Italy, before 1760. Several two-movement sonatas by the London Bach were published around 1780.[23] Mozart's earliest four-hand composition, the Sonata in C (K. 19^d, 1765) was written when he was in London with his father and sister Maria Anna. It may well be that their friendship with Bach provided the inspiration for this remarkable work by the nine-year-old. Most likely it was performed by Wolfgang and "Nannerl" on a two-manual instrument built by Tschudi (Shudi) in London for King Frederick the Great of Prussia.[24] Mozart's continued writing of four-hand sonatas (K. 358, 381) may well have been inspired by the existence of this brother-sister team, though some sonatas (K. 448, for instance) were intended for others. The well-known portrait of the Mozart family by della Croce, dating from 1780–81, shows the children, grown up by now, at the keyboard, with "Nannerl" playing the *primo* part.

K. 19^d is an attractive three-movement sonata—remarkable and enjoyable in itself, and not only because of the composer's tender age. *Primo* and *secondo* parts both contain melodic material and occasionally exchange parts. The second movement is a well-ordered minuet and trio. In the extensive rondo (C major, 2/4 time), a section in C minor is followed by the rondo theme's return, but this is interrupted, in mid-phrase, by the interpolation of an adagio in 3/4 time. There is opportunity for a cadenza, which then leads into the final statement of the theme.

[23]Cameron McGraw, *Piano Duet Repertoire* (Bloomington IN, Indiana University Press, 1981), p. 13. McGraw's book is an excellent source of information on four-hand music, from its beginnings to the present.

[24]Wolfgang Rehm, in the preface to *NMA* IX:24/2, p. vi f.

Della Croce portrait of Mozart family (father, holding violin; portrait of mother on wall). Austrian National Library.

A fine work indeed—but Mozart's later four-hand sonatas go far beyond it in length and depth, showing that the possibilities of this medium were of serious interest to him. K. 497 (1786), with its long adagio introduction full of chromaticism and dynamic variety, displays in all three movements qualities of harmony and part-writing admired in Mozart's mature works in other categories.

Four-hand compositions by contemporaries include a large number by Clementi, Vanhal, and Koželuch (who wrote a concerto for four-hand piano and orchestra). František Xaver Dušek (1731–99)—the friend at whose summer house in Prague Mozart stayed while working on *Don Giovanni*—wrote four-hand music, some of which was published at the time. Better known (and at times confused with Dušek) is Jan Ladislav Dussek (1760–1812), whose numerous four-hand compositions are again available today.[25] While Beethoven showed little interest in the genre, his highly esteemed Viennese contemporary Johann Nepomuk Hummel (1778–1837) did so substantially. But without a doubt it was Schubert whose many contributions assigned an important and lasting place to four-hand music.

[25]McGraw, *Piano Duet Repertoire*, pp. 72f. Dussek's piano music, though not his four-hand works, is discussed by Longyear, *Nineteenth-Century Romanticism in Music*, 2nd ed, pp. 86f.

OTHER SONATAS

As we have seen, the place and function of the violin in ensemble sonatas changed during the mid-eighteenth century. Gradually the Baroque sonata for violin and figured bass disappeared along with the trio sonata, their place being taken by the keyboard sonata to which was added an optional or, at any rate, less important violin part. One of the causes might have been the rising popularity of the piano and, related to this, the practice, growing during the late Baroque, of writing out keyboard parts completely instead of leaving the realization of the figured bass to the performer. Having complete control over the accompaniment, that is, the keyboard part, the composer now felt free to give important melodic material to the right hand. This amounted to an exchange between the violin part and the upper line of the accompaniment; the violin player now might accompany while the keyboard player led.[26] Sonatas of this kind were usually entitled "for the piano, with the accompaniment of a violin," and this, for some time, in fact they were. From 1750 to 1780 the custom was so widespread that publishers at times provided keyboard sonatas with a violin part when the composer had not done so. An advertisement in a Viennese newspaper of 1789 still refers to this manner of performance: "Wanted by a nobleman a servant who plays the violin well and is able to accompany difficult piano sonatas."[27]

An important (and in the nineteenth century often underrated) composer of violin sonatas was Luigi Boccherini (1743–1805). His reputation was well established by about 1770, both as a virtuoso cellist and as a composer of instrumental music. Burney's appraisal is to the point:

> [Boccherini,] who is still living at Madrid . . . has perhaps supplied the performers on bowed instruments . . . with more excellent compositions than any master of the present age, except Haydn. His style is at once bold, masterly and elegant. There are movements in his works . . . that place him high in rank among the greatest masters who have ever written for the violin or violoncello.

Burney gives special praise to the Italian composer's quintets, "in which invention, grace, modulation and good taste conspire to render them, well executed, a treat for the most refined hearers and critical judges of musical composition."[28]

---

[26]Regarding this development, see William S. Newman, "Concerning the Accompanied Clavier Sonata," *MQ*, 33 (1947), 327ff.

[27]Quoted in Geiringer, *Haydn*, p. 27.

[28]*A General History of Music* (1776–89), ed. Frank Mercer (New York: Harcourt, Brace and Co., 1957), II: 455f.

Of special importance in this development are Boccherini's sonatas, Op. 5. They were written and first published in Paris in 1768; other editions soon followed. The autograph's title is *Sei sonate per forte-piano con accompagnamento di un violino*, which describes the relation of violin and keyboard parts rather well (Example 7–12).

EXAMPLE 7–12. Boccherini, *Sonata,* Op. 5 (Gérard 29), from *Sei sonate di cembalo e violino obbligato*.

In the first edition's title the term *violino obbligato* is used instead, and in some of the other Op. 5 sonatas the violin does indeed have more to say, as in the two-movement sonata Op. 5 No. 3 (Gérard 27). In these works and in much of his later writing Boccherini appears as "a gentle, poetic musician, with a fresh turn of phrase, a subtle touch of fantasy, and a fine sense of clear form."[29]

The development of the Classic violin sonata can be traced by using Mozart's works as examples, from the Paris and London sonatas which offer little challenge to the violin player to the mature works in which the instruments participate on nearly equal terms. That the custom of adding violin parts to piano sonatas existed all through the Classic era appears from Mozart's late piano sonata K. 570, published with a violin part which, however, probably was not written by Mozart.

Among other composers whose works have a bearing on Mozart as

[29]Newman, *SCE*, p. 256.

a writer of sonatas was Johann Schobert (d. 1767), a German musician well established in Paris when the Mozarts journeyed there in 1763.[30] Though he was celebrated as a pianist and composer for that instrument, only a few of Schobert's sonatas are definitely for the piano alone, the others having string parts *ad libitum*. In some of his sonatas the violin part is indeed dispensable, providing little more than a doubling of the upper line of the keyboard part and occasional rhythmic accents. At other times, as in his Sonata Op. 14, No. 4, the violin part completes the harmony, imitates melodic lines in the keyboard part, or provides a patterned accompaniment. Schobert not only represents the fashionable Parisian manner, but he seems to have also been familiar with Mannheim style, which he is said to have transferred to the keyboard. He knew how to write a sighing, *empfindsam* melodic line (Example 7–13). Mannheim is also suggested by tremolo passages in the right hand with thematic material or passage-work in the bass, as in the first movement of Schobert's Op. 2, No. 1. Burney was aware of this when, in his *General History of Music,* he saw the chief innovation of Schobert's keyboard style in "the introduction of the symphonic style . . . upon the harpsichord."

EXAMPLE 7–13. Schobert, *Sonata,* Op. 14, No. 3, Menuetto (right hand of keyboard part).

Most of Schobert's sonatas consist of three movements of various types and in varying sequence, normally beginning with an allegro. This arrangement (rather than the two movements of John Christian Bach's violin sonatas) came to be preferred by Mozart as well. Occasionally Schobert included a movement for piano alone, a feature reflected in some variations-movements in Mozart's later violin sonatas; but generally speaking Schobert's musical personality is more evident in Mozart's youthful sonatas, written when the impressions of the early Paris journey were fresh in his mind.

Discounting the so-called "Romantic" sonatas, whose date and authenticity are doubtful, Mozart's Mannheim and Paris sonatas of 1778 are the first to show larger proportions and to involve the violin substantially. Six of these (K. 301–6) were published as "Opus 1" (not to be confused with the child prodigy's set of sonatas which had appeared as *Oeuvre I* in Paris in 1764). A seventh one, K. 296, was included in another set of six, pub-

[30]Schobert and other important, though lesser-known, Paris composers are discussed by Newman, *SCE,* pp. 626ff.

lished as Opus 2 in 1781. Its opening movement shows at once that melodic interest still lay predominantly in the piano part—so much so that from the beginning through the statement of the second theme the violin part has a harmonic and rhythmic rather than a melodic function. Later a cantabile phrase and bits of imitation suggest a more equal relationship. Elsewhere, particularly in the third movement, a bright rondo finale, Mozart lets the violin present most themes at one time or another.

Other sonatas in this set consist of two movements only, among them the well-known K. 304 in E minor, which is the most delicate and profound of these mostly unproblematic and optimistic works. Here a gentle, sweeping eight-measure theme, stated in unison, is foiled by four measures of forceful, staccato eighth-notes, elements of which appear, ingeniously transformed, through most of the movement. The opening theme reappears in various harmonizations (beginning of recapitulation; coda) and rhythmic patterns. The other movement, marked *tempo di menuetto* rather than *minuet*, is in the same minor key. Its mood takes us far away from any dance connotations. The repeat of the first section, after the trio in E major, contains further modifications; altogether the movement speaks a more subtle language than that of the courtly minuet.

In these sonatas Mozart still demands far more from the pianist than from the violinist, whose part lacks complicated passage-work and seldom rises above the third position. The keyboard player must possess substantial technical equipment if he wants to master a sonata such as K. 306 with its several cadenzas in the last movement.

Of the Sonata in G from the next set (K. 379) we learn that Mozart composed it between eleven o'clock and midnight on April 7, 1781, for a performance the following day. "Wrote down" rather than "composed" might be a more accurate way of putting it, since Mozart is known to have carried a composition in his head for some time before committing it to paper. In this instance, he relates, all that he had time to write down was the accompaniment—meaning, in the terminology of the time, the violin part. Certainly there is no evidence of haste in this substantial sonata, which consists of an extensive adagio leading into an allegro and a final *tema con variazioni*. The sonatas of this set show some complex and expressive writing. Violin parts are more demanding; soon after the set was published a reviewer pointed to their importance, which contradicted the allegation of the title page: "With accompaniment of a violin." Structurally, most of the opening allegros are simple. The short first movement of K. 376 serves as an example. Its first, second, and closing themes are clearly defined. The development begins with an eight-measure idea that grew out of the closing theme. After a few rather perfunctory modulations the recapitulation, which is quite literal, is reached, bringing the movement to an end without a coda. The rondo of this sonata is based on a theme which has the flavor of an Austrian folk song if it is not actually based on one (Example 7–14).

EXAMPLE 7–14. Mozart, *Violin Sonata*, K. 376, Rondo.

Allegretto grazioso

As in other categories of Mozart's instrumental music, the rondos are full of sparkle and surprise, as in that of K. 378, which begins in a lilting 3/8 rhythm, interrupted by a section in 4/4 time.

The remaining few sonatas, dating from 1784–88, reflect the continued trend to greater equality of the two instruments. Slow movements are extensive; the andante of K. 454 (in character close to an adagio) is particularly expressive and serious. Greater harmonic interest is illustrated by the adagio of K. 481. Extensive modulations take us from A♭ major through E♭ minor to D♭ minor (written enharmonically as C♯ minor), A major, and D♯ major which (returning in the same enharmonic fashion) becomes E♭ major, the dominant of A♭. Other movements also attain greater length and substance. The presto finale of the A Major Sonata, K. 526, exceeds by far the dimensions of other finales, but, aside from its length, it is the ceaseless energy and drive that make this last movement the culmination of the work. Such shifting of weight and importance from the first to the last movement can frequently be found in sonatas and other works by Beethoven.

Unlike Mozart, Boccherini wrote a great deal for the cello, including sonatas for cello and unfigured bass. Given the elaborate cello parts, most likely written for his own use, the light accompaniment seems just right: a bass line, perhaps discreetly reenforced by a chordal instrument such as a guitar. Example 7–15 shows what is expected of the soloist. The cello parts in Boccherini's string quartets and quintets also demand great virtuosity.

EXAMPLE 7–15. Boccherini, *Sonata for Cello and Bass in C Major* (Gérard 17), excerpt (cello part only) from first movement. Copyright 1970 by G. Schirmer, Inc., New York; ed. Analee Bacon.

BIBLIOGRAPHICAL NOTES

The most thorough and up-to-date coverage of the Classic sonata is found in *SCE*, chapters VI ("Style and Form") and XIV ("Haydn and Mozart") being specially important. *SCE* also includes extensive bibliography, giving much attention to the keyboard sonatas of Haydn (pp. 461ff and 827ff) and Mozart (pp. 482ff and 830ff) and providing chronological tables of their sonatas; Mozart's four-hand piano music is also discussed (pp. 489f, with further bibliography). E. and P. Badura-Skoda, *Interpreting Mozart on the Keyboard* (New York: St. Martin's Press, 1962; original German edition 1957), reflects the experience of two scholars and performers. A detailed and thoughtful study of Mozart's keyboard works, especially the sonatas, is H. Dennerlein's *Der unbekannte Mozart* (Leipzig, 1951). A. Hyatt King's *Mozart in Retrospect* (London: Oxford Univ. Press, 1955) contains a valuable chapter on "The Clavier in Mozart's Life." Arthur Hutchings contributed a chapter on Mozart's keyboard music to *MC*. A. Peter Brown's *Joseph Haydn's Keyboard Music: Sources and Style* (Bloomington: Indiana University, 1986), a thorough, scholarly study, deals with concertos and other works as well as sonatas, and discusses the keyboard instruments (including organ) for which Haydn composed.

Detailed information on keyboard instruments of the time can be found in *The New Grove Dictionary of Musical Instruments* (3 volumes, London, 1984), especially in the essay "Pianoforte, Germany and Austria, 1750–1800." Concerning the instrument for which Mozart wrote his keyboard music, see N. Broder, "Mozart and the Clavier," *MQ*, 27 (1941); C. Parrish, "Criticism of the Piano When It Was New," *MQ*, 30 (1944), and (also by Parrish) "Haydn and the Piano," *JAMS*, 1 (1948). A. Loft's *Violin and Keyboard: The Duo Repertoire*, I (New York: Grossman, 1973) includes discussion of eighteenth-century works.

Recent Clementi research has resulted in two major publications: A. Tyson, *Thematic Catalogue of the Works of Muzio Clementi* (Tutzing: Schneider, 1967), and L. Plantinga, *Clementi: His Life and Music* (London and New York: Oxford University Press, 1977). Clementi's most readily available works are the well-known sonatinas, the *Gradus ad Parnassum* (facsimile reprint, New York: DaCapo, 1980), and some of the later sonatas. Some earlier sonatas (Op. 7, No. 3; Op. 10, No. 3) have been edited by H. Albrecht (Lippstadt, 1953 and 1950). The 13-volume *Oeuvres complettes de Muzio Clementi* (Leipzig, 1804–ca. 1819) has been reprinted (New York, 1973). Clementi is also represented in *The London Pianoforte School 1770–1860* (New York: Garland, 1984– ; 20 volumes planned). Few keyboard works by Koželuch exist in modern editions; see *SCE*, p. 556.

EIGHT

THE CLASSIC CONCERTO

Sociological factors, discussed in an earlier chapter, account to a large degree for the favoring, ever since the late eighteenth century, of the solo concerto over the group concerto, the concerto grosso. As public concerts increased, the ability of outstanding virtuosos to attract large audiences assumed greater significance. Many Classic concertos were written with public performance in mind; the performer in many cases was the composer himself. In Mozart's time, display of instrumental virtuosity was not yet as important as it would become two generations later during the age of Paganini or Liszt; yet the soloist, while still *primus inter pares*, received more attention and more opportunities to display his skill than he had in concertos by Bach, Handel, or the *galant* composers.[1]

[1] Burney's evaluation of Christian Bach's keyboard concertos is characteristic: "Ladies can play them without much trouble." J. F. Reichardt published *VI Concerts pour le Clavecin à l'usage du beaux* [sic] *Sexe* (Amsterdam, 1774)—a title that would hardly be acceptable today.

We can trace the changing relation between the solo and tutti portions of a concerto by comparing works from the Baroque (Torelli's violin concertos, Op. 8 of 1709, or Vivaldi's violin concertos of about 1712) with those of early Classic composers and, finally, with the mature works of Haydn and Mozart. In many concertos from Vivaldi's age, the most important musical material is presented in the tutti portions.[2] The solo part may contain material that is new and even distinctive, but the difference is likely to lie in the elaborateness of the writing, the soloist embellishing material already heard or offering scales and arpeggios, rather than introducing new melodic, thematic material.[3] This still applies to Christian Bach's concertos (as in his Op. 1, No. 4, of 1763) and to those of Hasse (such as his flute concerto of 1760, published in *DdT*, volume 29). A keyboard concerto by Wagenseil shows a similar disposition, along with balanced distribution of musical weight between tutti and solo portions. The scoring is light, for strings and basso continuo accompaniment only. There are no brilliant display passages for the soloist.

Generally speaking, the solo sections now increase in length and importance, as in the violin concertos by Giuseppe Tartini (1692–1770). Various other ways of establishing contrast between tutti and solo sections are found, beyond soloistic display or the mere juxtaposition of a small and a large body of sound. The soloist and his music are increasingly featured in an effective, dramatic, even startling manner. Around the turn of the century, in the fully developed Classic concerto, the soloist frequently makes a bid for the listener's attention with a striking, dramatic initial statement, after the opening orchestral tutti.

The popularity of the concerto grosso was on the wane around 1750. Its place was taken to some extent by the sinfonia concertante, a group concerto close to the symphony in style and instrumentation, in which the several solo parts often had greater independence from each other than in the concerto grosso. The sinfonia concertante was especially popular in France and in Mannheim. Many Classic composers, including Haydn and Mozart, wrote such works, such as Mozart's sinfonia concertante for oboe, clarinet, horn, bassoon, and orchestra, K. Anh. C 14.01 (authenticity doubtful), which is, perhaps, another version of a lost work written for Paris; or K. 364 for violin, viola, and orchestra. This work, especially, points the way to the double and triple concertos of the nineteenth century.

The sinfonia concertante also had an important place among the works of Ignaz Pleyel (1757–1831), an Austrian composer neglected today, though violinists still enjoy playing his duets. Pleyel had been Vanhal's stu-

---

[2] For a discussion of Vivaldi's concertos, see Palisca, *Baroque Music*, pp. 149ff., and Pincherle, *Vivaldi*, (New York: Norton, 1957) pp. 141ff.

[3] See, for instance, the first movement of Vivaldi's violin concerto, Op. 9, No. 10, in which the theme of the opening tutti and each of its repetitions are answered by the soloist with passages in arpeggiated chords.

dent in Vienna and Haydn's in Eisenstadt. A successful career took him to
Germany, France, and other places. His life (including his experiences during the French Revolution) was rich and colorful, with ventures into the
fields of publishing and instrument building and selling. In 1792 Pleyel was
brought to London by the *Professional Concert*. For the occasion he wrote
a sinfonia concertante in F major (Benton No. 113) for two solo violins, viola, cello, flute, oboe, bassoon, and orchestra. It is a brilliant work with
much virtuoso writing, especially for the first violin. Haydn, at Salomon's
urging, had gone to London for the same season; the result was a rivalry
that probably had not been either composer's intention. At any rate, Haydn
also supplied such a work (Hoboken I: 105) with oboe, bassoon, violin, and
cello as concertante instruments. Salomon himself played the solo violin
part.[4] An elaborate cadenza for the four soloists occurs in the first movement. In the rousing finale, Haydn delays the first full statement of the
rondo theme until measure 35. Before that, the allegro is interrupted twice
by passages in accompanied-recitative style (the solo violin being the
"singer"), blocking, as it were, the forward thrust of the movement.

Many late-eighteenth-century composers contributed works to this
genre, sometimes for unusual combinations of instruments. A sinfonia concertante by Koželuch is scored for piano, mandolin, trumpet, contrabass,
and orchestra. It was performed at a concert on December 22, 1798, conducted by Haydn.

The sinfonia concertante's popularity did not last beyond the early
nineteenth century, and even during the Classic period the solo concerto
was far more widely cultivated. For the solo concerto, as for the sonata, the
favored instruments were the violin and the clavier, the latter usually
meaning the piano rather than the harpsichord. The number of concertos
for other melody instruments, both strings and winds, is much smaller.
That there are few significant viola concertos from the eighteenth century
should not surprise us in view of the subordinate position of that instrument, but even the cello's repertory is small.

As the solo concerto's popularity increased during the Classic period, the concerto acquired some of the formal characteristics of symphony
and sonata. The three-movement arrangement of the Baroque solo concerto
remained the norm; the minuet, lacking opportunities for soloistic display,
remained outside the concerto realm, although last movements of concertos
occasionally applied the tempo and style of the minuet to rondo structures.
In the first movement, elements of sonata form were adapted to the concerto principle of contrasting bodies of sound. The main themes, usually
two but often more, are presented in the opening tutti. To avoid digression
from the principal key before the soloist's entrance all themes are stated in
the tonic. A clear-cut cadential progression brings the orchestral introduc-

[4]S. Gerlach in preface, *Haydn: Werke*, Reihe II (Munich, 1982).

tion or ritornello to a close. The manner in which the solo part then begins and the material that it displays vary a great deal. Quite often, especially in Mozart's concertos, the soloist enters with a theme that has not been previously heard, and throughout the movement this theme and others may appear in the solo part only. Because of this the term "double exposition," frequently applied to first-movement form in Classic concertos, is not altogether valid.

The soloist participates in the "exposing" and "developing" of themes, and the relation between solo and tutti sections becomes far more flexible and subtle, appealing to the listener with much that is unexpected. To have the soloist accompany the orchestra is but one way of achieving variety in the solo-tutti relation; to have a theme or phrase begun by the soloist and concluded or echoed by the orchestra is another. After the soloist's entrance the overall harmonic scheme of sonata form may be found: contrasting themes occur in the dominant or the relative major; the exposition ends in that key; the development is likely to bring much modulation; and the recapitulation will stress the tonic. In all of this the ritornello principle of the Baroque concerto is not discarded, since the orchestra may repeatedly return with the same refrain.[5] A cadenza may occur in several places, but later Classic composers most frequently placed it at the end of the recapitulation, that is, at the end of the last orchestral section, in which case the cadenza is followed by a short orchestral coda. The cadenza customarily appears as a free and unaccompanied interpolation or interruption of a standard cadential progression, after a $^6_4$ chord held by the orchestra (Example 8–1). Though a cadenza ought to give the impression of spontaneity, of on-the-spot improvisation on a theme or themes from the movement just played, by the late eighteenth century these "improvisations" frequently were written out and rehearsed beforehand. Some composers, including Emanuel Bach and Mozart, occasionally wrote down cadenzas for

EXAMPLE 8–1. (a) Basic Classic cadence. (b) Classic concerto cadence, with interpolated cadenza.

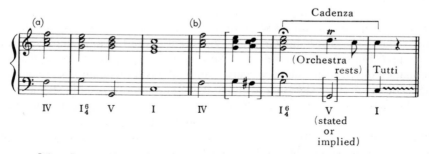

[5]The relation of Classic concerto form to "sonata form" is discussed by J. R. Stevens, "An 18th-century Description of Concerto First-Movement Form," *JAMS*, 24 (1971), 85ff., and the same author's "Theme, Harmony and Texture in Classic-Romantic Descriptions of Concerto First-Movement Form," *JAMS*, 27 (1974), 25ff.

their own use or that of their pupils, thus providing us with guidelines as to what a cadenza from that age sounded like—guidelines which many nineteenth- and twentieth-century virtuosos overlooked. Beethoven once encouraged his pupil Ries to write a cadenza for his piano concerto, Op. 37, and Beethoven himself composed cadenzas both for his own concertos and for Mozart's D Minor Concerto, K. 466.[6]

In Classic concertos one or several cadenzas occur in each of the three movements. No doubt they were intended to be of modest length in order to preserve the balance of the movement as a whole.[7] Later the number of cadenzas decreased (leaving, in some nineteenth-century concertos, only one cadenza, in the first movement), and they came to be regarded primarily as vehicles for the display of highest technical (rather than improvisatory, that is, musical) skill.

Formal arrangements of the second and third movements of concertos correspond largely to those of the contemporary symphony, with such modifications as the concerto principle suggests. Two-part or three-part song form, or theme and variations form, are frequently encountered in the andante or adagio movement. The last movement in the majority of works, and sometimes the second movement as well, is a rondo. A favoring of some kind of rondo structure for the concerto's conclusion is not unusual. A happy ending seemed desirable within the Classic aesthetic; the formal arrangement of the rondo as well as the nature of the rondo themes helped to create such an effect. Furthermore, the rondo principle of different couplets and a refrain, an age-old device in vocal music, seemed naturally suited for the solo-tutti deployment of forces in the concerto. Rondo themes thus tend to be lighter than first-movement themes, and the experienced listener can be reasonably certain that a movement with a main theme as shown in Example 8–2(a) or 8–2(b) will be a rondo.

EXAMPLE 8–2a. Boccherini, *Cello Concerto* (Gérard 482).

EXAMPLE 8–2b. Mozart, *Piano Concerto in B♭ Major*, K. 450, Third Movement.

Allegro

[6]E. Badura-Skoda, "Performance Conventions in Beethoven's Early Works," *Beethoven—Performers and Critics* (Detroit, 1980), pp. 56f. The article includes facsimile reproductions of two of Mozart's own cadenzas.

[7]Cadenzas from Haydn's time for his keyboard concertos are discussed and printed in *Haydn: Werke*, XV/2, pp. 159ff and 198ff.

The Classic concerto saw the same growth in orchestral resources that occurred in the symphony. Many early examples by Christian Bach and others were scored for an accompaniment of two violins and figured bass only; twenty years later, concerto accompaniments frequently called for a full wind section including clarinets, horns, even trumpets and timpani. Exploitation of these orchestral timbres, especially in the wind section, became characteristic of Mozart's scoring in his mature concertos. It was one of his ways of maintaining balance between orchestra and soloist— a balance that otherwise might have been easily upset by florid and brilliant solo writing.

MOZART'S VIOLIN CONCERTOS

In today's concert repertory the Classic concerto is represented mainly by Mozart's works. Although the list of concertos attributed to Haydn is not inconsiderable, it includes several lost and spurious works. With the possible exception of his last concerto (for keyed trumpet), two cello concertos, and one or two keyboard concertos, the authentic works have not found lasting favor with performers or public. As pointed out earlier, Haydn did not consider himself an outstanding performer on the clavier or other instruments. Many of Mozart's concertos, on the other hand, owe their existence to his own needs as a violinist and pianist. It is possible that his violin concertos were written for Brunetti, the Salzburg concertmaster, but performances by the composer are known to have taken place as well. When Mozart, around 1777, lost interest in violin-playing, at least as far as concertizing was concerned, father Leopold (the violin teacher!) gently reproached him—"You don't even realize how well you play!"—and admonished him to continue. Nevertheless, the piano henceforth had a strong attraction for Wolfgang, a change which violinists may deplore but which gave to the world some of the most satisfying keyboard concertos of all times.

In the authentic violin concertos, all written in 1775, Mozart shows himself well acquainted with the reigning Italian and French styles. The Italian school of violin playing, continuing a strong Baroque tradition, was well represented in Salzburg and throughout Germany and Austria. Pietro Nardini (1722–93) and Luigi Boccherini (1743–1805) were among its outstanding practitioners; their graceful, elegant melodic style speaks from Mozart's best-known violin concertos (the last three) and also from the more violinistic divertimentos (see Chapter 9).[8] Yet here, as so often,

---

[8] A violin concerto in D major, allegedly by Boccherini and published in 1924, contains surprising similarities to Mozart's violin concertos, K. 218 and 219. Its authenticity has always been doubtful, and cogent reasons exist for considering it a forgery. Yves Gérard, compiler, *Thematic . . . catalogue of the works of Luigi Boccherini* (London, 1969), pp. 564ff.

Mozart's imagination carries his works beyond any models, especially in regard to harmony and formal disposition. The integration of tutti and solo portions, while not yet as ingenious as in the later piano concertos, shows many touches of Mozart's inventiveness. In the A Major Concerto the opening tutti theme reappears with the entrance of the solo violin, the two themes being ingeniously combined (Example 8–3). A concluding flourish in a tutti section is picked up by the soloist and developed into thematic material (Example 8–4). In the last movements of these concertos Mozart

EXAMPLE 8–3. Mozart, *Violin Concerto in A Major*, K. 219, First Movement.

EXAMPLE 8–4. Mozart, *Violin Concerto in A Major*, K. 219, First Movement.

uses the title *rondeau*, mindful of their French character. A *galant* mood prevails, but there are surprise interpolations of folk, or folk-like, melodies. Surprise must also have been caused by the *alla turca* section which suddenly interrupts the gentle rondeau *(tempo di menuetto)* of K. 219—"Turkish" music Mozart had arranged for a ballet, *Le gelosie del serraglio*, about 1772.

An orchestra consisting of strings with two oboes (replaced, in some middle movements, by flutes) and horns was sufficient for the violin concertos; it was enlarged for the piano concertos of the following decade.

The *Sinfonia concertante* in E♭, K. 364, was written several years after the violin concertos. In effect it is a double concerto for violin and viola, on the same expressive level. The viola is treated as an equal to the violin; Mozart provided for its equality in sound by writing its part in D major, requiring the instrument to be tuned a half-tone higher than the violin.

Since cadenzas (at least in eighteenth-century concertos) could not be improvised simultaneously by both instruments, Mozart provided them, thereby giving us an idea of the amount and kind of music he considered suitable for a violin or viola cadenza.

MOZART'S PIANO CONCERTOS

Of all the instruments for which Mozart composed concertos (and these include a number of wind instruments), the clavier received his most constant attention. His enthusiasm for the (then still fairly new) piano has been mentioned before; it inspired him to write piano concertos all through his life, among them some of his most beautiful and profound compositions. The ten-year-old boy, probably with some help from his father, fashioned keyboard concertos out of sonatas by the "London" Bach by providing tutti sections and cadenzas, and by making the necessary adjustments in key relationships. Individual sonata movements by Schobert and others were similarly adapted to provide performing repertory needed by the Mozarts on their travels. John Christian—rather than Emanuel—Bach, and Wagenseil are among the more immediate models for Mozart's first original concertos, beginning with K. 175 of 1773. Their characteristic "singing" themes owe much to the expressive possibilities of the new instrument, possibilities that were bringing about a reorientation in the manner of playing keyboard instruments as well, with legato rather than non-legato playing becoming the norm. In a group of concertos written in 1776–77, K. 271 is the most substantial. The soloist makes a surprise appearance at the opening: the first two measures of the theme are stated in unison by the orchestra; the soloist completes the thought. This procedure is repeated; only then does the orchestra embark on the customary opening tutti, at the end of which the piano eases in again with a long trill.

In general character these concertos are understandably close to the violin concertos that were written a year or two before, including, in K. 271, the insertion of a contrasting section in the final *rondeau.* Mozart goes one step further: he interpolates what amounts to a separate movement, a *menuetto* marked cantabile, with several free, cadenza-like passages. The entire rondeau abounds in such improvisatory material and includes several tempo changes.

After Mozart settled in Vienna he viewed the writing and performing of piano concertos as the most promising avenue to public recognition. Here he showed himself to be far ahead of his contemporaries in technique as well as in musical imagination. His playing was widely admired for its sensitivity, delicate touch, and fluency—qualities for the display of which his concertos provide ample opportunity. At the same time he did not wish to put himself musically beyond the reach of his public, and he seems to have taught some of his concertos to his better pupils. Concerning some of the early Viennese concertos, including K. 413, he wrote to his father that they were a "happy medium between the too easy and the too difficult," and that they contained brilliant writing and should please connoisseurs and others. Brilliant keyboard parts certainly are much in evidence, frequently consisting not of mere passage-work but of melodically meaningful figuration. Equally or more striking, however, is the profusion of ideas, the great wealth of themes. In some movements no one theme can be said to be the principal one. In the opening tutti of K. 482 one might count seven distinct musical ideas before the entrance of the solo brings yet another theme. Occasionally several motifs or themes are related; in K. 503/I they are unified by a pattern of three repeated eighth notes, common to several themes. Aside from the wealth of ideas, the listener marvels at the ingenuity of their deployment and the complex, subtle, ingenious ways in which soloist and orchestra collaborate. That in Mozart's concept of the concerto they are equals is evident from their frequent sharing of themes, as in K. 466/I, one of his most popular concertos (Example 8–5). Lively give-and-

EXAMPLE 8–5. Mozart, *Piano Concerto in D Minor*, K. 466, First Movement.

take between solo and tutti is frequent, including short interjections of one measure or less. The number of tutti and solo sections is larger than in the earlier Classic concerto. Themes recur in varied order and distribution, so that few movements reveal what one might consider a standard pattern. Melodic ideas are offered in such abundance that we hardly take notice of the fact that Mozart's developments are on a more modest scale than in his symphonies from the same years. His harmonic vocabulary, on the other hand, is as rich as in any of his other compositions, using devices and establishing moods generally associated with later, Romantic music (Example 8–6).

EXAMPLE 8–6. Mozart, *Piano Concerto in E♭ Major*, K. 449, Second Movement.

EXAMPLE 8–6. *Continued.*

What, specifically, causes these works to be outstanding? Aside from qualities already mentioned it would seem to be the satisfying variety within a generally understood and anticipated pattern. We can point to specific instances of melodic freshness—the way a phrase veers and departs from the expected completion, or is chromatically altered upon its repetition, making an elegant gesture out of a routine motion (Example 8–7).

EXAMPLE 8–7. Mozart, *Piano Concerto in D Major,* K. 537, First Movement.

Furthermore, we can point to lively contrapuntal writing, often already found in the opening ritornello, or in the solo part, or involving both. Unexpected interpolations have been noted in K. 271; they also occur at times in movements in theme and variations form. But Mozart startles us with a greater variety of procedures in these final rondos. Here he is not above providing melodies which, with their *opera buffa* lightheartedness, seem to make fun of those serious moods that have already been established. Such a mood characterizes the refrain from the last movement of K. 482; it is reinforced in the couplet that follows, boisterously given out by one clarinet with a jolly accompanying figure provided by another (Example 8–8). This

EXAMPLE 8–8. Mozart, *Piano Concerto in E♭ Major,* K. 482, Third Movement.

finale and others are full of surprises involving sudden changes of key, meter, and tempo. At times, as in K. 482, these contrasts are intensified by complete changes in timbre, the andantino cantabile here being given over entirely to wind instruments. In the first movement of this concerto the winds had already been given a prominent place in the presentation of thematic material (Example 8–9). Mozart knew that the special attention he

EXAMPLE 8–9. Mozart, *Piano Concerto in E♭ Major*, K. 482, First Movement.

gave to the wind instruments was something that few other composers had tried. In this way, too, he showed his essentially symphonic concept of the concerto.

Finales in theme-and-variations form are rarer than rondos; they occur in K. 453 and K. 491 in C minor. In the latter, we have the customary variation in major with much importance given to bright woodwind writing. After the cadenza a final variation brings a change to rapid 6/8 time. A presto finale also provides a brilliant ending for K. 453.

Mozart's last piano concerto, K. 595 of 1791, lacks some of the brilliance of its immediate predecessors—a statement which also applies to the Clarinet Concerto, K. 622, Mozart's last work in concerto form. Both have been noted for their more subdued mood and lack of soloistic display. K. 595 has with some justification been called introspective—not a value judgment but a realization of its beauty and appeal on a more intimate level. If one looks for reasons in the circumstances of the composer's life during these terrible last years, one must, at the same time, be mindful of the many works or movements that breathe a different air—even the rondo finale (K. 595), which returns to serenity and amiability. Once more it is the great variety of experience, the universality of meaning encountered in these concertos that cause us to view them, and their composer, as representing the essence of Classicism.

BIBLIOGRAPHICAL NOTES

Several concertos for keyboard and strings by Wagenseil are available: in C major (ed. Walter Upmayer [Berlin, 1936]; D major (ed. E. F. Thom [Leipzig, 1964]; and A major (ed. H. Bemmann and H. Ruf [Wolfenbüttel, 1964]).

Among special studies of Mozart's keyboard concertos, those by C. M. Girdlestone (*Mozart and His Piano Concertos* [London, 1948]) and A. Hutchings (*A Companion to Mozart's Piano Concertos*, 2nd ed. [London, 1950]) should be mentioned, along with chapters 16 and 17 in Einstein's *Mozart*, and contributions by F. Blume and H. C. R. Landon in *MC*. See also "The Concertos: Structure and Style," in A. Peter Brown, *Haydn's Keyboard Music* (Bloomington, IN: Indiana University, 1986).

Keyboard concertos by J. C. Bach, Hummel, Pleyel, Wagenseil, and contemporaries are available in modern editions. See M. Hinson, *Music for Piano and Orchestra* (Bloomington, IN: Indiana University, 1981). Among performing editions of Boccherini cello concertos are G. 474 (Milan, 1960), G. 476 (Frankfurt, 1977), and G. 477 (Mainz, 1968).

NINE

CHAMBER MUSIC, DIVERTIMENTO, SERENADE

DEFINITIONS AND CATEGORIES

Musical terminology is notoriously inaccurate and inconsistent. The term "symphony" shows this clearly, and a similar variety of meanings makes it impossible to define "chamber music" in one short sentence. *Musica da camera*, as a concept of the Baroque era, took in virtually all music that was neither church music *(musica da chiesa)* nor theatrical music (opera); it thus included what today goes under the name of orchestral music as well as "chamber music" in the modern sense. This situation still existed, to some extent, in the later eighteenth century—understandably so since princely chambers were the setting in which a symphony, a string quartet, or a secular cantata might be heard.

Today chamber music is usually defined as music in which there is only one player to each part. This definition works for most chamber music

Palace of the Archbishop *(Residenz),* Salzburg: conference room. Much of Mozart's instrumental music was written for performance in these chambers. Museum Salzburg.

of the Classic period, though we cannot always be sure of the composer's intentions. Some of the earlier flexibility still existed, according to which various decisions, including the number of players to be used, were left up to the person in charge of a particular performance.

By the time Haydn and Mozart wrote their mature works of chamber music, certain standard combinations of instruments had evolved. Among these the string quartet became most important, and it has maintained this position to the present day. Other popular combinations included the string trio (two violins and cello; or violin, viola, and cello) and the string quintet (usually with two violas; occasionally with two cellos). The piano trio (violin, cello, piano) and piano quartet (with a viola added) achieved importance late in the eighteenth century but, together with the piano quintet (string quartet and piano), figured more prominently in nineteenth-century music.

While we must acknowledge the importance of standand combinations in Classic chamber music, we should not overlook the wealth of music for other small combinations of instruments, including wind instruments. Hoboken's thematic catalog of Haydn's instrumental works provides ample documentation, since works are listed there according to categories such as string trios, divertimentos for four or more instruments, and so forth.

Works written for one combination were frequently published in other arrangements as well, with or without the composer's blessing. All this variety underlines the importance of chamber music in the musical life of the age, its place still being the home rather than the concert hall. Those of us whose knowledge of chamber music stems largely from recitals and phonograph records may find it hard to imagine the importance of the family string quartet, and of *Hausmusik* in general, in eighteenth- and nineteenth-century musical life, especially in Austria and Germany. All parents who could possibly afford it included music lessons in their children's education. One chronicler of Vienna's musical life in 1808 found words of special (and no doubt exaggerated) praise for this tradition:

> The parents' birthdays are celebrated with music . . . no special occasion goes by without being enhanced by this art form. . . . In this great capital city, on any given evening, one would find few homes in which families did not entertain themselves with a string quartet or a piano sonata, in preference to card playing, formerly so much in vogue.[1]

Understandably, some music written for home use may not have great appeal in the concert hall today. This applies to the duet repertory of the age—the hundreds of duets (original and arrangements) for violins and for flutes, for violin and viola, and, less numerous, for violin and cello. Boccherini, Joseph and Michael Haydn, Mozart, and Pleyel are among the well-known composers of duets. Those by Vanhal and other lesser figures were also printed and widely played at the time.

TOWARD THE STRING QUARTET

String music with four essential parts or musical lines was known during the Baroque era under names such as *sinfonia a 4* or *sonata a 4*. Works of this nature often used several players on each part, employed a figured bass instrument, and, as in the Baroque suite, varied greatly as to number and sequence of movements, all of which were likely to be in the same key. Haydn's early chamber music shows this loose organization and also flexibility in the choice of titles. Until about 1765 he used terms like "divertimento" and "quadro" for works that varied greatly in scoring, number of movements, length, and form. Hoboken shows that one of Haydn's early divertimentos existed in many contemporary copies, entitled variously Divertimento, Gassatio or Cassatio, Quartett, Quadro, Notturno, and

[1]"Übersicht des gegenwärtigen Zustandes der Tonkunst in Wien," *Vaterländische Blätter für den österreichischen Kaiserstaat,* I (1808), 39 ff.

Sonata. Gradually Haydn and others introduced distinctions on musical grounds: the light and purely entertaining ensemble music retained the old titles while more serious works, making greater demands on player and listener, were normally (but not always) called trio, quartet, and so forth.

The trio sonata for two violins and figured bass, the most popular chamber music combination of the Baroque, was another predecessor of the Classic string quartet. In performance it required four instruments, since the bass part was realized by both a melody and a chord instrument. In chamber music as in orchestral music the figured bass gradually disappeared, its harmony-supplying function being absorbed by more active voices. The viola, a middle-range instrument, slowly assumed an essential position in chamber music, so that two violins, viola, and cello emerged as a particularly serviceable combination. In view of the earlier importance of the trio sonata it is not surprising that Haydn wrote string trios before turning to the quartet for the first time. Some of these called for "basso" rather than specifying the cello, and quite possibly a (keyboard) figured bass instrument was still used; parts for such are included in some early editions.

Other early chamber music works by Haydn (for example, a divertimento for two violins, two English horns, two bassoons, and two horns, composed before 1767) have a structure that became a favored form for divertimentos: five movements of which the second and fourth are minuets. This is the plan of Haydn's earliest string quartets—works which were written for the enjoyment of the participants rather than the listeners. Their origin is linked to the name of Karl Josef von Fürnberg, a nobleman and music lover who, around 1755, invited Haydn to his castle, Weinzierl (near Melk in Lower Austria), to provide some professional leadership for the summer's musical activities. Three other string players were available, including the local parson. Quite possibly young Haydn began to write string quartets for the simple reason that this was the available combination at Weinzierl. At any rate, from then on the string quartet assumed the foremost place in his chamber music.

The quartets of Op. 1 and Op. 2 have much in common.[2] Most of them are simple enough so that amateurs could participate successfully. All but one of them consist of five short movements. The outer movements are bright; their melodic ideas are simple, often (as in Op. 1, No. 1) based on

[2]Of the so-called Op. 3 quartets, at least two may have been written by Romanus Hoffstetter (1742–1812), although as late as 1975 the provenance of these quartets was discussed at length without arriving at definite proof of Hoffstetter's authorship (*Haydn Studies,* ed. J. P. Larsen, H. Serwer, and J. Webster [New York: Norton, 1981], pp. 95ff). The total number of Haydn's string quartets, traditionally set at eighty-three, has been revised, for this and other reasons. Geiringer (*Haydn,* pp. 211ff) considers sixty-eight to be the correct number. See also P. Griffiths, *The String Quartet* (New York: Thames and Hudson, 1983), pp. 11f.

triads, stated in vigorous unison. The viola as yet is not independent and often follows the bass line an octave higher. Doubling of this kind, contrary to the practice of the Baroque *sonata a 4,* brought criticism. The minuets are still close to the dance, without the surprises, serious moods, or rhythmic complications found later. In the slow movements the first violin becomes a singer with a graceful, lyrical melody, discreetly accompanied. At times the singer is a prima donna, as in the elaborate adagio of Op. 2, No. 2, with two cadenzas on the customary $^6_4$ chord stressing the soloistic nature of the movement. The dimensions of Haydn's early quartets are small: an entire five-movement work may take no longer to play than the first movement of a quartet written toward the end of his career.

Haydn's Op. 9 quartets, dating from about 1768, show the emergence of a distinctive style. Florid first violin parts are a reminder that an accomplished virtuoso, Luigi Tomasini, had by this time joined Prince Esterházy's musical establishment. To be sure, the first violin had led in Op. 1–2 also, but its technical requirements were much more modest. Paradoxical though it may sound, the Tomasini parts are more soloistic, yet they dominate the proceedings less. In other words, second violin, viola, and cello now participate at least occasionally with material of thematic importance, as in Op. 9, No. 2, where the last movement's main theme returns in the cello. Even when the lower parts are not thematically involved, they show greater independence from each other, resulting in a more varied texture. It seems that Haydn was aware of the new qualities of his Op. 9; later in life he wished his official list of string quartets to begin with these. The minuets in Op. 9 still precede the slow movements.

The quartets of Op. 17 and Op. 20 followed in close succession (1771 and 1772); they continued and intensified the stylistic developments noted before. In Op. 17 balance and integration of all four parts are achieved with more success than earlier; this in spite of the fact that Tomasini continued to be favored with virtuoso first violin parts. Naturally, when Haydn writes a passage such as the following (Example 9–1), the lower instruments retire to the background:

EXAMPLE 9–1. Haydn, *String Quartet,* Op. 17, No. 5, First Movement.

Allegro

Elsewhere, as in the minuet of the same work, they answer and imitate. In general, the increased use of imitation, of counterpoint, reflects Haydn's intention of giving greater equality to all parts. The expressive range is increased; "dark" movements in minor keys are not uncommon during this period. Elements of "storm and stress" are much in evidence in the Op. 20 quartets: restless melodies, sudden shifts in rhythmic patterns and accents, frequent outbursts of intense emotion. The adagio of Op. 20, No. 2 with its violent unison passages speaks this language, as does the serious opening of Op. 20, No. 5.

Contrapuntal writing is prominent in these quartets, and not only in the famous finales of Op. 20, Nos. 2, 5, and 6, which are fugues with four, two, and three subjects respectively. After Op. 20, Haydn no longer considered the string quartet a medium for strict polyphony; on the other hand these works prepared the ground for the greater freedom in part-writing which was to be a landmark of the mature Classic style. Mozart soon came to know and esteem Haydn's Op. 20; as often, such esteem was reflected promptly in his own compositions, in this case the quartets which Mozart wrote in 1773, K. 168–173.

HAYDN'S LATER QUARTETS

The ten-year gap that separates Op. 20 from the next group of quartets is generally interpreted as a sign of the composer's dissatisfaction with the style he pursued in this medium up to that time, or of his having explored a certain road to its end. In a letter dated December 3, 1781, Haydn referred to the new quartets of Op. 33 as having been written in "an entirely new, very special manner." This often-repeated statement has resulted in some exaggerated claims as to their revolutionary nature. They are not revolutionary, but they do incorporate to a far greater degree than ever the principle of thematic fragmentation, manipulation, and development. This principle, already discussed in connection with the symphonies, becomes the outstanding characteristic of Haydn's "new manner"—in fact, it has remained the touchstone of good quartet-writing to the present day. The good part-writing found in the Op. 33 quartets, meaning the integration of the four instrumental lines, was widely praised. Goethe's comparison of a string quartet with a conversation among four intelligent people has become famous since it describes so well this important stylistic feature of Classic chamber music. An intelligent conversation requires participants who are intellectual equals, or near-equals, and a performance of a late Haydn quartet requires capable players for all four parts. An early nineteenth-century observer claimed that in amateur circles the later quartets were not played as much since it was often hard to find four equally strong players, and that for this reason the quartets of Ignaz Pleyel were found more accessible, though admittedly on a musically lower level.

In Op. 33 Haydn had substituted the term "scherzo" for the customary "menuetto." Except for a slightly faster tempo the movements in question are scherzi in name only. Haydn himself might have felt that though their mood was lighter and less courtly it was not basically different; at any rate he did not use the term "scherzo" in any of his remaining quartets.

The years after Op. 33 saw the unfolding of the touching friendship between Haydn and Mozart in which each gave to and learned from the other. Many music lovers of our day must wish that they could turn back time to be present at the memorable gatherings described by Michael Kelly in his *Reminiscences* (London, 1826)—gatherings which took place at the Vienna apartment of Stephen Storace, whose sister Nancy was a well-liked singer at the opera:

> Storace gave a quartet party to his friends. The players were tolerable, not one of them excelled on the instrument he played, but there was a little science among them, which I dare say will be acknowledged when I name them:
>
> | | |
> |---|---|
> | The First Violin................ | Haydn |
> | The Second Violin.............. | Baron Dittersdorf |
> | The Violoncello................. | Vanhall |
> | The Tenor [viola] .... | Mozart |
>
> A greater treat . . . cannot be imagined. . . . After the musical feast was over, we sat down to an excellent supper, and became joyous and lively in the extreme.

Haydn dedicated the six quartets of Op. 50 (1787) to King Frederick William II of Prussia. As we might expect, the cello parts pay tribute to the royal patron: he must indeed have taken his playing seriously to do justice to some demanding passages. In these quartets the independence of parts is again to be noted, particularly in the slow movements. Haydn's custom of building an entire movement on motivic material derived from one theme is illustrated by the opening allegro of Op. 50, No. 6 (Example 9–2).

EXAMPLE 9–2. Haydn, *String Quartet*, Op. 50, No. 6, First Movement.

This theme is soon fragmented; its first six notes are used extensively and much is made of their melodic and rhythmic quality. In measure 37 a cadence turns out to be deceptive and leads to further modification of the principal theme (Example 9–3). A closing theme is introduced during

EXAMPLE 9–3. Haydn, *String Quartet*, Op. 50, No. 6, First Movement.

the last measures of the exposition. The development that follows has to be heard, preferably with score in hand, in order to appreciate the ingenuity with which the opening theme of the quartet, and only this theme, is manipulated; it occurs in some form or other in virtually every measure. This movement and the following poco adagio also show well the increased harmonic variety that is one of the more tangible ways in which Mozart's influence appears in the quartets from Op. 50 on.

Much has been said about humor in Haydn's music: it is a prominent and cherished ingredient of many Haydn quartets, particularly the finales. The last movement of Op. 54, No. 1 (1788) is typical; its main theme falls into what the listener expects to be two phrases of eight measures each. But the second phrase ends unexpectedly and inconclusively on a diminished seventh chord, followed by an apparent continuation of the theme, to be cut off after three notes, piano (Example 9–4).

EXAMPLE 9–4. Haydn, *String Quartet*, Op. 54, No. 1, Finale.

Only then does the theme reach its conclusion. The repeated-note figure produces more humorous effects later in the movement, when it is coupled with harmonic and dynamic changes that are abrupt to the point of being grotesque (Example 9–5).[3]

EXAMPLE 9–5. Haydn, *String Quartet*, Op. 54, No. 1, Finale.

[3]See also S. Paul, "Comedy, Wit, and Humor in Haydn's Instrumental Music," *Haydn Studies*, pp. 450ff.

Other qualities that distinguish Haydn's later quartets include greater variety in the key relationships between movements, as in Op. 74, No. 3 (first movement in G minor, ending in G major; second movement in E major—a very expressive and chromatic largo); Op. 76, No. 5; or Op. 76, No. 6 in E♭ major, in which the second movement is a fantasia in B major. Harmonic variety is increased when Haydn modulates, within this movement, to B♭ and A♭ major before returning to B major.

Slow movements in theme and variations form occur more frequently in Haydn's later chamber music. Op. 76, No. 3, one of Haydn's best known quartets, thus acquired its popular name, the "Emperor" Quartet. That he was asked to write a hymn for the birthday of Emperor Francis in 1797 shows the esteem in which Haydn, then sixty-five years old, was held. Haydn took his commission seriously. This was to be a surprise homage upon the Emperor's arrival at the opera. Leaflets containing the text were distributed among the audience, whose singing of the new hymn moved the monarch visibly. The hymn, its text based on the English "God Save the King," was commissioned and printed by Austrian government authorities. It was ordered to be sung throughout Austria on the same day. For the rest of his life Haydn remained very fond of this melody. Playing it several times, with great feeling, was his last musical activity a few days before his death. The variations that he composed for the quartet have the same beauty, the "noble simplicity," that characterizes the melody; in a sense they are among the best examples of Classic style. Each variation preserves the melody, which is entrusted in turn to all four instruments, but each statement presents a different appearance. Subtle modifications are introduced in the accompaniment, which becomes quite chromatic and rhythmically complex in the last variation, without for a moment dispelling the sense of serenity and quiet dignity suggested by the theme.

Haydn's gift for simple melody, revealed here and elsewhere, has inspired many attempts to show that he borrowed melodies, especially from folk songs. Although such a procedure would have been considered neither unusual nor reprehensible in the eighteenth century, Haydn seldom consciously incorporated actual folk melodies in his compositions. Instead, he seems to have assimilated the essential qualities of much of the music sung by the "folk" around him, starting with his childhood days. Though a court composer most of his life, Haydn succeeded in maintaining rapport with his people without deliberately trying to be popular.

OTHER CHAMBER MUSIC BY HAYDN

In comparison with his string quartets, Haydn's numerous other chamber works are of secondary importance. The many baryton trios, written for Prince Nicholas, come to mind: they are largely *galant* music.

Haydn's *Emperor Hymn*—autograph. Austrian National Library.

When, around 1775, the Prince lost interest in his favorite instrument, the stream of trios and other baryton works soon ran dry. More lasting was Haydn's concern with the piano trio. In this category he produced the first works to maintain themselves in the repertory to this day. Melodic interest, especially in the early trios, is fairly evenly divided between violin and right-hand piano part. The cello rarely assumes melodic significance or independence, doubling the left-hand keyboard part instead. A three-line texture is thus typical: there are few full chords for the piano, even at cadences. The Trio in A♭ Major (Hoboken XV:14) was performed in London in 1792 as a "New Sonata Piano Forte, with a Violin and Violoncello," though the violin part is substantial.[4] Still, the piano contributes the most, especially in the adagio. Among these later trios, Hoboken XV:25, with the *Rondo all'ongarese* ("Gipsy Rondo"), has always been a favorite.

MOZART'S STRING QUARTETS

For Mozart, too, the string quartet was a favored medium of expression. Of the more than sixty original Haydn quartets, thirty, for better or for worse, have become known as "the celebrated quartets"; of Mozart's considerably fewer contributions ten have achieved this status, beloved by

[4]W. Stockmeier, Preface to *Haydn: Werke*, XVII/2 (Munich, 1974), p. vi. See also M. Rolf, "Stylistic Influence in the Early Haydn Piano Trios," *Haydn Studies*, pp. 459ff.

chamber music players everywhere and constantly performed today. The first six of these[5] were published in 1785; they are generally known as the "Haydn Quartets" because of the touching dedication to the older composer. They present many features that are characteristic of Classic style in general: the nature and development of ideas, the harmonic idiom which is expressive and at times dramatic, and the lightness of texture with its happy mixture of homophony and counterpoint. Mozart was aware of the significance of these works, written after a pause (in quartet composing) of approximately ten years. In the dedication he calls them the "fruit of long and tiring efforts"—a statement the sincerity of which is clearly reflected in the autograph's appearance. It contains far more extensive changes than were customary for Mozart, who usually had a detailed concept of the music in his head before putting pen to paper. He evidently intended to make these works, which were not commissioned, something very special, worthy of being dedicated to his friend. Nevertheless, they are not imitations of Haydn's style; Mozart's individuality shows itself in many ways, especially in his harmony. No better example exists (and none has been more frequently cited) than the introduction to the last of these six quartets, K. 465, the "dissonant" quartet. Slow introductions are rare in Mozart's chamber music, and this is the only occurrence in the mature quartets. The successive entrances of the four instruments are most startling: after the cello's repeated C, the viola, second violin, and first violin enter on A♭, E♭ and A♮ respectively. What happens in these measures can be satisfactorily explained in terms of functional harmonic analysis, but they caused headaches to many stalwart nineteenth-century teachers of composition, at least one of whom felt called upon to publish a "correction" of Mozart's score.[6] Aside from the controversial eight opening measures, the entire slow introduction is a good example of Mozart's expressive chromatic harmony. Here Haydn clearly learned from his younger colleague.

Mozart's last three quartets appear in most modern editions with the notation "dedicated to the King of Prussia." During a visit to Berlin in 1789, Mozart apparently conceived the plan of writing six quartets for Frederick William II, though it is doubtful that an actual commission by the King was involved. Three quartets (K. 575, 589, 590) were probably begun soon after Mozart left Berlin and completed after his return to Vienna, but the plan of dedicating them to the King was given up. In the cello parts of these three works Mozart gave his royal patron ample opportunities to shine. The cello is treated as a melody instrument throughout; often the first statement of an extended cantabile theme is entrusted to it,

---

[5]K. 387, 421, 428, 458, 464, and 465.

[6]The passage in question, and the criticism by Fétis (1829) and others, formed the subject of a long essay by Gottfried Weber, "Über eine besonders merkwürdige Stelle in einem Mozartschen Violinquartett aus C," *Caecilia*, 14 (1832), 1–49, 122–29.

exploiting a high register challenging for the most seasoned player.[7] The resulting near-equality of cello (and viola) with the violins reminds us that these are examples of Mozart's late chamber-music style, written after his last symphonies.

OTHER CHAMBER MUSIC BY MOZART

To appreciate Mozart's achievement in the field of chamber music one must listen to his late string quintets as well: K. 515 and 516 (1787), K. 593 (1790), and K. 614 (1791). No commission or other reason is known for the composition of these works, which contain much that is as eloquent as his quartets and on the same expressive level. Aside from Mozart's own earlier quintets, models existed in works by Michael Haydn and Boccherini; in these, divertimento qualities were dominant. The inclusion of a second viola makes for a texture that is fuller, darker, and warmer at the same time, qualities that Mozart used to best advantage in these, his last major works of chamber music. K. 516, like earlier works in the key of G minor, strikes us at times as gentle and melancholy but also rises to great intensity. Extensive modulations in the slow movement and the adagio introduction to the finale contribute to these qualities. In the first movement of K. 593 the slow introduction returns just before the coda—a procedure to be found more frequently in Beethoven's writing.

Certain other late works of chamber music should be mentioned. The quintet for clarinet and strings, K. 581, one of the few great compositions for this combination of instruments, accords a prominent place to the versatile wind instrument without thereby reducing the strings to an accompaniment function. This late work (as well as the clarinet concerto K. 622 mentioned earlier) was inspired by the fine playing of Anton Stadler (1753–1812) whom Mozart befriended late in life—circumstances similar to those that brought about the creation of Brahms's last works of chamber music with clarinet.

The string trio for violin, viola, and cello, K. 563, is a full-fledged, profound work of chamber music; its title "divertimento" is justified primarily by its external form: six movements including two minuets.

Among Mozart's piano trios we find some that are close to the Rococo in mood, with the same favoring of the piano part that characterizes Haydn's works. Others, especially K. 502 in B♭ and K. 542 in E, come closer to the standard of chamber music set in the string quartets of the same period, though the very different timbre of the piano precludes any

[7]See A. Tyson, "New Light on Mozart's 'Prussian' Quartets," *The Musical Times*, 116 (1975), 126–30.

real blend with the sound of the two string instruments. In two other works Mozart added a viola to these forces, and the group of three string instruments asserts itself quite successfully against the piano. Of the two piano quartets, K. 478, once more in the "fateful" key of G minor, has achieved greater popularity. Its dramatic opening movement immediately sets the work apart from much other late eighteenth-century chamber music with piano. Mozart's keyboard part stands out much of the time—its difficulty must have put it beyond the reach of most amateurs—yet it avoids, for the most part, concerto-like display. Mozart's G Minor Quartet represents the first substantial contribution to the medium of the piano quartet, which was to be cultivated more extensively by nineteenth-century composers.

BOCCHERINI'S CHAMBER MUSIC

The compositions of Luigi Boccherini include many trios for two violins and cello, about 90 string quartets, 125 string quintets, and many chamber works for other combinations, as well as about 30 symphonies. A fair amount of his chamber music has again become available. Much of it is charming, displaying graceful melodic writing and much variety in the formal design of multi-movement works.

Boccherini, who has been called the greatest cellist of the Classic period, concertized extensively in many countries. His many string quintets, with two cellos, are indicative of his mastery of that instrument; they contain prominent cello parts, rhythmically complex and highly ornamented. Good examples are the quintets Op. 11, No. 5 (Gérard 275, 1771, with the celebrated minuet) and Op. 51, No. 2 of 1795 (Gérard 377), the later containing a second movement with characteristically elegant, lilting melodic lines (Example 9–6).

EXAMPLE 9–6. Boccherini, *Quintet,* Op. 51, No. 2, Second Movement.

Andantino con innocenza

Boccherini's style, here and elsewhere, is individual; his development took place apart from the mainstream of Classic music in the north. Though a successful composer during his lifetime, he was soon overshadowed by his three great contemporaries. The writer of the obituary that appeared in the Leipzig *Allgemeine Musikalische Zeitung* of August 21, 1805 may have accurately summed up Boccherini's place in contemporary music:

> [He was] truly one of the most distinguished instrumental composers of his country, Italy. Unlike the majority of his compatriots he advanced in step with the times and with the development of the art of music in Germany. . . . [From Haydn] he assimilated into his own work all that he could without denying his own personality. Italy ranks him, for his quartets and similar music, at least as high as Haydn; Spain, where he spent the greater part of his creative life, in many of his works actually prefers him to the German master, who in that country sometimes is considered too learned. France, without wishing to place him on the same level as Haydn, has high esteem for him, while Germany, with its present preference for all that is more difficult, more artful, more learned, appears still to know him too little. He distinguished himself in the cause of Italian, Spanish (and probably also French) instrumental music, being the first to write string quartets in which each instrument was given an important part. He was, at any rate, the first to succeed there with this kind of writing. Boccherini (and soon after him Pleyel, with his early works) created quite a stir there with his chamber music—sooner, certainly, than Haydn, of whose music the public was still afraid.

DIVERTIMENTO AND SERENADE

While the term "string quartet" refers to a specific chamber-music grouping, other terms are less exact. Should Mozart's divertimentos and serenades be discussed in this chapter? Some of them clearly require only one player for each part; others demand, with equal clarity, somewhat larger forces—the kind of group which today is often called a chamber orchestra. For still others no unequivocal answer is possible: the composer himself may have considered either manner of performance possible. A work such as the Divertimento, K. 334, with a very florid first violin part, today may be performed successfully by an orchestra—an entire first violin section playing in flawless unison—but it is doubtful that this was possible or intended with the musicians available in Salzburg around 1780. Since many of these works are chamber music in the modern sense, it seems best to consider the divertimento in general, and related types, in this chapter rather than in the one dealing with symphonic music.

Before the Classic period the terms "divertimento," "serenade," "notturno," and "cassation" were in general use to designate music of a light, entertaining character, referring to the function of the music rather than its form or instrumentation. Music of this nature was welcomed for many social purposes, both indoors and outdoors. Today the term "dinner music" may suggest music of a superficial, inferior quality, not meant to be listened to attentively. A great deal of music by respectable Baroque composers was written for such lowly functions as well as for garden parties, weddings, birthday, and name-day celebrations. Classic composers continued this tradition in their divertimentos and serenades.[8] Mozart's "Haffner" Serenade goes back to such an occasion, a wedding.

The term "serenade" may have predominantly amorous connotations for some—a young man singing under the window of the lady of his affections—but happily the custom of serenading extended to a greater variety of occasions in the eighteenth century. Mozart writes of one such occasion, late on the eve of his name day in 1781, when some friends surprised and honored him by performing under his window his own Serenade in E$\flat$ Major, K. 375; a surprise which apparently gave a much-needed lift to his spirits. Outdoor serenading of this kind was a widespread summer custom, often commented upon by travelers, in Germany, Austria, and Bohemia. Having concluded one performance, the musicians might move on to several other places, repeating their playing and hoping to receive some payment each time.

Whether the music was intended for indoor or outdoor performance often can no longer be established today. Style and instrumentation do not seem to have been seriously affected by location: strings participated in outdoor, winds in indoor, performances. Those serenades that Mozart composed during the winter months (e.g., the *Serenata notturna*, K. 239) surely were not meant to be open-air music, yet their style does not distinguish them from many that are known to have added charm to some happy summer function.

Nor does it seem possible to make any consistent distinction between divertimento, serenade, and so forth, according to instrumentation, except that works called divertimento are frequently in chamber style whereas (at least Mozart's) serenades generally call for a small orchestra or wind ensemble. Both vary greatly as to number and type of movements. Most works have from three to eight movements; the number may grow to ten if one counts the marches which in many cases were intended to begin and end the composition.

Among Boccherini's contributions to this genre are six *divertimenti notturni* (Gérard 467–472; 1787–88) for various combinations of string and wind instruments. Gérard 470, an octet (1798), was also published as a *sin-*

---

[8]Other terms with the same or related meanings were *Finalmusik, Nachtmusik,* and *Gran Partita.* The origin of *cassation* is uncertain; a possible derivation is from the German *Gasse,* "street." J. Webster discusses the complex terminology in detail in "Towards a History of Viennese Chamber Music in the Early Classical Period," *JAMS,* 27 (1974), 212–47.

fonia concertante. The Quintet No. 60, *La musica notturna delle strade di Madrid* (Gérard 324, 1780), has been popular both as a chamber work (two violins, viola, two cellos) and in performance by a string orchestra.

Within its flexible number and organization of movements the Classic divertimento displays some favored arrangements, especially a five-movement form in the following sequence: (1) fast movement; (2) minuet and trio; (3) slow movement; (4) minuet and trio; (5) fast movement. Yet the variants are too numerous to consider this a norm. Some divertimentos have no minuet; others have one minuet, as in symphony and quartet, and some minuets have two trios.

To begin and end a divertimento with a march seems appropriate in open-air music; it gives the musicians an opportunity to make their entrance and departure pleasant and effective. The custom extended to works with strings as well: K. 251 ends with a *Marcia alla francese,* though we may well wonder whether in such instances the performers (including the string bass!) played while marching away. In many modern editions (including the older complete Mozart edition) the marches have been separated from the divertimentos or serenades for which they were intended.

To supply dinner music for the Archbishop seems to have been the function of many of these divertimentos. Their light nature is reflected in their harmonic and formal simplicity. Examples of the "diverting" spirit can be found in many divertimentos for winds, especially among the early ones. A carefree spirit asserts itself in some of their folk-like themes (Examples 9–7a and 9–7b).

EXAMPLE 9–7a. Mozart, *Divertimento in E♭ Major,* K. 166 (1773).

2 Oboes

EXAMPLE 9–7b. Mozart, *Divertimento in F Major,* K. 213 (1775).

Oboe I

The wind divertimentos K. 166 and K. 186 include clarinets. They may have been written for a patron in Milan rather than for performance in Salzburg (where clarinets were not yet used). Both include some material borrowed from other composers. K. 187, a set of many short, festive movements, at one time was thought to have been written for the anniversary of the Archbishop's enthronement in 1773, but it is no longer considered authentic. This "table music" calls for two flutes, five trumpets, and four timpani and consists of eight (originally ten) pieces. They are all simple and short—ceremonial music to provide the background for a public function. K. 188, for the same unusual combination of instruments and most likely authentic, is similar in character.

From 1775 to 1777 Mozart wrote many wind divertimentos for Salzburg. They tend to be simpler and shorter (and are less well known) than those from the same period that include strings (such as K. 251). K. 213, for woodwind sextet, is one of these carefree divertimentos and consists of four movements (allegro-andante-minuet-contredanse en rondeau). But Mozart also left more substantial wind music, for small and large ensembles. K. 439[b] (Vienna, probably 1783), for two bassett horns (or clarinets) and bassoon, is distinguished by lively part-writing, the three woodwind instruments producing a beautiful timbre. This is unproblematic, happy (but not superficial) music, delightful to players and audiences today.

Great variety of instrumentation is found in the Classic divertimento, perhaps somewhat greater than in the serenades. A cursory examination of the works listed in Group II of Hoboken's Haydn catalog will verify this. The more esoteric combinations are represented by Haydn's notturni for two "Lyre organizzate" (an instrument related to the hurdy-gurdy, with added organ pipes activated by small bellows[9]), two violas, bass, two clarinets, and two horns; and the well-known "Toy" Symphony of disputed authorship.

Among Haydn's wind divertimentos we find a group of six *Feldparthien* (i.e., outdoor music) written, perhaps, for the military band of his Prince.[10] Several of these begin with a march. One of the *Feldparthien* includes the *Chorale St. Antonii* which has become well known as the theme for a set of orchestral variations by Brahms (Op. 56a, 1873).

Mozart approached the divertimento with no standard combination of instruments in mind: there are examples for strings alone, for winds, and for manifold combinations of the two, in many cases presenting us with a delightful freshness and variety of timbres within one composition. K. 131, after a fully scored opening movement, brings an adagio for strings only, with a cantabile violin solo. The minuet, also for strings, has three trios: one for four horns only, one for flute, oboe, and bassoon (a real "trio"), and one for the combined forces of the first and second trios. Since the minuet is to be played after each trio, there are constant contrasts of timbre. After the last repeat of the minuet, Mozart writes a coda using, for the first time, all the instruments heard so far. Similar variety is provided in the second minuet, which includes a second trio for the unusual scoring of oboe, viola

[9]Illustration in *Grove 6*, 11:22.
[10]The authenticity of the six is dubious. Landon, *Chronicle and Works*, I: 271.

1 and 2, and bass. It is a pity that Mozart's divertimentos are seldom heard; his ingenious handling of tonal resources alone should be sufficient cause to change this.

Serious moods are not lacking in the divertimentos. The *Gran Partita* for thirteen wind instruments, K. 361, furnishes a fairly well known example. In this extensive work all instruments, including basset horns, display their characteristic tone qualities. In a number of other divertimentos the first or solo violin part provides the most striking timbre—a part which Mozart in some instances had written for himself. K. 287 for strings and two horns is such a composition. Describing his participation in a performance, Mozart writes that "everyone made big eyes. I played as though I were the greatest violinist in Europe." In this and some other divertimentos the first violin part goes technically as far as or beyond anything Mozart requires in his violin concertos—a fact generally unknown to violinists in search of challenging repertory from the Classic period.

Among Mozart's serenades for strings only, K. 525 has become famous as *Eine kleine Nachtmusik*. Several larger serenades call for a division into two to four small orchestras, making possible all sorts of echo effects and other spatial arrangements (*Serenata notturna*, K. 239; Notturno, K. 286). They must have delighted the guests at garden parties or palace festivities where the several groups of musicians probably were stationed in small pavilions or in adjoining rooms.

Several of Mozart's larger serenades present an unusual formal aspect: they include a central section of three movements with a solo violin part—a concerto within the serenade that is set off from the surrounding movements by its tonalities as well. Thus in K. 203 the outer movements, all in D and G, form one harmonic entity while the three central movements, with a *violino principale* part, are in B♭ and F.

Both Mozart and his father composed serenades which, under the designation *Final Musik*, served during the festivities marking the end of the school year at Salzburg's Benedictine University in early August. Students commissioned such works, to be performed in honor of their professors, and several Mozart serenades—composed in July or early August but otherwise unidentified—undoubtedly served this purpose.[11] K. 100 and 185 are among these; the former, of rather modest dimensions, achieves variety of sound by giving prominent passages to several wind instruments. K. 185, with the march, K. 189, is considerably longer and brings varied instrumentation in each of its many movements.

Concertante writing is so frequent that it may be considered an essential characteristic of the Classic divertimento and serenade. It may occur

---

[11]The festivities also included theatrical performances with music. *Die Schuldigkeit des ersten Gebots*, the first act of which was composed by Mozart, is one of these didactic oratorios. See the description by F. Giegling, Preface to *NMA* I:4/i.

in any movement, including minuet and especially trio; in cantabile movements, theme and variations movements, and rondos. It appears, as we have seen, in intimate chamber works and also in the larger serenades, symphonic in concept, such as K. 250, the rather lengthy "Haffner" Serenade.

Among later composers of chamber music for winds, Anton Reicha (1770–1836) should be mentioned because of his major contributions to the repertoire of the woodwind quintet (flute, oboe, clarinet, bassoon, horn). While employed in Bonn, Reicha became a friend of Beethoven and made the acquaintance of Haydn. After a stay in Vienna from 1801 to 1802, he settled in Paris in 1808, where his pupils included Berlioz and Liszt. In his autobiography Reicha explained that woodwind instruments now were greatly improved, but that other composers knew too little of their technique to show them off to advantage.[12] Reicha's woodwind quintets Op. 88 and 91, first published in 1817–19, achieved great popularity, with several editions appearing during his lifetime. They favor the four-movement arrangement typical of Classic chamber music, present technical challenges for all the instruments including the (valveless) horn, and generally display variety and imagination.

MUSIC FOR LARGER WIND ENSEMBLES

In wind music from the late eighteenth and early nineteenth centuries no clear dividing line can be drawn between "chamber" and "band" music. Mozart's large serenade K. 361, mentioned above, has companion pieces (the serenades K. 375 and K. 388) that are similar in scope but scored for fewer players. The latter, in C minor, is an especially dramatic and passionate work, as moving as many of Mozart's symphonies or string quartets. Serious or light, wind-ensemble music formed an important part of the repertory of this age. Some credit for this goes to Emperor Joseph II who, in 1782, ordered the formation of a *Harmonie* or wind band, according to a standard instrumentation of paired oboes, clarinets, horns, and bassoons. Such imperial support of wind music led other noblemen to follow suit and, at least for a few years, there was a flourishing of wind music in Austrian realms and beyond.[13] A chronicler in 1796 deplored that fewer and fewer noblemen maintained their own orchestras, "whether due to a cooling off of their love of art" or other (probably meaning financial) reasons, citing one prince who had "reduced his orchestra to a *Harmonie*."[14]

---

[12]J. G. Prodhomme, "From the Unpublished Autobiography of Antoine Reicha," *MQ*, 22 (1936), 339ff.

[13]See N. Zaslaw, preface to *NMA* VII:17/2, pp. viii ff.

[14]*Jahrbuch der Tonkunst von Wien und Prag* (Vienna, 1796), pp. 77f.

Around 1800 the extensive wind-band repertory consisted of original compositions (including some by Mozart's alleged rival, the court Kapellmeister Salieri)[15] and a vast number of arrangements or transcriptions, especially of operatic excerpts or entire operas. Johann Nepomuk Wendt (or Went, 1745–1801) transcribed many opera and ballet scores for various Viennese wind ensembles. If a new opera was successful, such transcriptions appeared quickly and often became very popular. Mozart was eager to make one of his own opera *Die Entführung aus dem Serail* before someone else could derive profit from doing so. Wenzel Sedlak (1776–1851) was equally successful in this field. His transcription of Beethoven's *Fidelio*, authorized by the composer, was published in 1814, the year the opera itself (third version) appeared on the stage. Sedlak knew his craft. The eleven excerpts, scored for nine wind instruments, are melodic ones (mostly from Act I) rather than the more dramatic scenes that rely on text declamation for their effect.

BIBLIOGRAPHICAL NOTES

Valuable essays on the chamber music of individual composers can be found in *Cobbett's Cyclopedic Survey of Chamber Music* (2 volumes, London, 1929; supplement, 1963). Newman's *SCE* deals only peripherally with chamber music other than sonatas but does discuss Haydn's piano trios. Detailed studies incorporating recent research include J. Webster, "Towards a History of Viennese Chamber Music in the Early Classical Period," *JAMS*, 27 (1974), 212–47; P. Griffiths, *The String Quartet*, Part I, (London, 1983); and R. Barret-Ayres, *Joseph Haydn and the String Quartet* (New York: Schirmer, 1974).

Grove 6 has articles on most categories of chamber music, including "Cassation," "Divertimento," and "Serenade." There is a chapter "The Divertimento and Cognate Forms" in *NOHM*, 7. Scholarly publications in German are L. Finscher, *Studien zur Geschichte des Streichquartetts*, vol. 1 (Kassel, 1974), and G. Hausswald, *Mozarts Serenaden* (Leipzig, 1951). Hausswald's *The Serenade for Orchestra* (*Anthology of Music, volume 34;* Cologne, 1970) is an overview of the genre including nineteenth- and twentieth-century examples. See also the contributions in *MC* by H. Engel ("The Smaller Orchestral Works"), D. Mitchell ("The Serenades for Wind Band"), and H. Keller ("The Chamber Music").

Yves Gérard has clarified matters of Boccherini chronology and authenticity in his *Thematic, Bibliographical and Critical Catalogue of the Works of Luigi*

---

[15]Salieri's *Armonia per un tempio della notte* was composed or arranged by Maelzel for a musical clock or automaton (see p. 229) which was located in a grotto (the "Temple of Night") in the park of a castle near Vienna.

Boccherini (London: Oxford University Press, 1969), but many questions remain unsolved. A complete edition of Boccherini's works was begun in 1970; the first nine volumes contain string quintets. Much of the chamber music is available in modern performing editions. Reicha's woodwind quintets have been reissued by several European publishers.

TEN

THE ART SONG (LIED) BEFORE SCHUBERT

To most singers the term *Lied* means nineteenth-century German solo song, beginning with Schubert's Lieder, with Schumann, Mendelssohn, Brahms, and others continuing and developing the genre. However, while the Lied was not central to the work of Classic-period composers, some of their contributions are substantial; singers who investigate the art song in its development from the mid-eighteenth century to Beethoven may discover some fine additions to their repertory. At the same time such study will show that Schubert's Lieder have ties to the past and to the work of composers around him.

Much of this development can be understood in terms of text-music relationships; the relative importance of poetry and music is a subject that comes up frequently in discussions of song and opera, during the Classic period and beyond. The development of the piano also had a bearing on the style of the Lied: its new, expressive possibilities made it the favored accompaniment instrument.

178

In some songs by C. P. E. Bach we have already encountered an intentionally simple, folk-like style—songs in which a melody, repeated for many verses, is supported by an extremely simple accompaniment, given to the keyboard player's left hand. (See p. 30.) Neither the texts nor the music of such songs probed great emotional depths or dealt with complex thoughts, and much of the poetry was by minor German writers of the time, forgotten today even in their own country.

The term "classic," in the general meaning described in an earlier chapter, extends to German literature as well. In the late eighteenth century Johann Wolfgang von Goethe (1749–1832) emerged, above all others, as the writer whose work in many categories (novel, drama, poetry) acquired a place of lasting distinction in German and world literature. Goethe's poetry inspired virtually all the great Lieder composers and many lesser ones.[1] Interestingly enough, the poet himself was not happy with many of the musical settings we esteem most highly today. The reasons, again, have to do with different views (his, his contemporaries, and ours) of the functions and relative importance of text and music.

Goethe and other writers expressed their views in conversations, letters, and essays; some composers also put their thoughts in writing. J. A. P. Schulz, in the preface to his *Lieder im Volkston* (Part II, 1785; see p. 29), stated the rationale for his collection of simple songs: he selected only those texts that called for folk-like treatment and endeavored to match those with melodies that were simple and easily learned and remembered, even by untrained lovers of singing. A good example is his "Der Mond ist aufgegangen" (1790; text by Matthias Claudius, 1778), still found today in many German folk-song collections. Melodies in an equally simple idiom occur in some of the theater music of the age, especially the popular ariettes of French *opéra comique* and the German *Singspiel*.

SONGS OF THE "SECOND BERLIN SCHOOL"

Other composers of the "Second Berlin School" contributed songs in this style, with simple, diatonic melodies, strophic form (i.e., identical music for each of the verses of text), and light, often minimal accompaniment. But the same composers, and others of their generation, also wrote Lieder that go beyond this. Reichardt, Zelter, and Zumsteeg represent this development; they were inspired largely by the rise of German classic poetry. In addition to Goethe, leading contributors of song texts were Johann Gottfried Herder (1744–1803) and Friedrich Schiller (1759–1805).

[1]Friedländer lists about two hundred settings of Goethe poems by eighteenth- and nineteenth-century composers in *Das deutsche Lied im 18. Jahrhundert*, vol. III (Hildesheim, 1962), 152ff.

Johann Friedrich Reichardt, whose writings on music we have encountered earlier, had close contacts with Goethe, whom he admired; the poet, in turn, was glad to have a composer-companion with whom he could discuss musical subjects. A wealth of Goethe songs resulted. Earlier, Reichardt had published a collection of songs to texts by Klopstock, Stolberg, Claudius, and Hölty (1779). His objective then had been to compose melodies that would be suitable for all the stanzas of a poem; more variety distinguishes his later songs, though traditional strophic form continues to be found. Reichardt composed Goethe's "Veilchen" (published 1783) several years before Mozart's well-known setting. Unlike Mozart, Reichardt set all three verses to identical music. The keyboard part is of the older *Klavierlied* style: a spare bass that merely outlines the extremely simple harmonies and a right hand which doubles the melody and has a few additional notes. The only way in which monotony can be avoided in such simple strophic songs is through the singer's interpretation of the text's changing emotional content—indeed, that is imperative in songs with many stanzas. Goethe himself once made this recommendation to the interpreter of one of his songs.[2]

EXAMPLE 10–1. Reichardt, "Das Veilchen," beginning.

[2]W. Salmen, in the preface to his edition of Reichardt's songs, *Das Erbe Deutscher Musik*, 58 (Munich, 1964), v f.

Reichardt's settings of Goethe's *Lieder, Oden, Balladen und Romanzen mit Musik* appeared in 1809–11. His "Erlkönig" (1794), simple and strophic, pales in comparison with Schubert's famous Lied.[3]

But there are other ballads by Reichardt that in mood and importance of the keyboard part come closer to Schubert's "Erlkönig," such as "Johanna Sebus" (published 1809; there is an incomplete setting of the same text by Schubert) in which the breaking of a dam and the resulting flood are pictured in the piano accompaniment (Example 10–2):

Other Goethe songs display distinctly Romantic qualities. In "Tiefer liegt die Nacht" a gloomy mood is convincingly painted. Expressive chromaticism and a sensitive, varied accompaniment help to make this a great

EXAMPLE 10–2. Reichardt, "Johanna Sebus," beginning. Copyright Arno Volk Verlag, Cologne, 1957. Printed by permission.

[3]The beginning of Reichardt's version is given in *Grove 6*, the entire song in Friedländer, *Das deutsche Lied*, 3: 200f. The text also inspired Corona Schröter (1782), Zelter (1807), and later composers.

song. There are others—"Rhapsodie," for instance, based on the text (*Harzreise im Winter*) well known through Brahms's "Alto Rhapsody"—in which Reichardt writes a keyboard part that is free, varied, and full, with much chromaticism and some enharmonic changes (Example 10–3).

EXAMPLE 10–3. Reichardt, "Rhapsodie."

Reichardt also composed two versions of "Nur wer die Sehnsucht kennt" from Goethe's *Wilhelm Meister*—a text that inspired many later composers.[4] Here, too, the text is closely observed, as in the startling harmonic changes at the words "Es schwindelt mir" (Example 10–4).

Also a friend of Goethe, Karl Friedrich Zelter (1758–1832) endeavored to provide settings in a style to the master's liking: in strophic form but with melodic variants that would reflect changing moods and word meanings. "Um Mitternacht" is an example of this technique: the accompaniment remains the same for all verses but the melody is varied slightly by the composer and, in performance, might be varied further by the singer. Goethe, it is well known, preferred Zelter's songs to settings of the same texts by Schubert (e.g., those from *Wilhelm Meister*), feeling, no doubt, that Zelter's music did not overwhelm or distract from the poetry. Whether Goethe appreciated Zelter's repetitions of individual words and phrases (in

---

[4]Reichardt's melodies for several of the *Wilhelm Meister* songs were included in the first edition of the novel (1795).

EXAMPLE 10–4. Reichardt, "Sehnsucht."

one version of "Kennst du das Land") is another matter. Yet Zelter, too, wrote songs that come close to Schubert's in style—"Rastlose Liebe," is one, with its accompaniment that is completely independent of the vocal melody and well expresses the meaning of the text ("Through snow, rain, wind: onward! onward!"). This and other songs are "through-composed," i.e., employ different music for each verse.

Johann Rudolf Zumsteeg (1760–1802) shows similar diversity in his songs. During his school years he became a friend of Schiller, next to Goethe the foremost representative of German literary classicism. Zumsteeg composed many texts by Schiller, including some ballads (long, dramatic tales of adventure). "Ritter Toggenburg" is one of these. Zumsteeg treats the ten verses with much variety, with numerous key and tempo changes, a section in recitative style, interludes for the piano, and changes in accompaniment patterns to reflect changing text meanings. Through his ballads in particular Zumsteeg made a profound impression on the young Schubert, who was fond of singing Zumsteeg's Lieder and composed settings of some of the same texts, including "Ritter Toggenburg." Similarities are obvious in their settings of "Nachtgesang," also of "Hagars Klage."[5]

---

[5]The new complete edition of Schubert's works includes both Schubert's and Zumsteeg's "Hagars Klage." See *Neue Ausgabe sämtlicher Werke* (Kassel, 1969), IV/6, 3–21 and 186–94.

Throughout this period and well into the nineteenth century the art song was thought of as music for the home—for small gatherings, for a circle of friends. As we turn to the songs of Haydn and Mozart this should be kept in mind, for it may help explain why these composers, especially Mozart, considered their songs less significant than most of their other works. For Mozart, anxious to make a name for himself in Vienna and beyond, operas, symphonies, and especially piano concertos were appropriate vehicles for his ambition, while he might write a song merely to please a friend. Haydn's songs, in Vienna and London, were written for similar purposes. If they acquired some popularity late in his life, this was in part due to the position of eminence he had achieved. Only a few of them, however, remained in the nineteenth-century repertory. The low quality of many of the texts is all too apparent; most of the poets are forgotten today. Some verses are naive or trite; others are overly complex in language and in the sentiment expressed. No texts by Goethe appear; In the Vienna of the 1780s Haydn may not have been familiar with his poetry.

Most of Haydn's "early" songs—he was almost fifty years old when the *Lieder für das Clavier* appeared in 1781 and 1784[6]—are still written on two staves, as in "Gegenliebe" (Example 10–5). In this song and others

EXAMPLE 10–5. Haydn, "Gegenliebe," beginning.

the collection there are brief keyboard interludes. These usually occur at logical places, between lines or phrases of text. Indicative of a lack of concern with text-music relationships in strophic songs is Haydn's treatment of "Zufriedenheit" (1784). Here a two-bar interlude makes sense in verses 1–3, but awkwardly breaks up a line of text in verse 4. Other strophic songs, while avoiding this problem, express very different emotions in successive verses sung to identical music. In songs such as "Die Verlassene" (1781), with seven verses, a great deal depends on the interpretive skills of the singer, who must bring out these differences.

---

[6]The term "Clavier" often meant "clavichord," which was popular not only in North and Central Germany but also in Austria, where it was frequently used for song accompaniment. Editions marked "beim Clavier zu singen" or "Lieder für das Clavier" may indeed have been intended, primarily, for the clavichord. H. Walter, "Haydns Klaviere," *Haydn-Studien,* II (1970), 261. Gradually, "clavier" also came to mean "fortepiano."

Haydn's journeys to England resulted in two sets of songs—the "Original Canzonettas" (1794 and 1795). Most of the English texts are by Anne Hunter, the wife of a surgeon who had befriended the composer. A more profound musical language distinguishes these canzonets: they are longer, more substantial, and varied. "Fidelity," 121 measures long, contains changes in tempo, key, and accompaniment patterns. "Despair" has an eloquent melodic line suitably representing the poem's message. In this and other canzonets Haydn provided careful dynamic markings suitable for the fortepiano, the keyboard instrument he now preferred. The three verses of "Pleasing Pain" are set in modified strophic form: the second verse contains changes in both melodic and accompaniment patterns, to reflect textual changes. In this and some other canzonets the keyboard part assumes greater importance, both in the introductions, now fairly long, and throughout. Best known among the canzonets are "A Pastoral Song" ("My Mother Bids Me Bind My Hair") and Haydn's only Shakespeare song, "She Never Told Her Love." In "The Wanderer" the text's romantic flavor is well brought out in the chromatic vocal line.

Among the canzonets and the few other songs from Haydn's last years some are rewarding to singers today, especially when heard in the intimate setting for which, like art songs in general, they were intended. Even those that have less appeal to today's performers and listeners help us obtain a good picture of the state of the art song just before its great flowering began.

MOZART'S SONGS

Aside from dramatic and sacred music, Mozart left a fair number of compositions for solo voice and various kinds of accompaniment (keyboard, mandolin, orchestra). Only a small number of these has a place in the development of the art song. There are concert arias, some conceived on a large scale and, as the name implies, intended for a different public and for the trained, operatic voice. But the more intimate song with keyboard accompaniment also occupied Mozart, if only occasionally and briefly, throughout his life.

In editions that appeared during his lifetime, the titles reveal no consistent distinction: "Das Veilchen" (K. 476) and "Das Lied der Trennung" (K. 519) were advertised in Vienna in 1789 as *Zwey Deutsche Arien,* while a year later "Das Veilchen" appeared in Bonn as *Ein deutsches Lied.*

Much of what has been said about Haydn's songs is again relevant. The texts set by Mozart vary greatly in substance, most of them stemming from minor poets, of his day and earlier; a few authors cannot be identified.

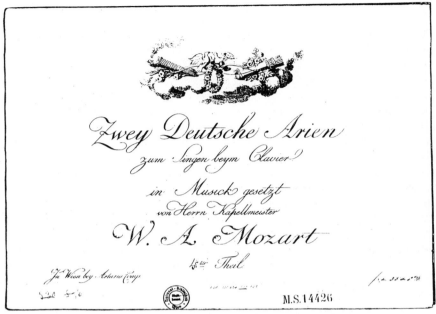

Zwey Deutsche Arien
zum Singen beym Clavier
in Musick gesetzt
von Herrn Kapellmeister
W. A. Mozart
ter Theil

M.S.14426

Two Mozart songs, Vienna, 1789. Austrian National Library.

One might say that a Mozart could transform less-than-great verses into great music, and indeed songs such as "Abendempfindung" prove the point. Yet Mozart's only Goethe song, "Das Veilchen," became his most beloved composition in this genre.

Though it has been claimed that Mozart's Lieder "have nothing to do with folk song,"[7] some do display a simplicity of line, rhythm, and structure that suggests a folk idiom. In the last year of his life Mozart contributed three songs to a collection "For Children and Friends of Children"; they display these qualities. "Sehnsucht nach dem Frühlinge," K. 598, has maintained the status of a German folk song to the present day—a position perhaps comparable to that in the United States of some of Stephen Foster's songs (Example 10–6).

A similar, unassuming (though less "folk-like") style is found in other songs by Mozart, beginning with "An die Freude," K. 53, written by the composer at age eleven. Melody and bass line only are given, for the first verse of a seven-verse poem. Other strophic songs, musically more extended, have as many as nineteen verses.

Various occasions inspired Mozart to write songs—to please his

[7]Einstein, *Mozart: his Character, his Work* (New York: Oxford University Press, 1945), p. 375.

EXAMPLE 10–6. Mozart, "Sehnsucht nach dem Frühlinge," beginning.

friend Gottfried von Jacquin ("Das Traumbild," K. 530) or to contribute to an almanac (K. 390–92) or song anthology (K. 596–98); he set patriotic poems dealing with the Turkish War of 1787–92 ("Lied beim Auszug in das Feld," K. 552; was he attracted by the "enlightened" sentiments of the text?). One song, though from the Salzburg years, appears to have been occasioned by Masonic rites ("O heiliges Band der Freundschaft," K. 148). Few of these can be called "Lieder" in the sense in which we use the term today, implying certain approaches to text treatment, vocal style, and role of the keyboard part; one is "Abendempfindung" (K. 523; 1787). The poem, by an unknown author, establishes an elegiac, sentimental mood well captured in Mozart's extended melodic line, varied through the poem's six verses. Quite dramatic (beginning with the piano's opening phrase, which is repeated at intervals throughout) is K. 520 of the same year: "Luise, On Burning the Letters of Her Unfaithful Lover." Text meaning is effectively reflected throughout this short but intense song, in melody, harmony, and accompaniment pattern (Example 10–7).

These qualities also distinguish "Das Veilchen." Goethe's poem appeared in 1775 but was probably known to Mozart later through a setting by the Viennese composer Friberth, published in 1780.

EXAMPLE 10–7. Mozart, "Als Luise die Briefe ihres ungetreuen Liebhabers verbrannte," K. 520, excerpt.

EXAMPLE 10-7. *Continued.*

er sang nicht mir   al - - lein.

Mozart's version has been called a *scena,* meaning that it is divided into musically different sections. These include two brief recitatives. The music, both voice part and accompaniment, closely matches the different emotions evoked by the story as it unfolds. The "light step and cheerful mood" of the shepherdess—her singing as she walks across the meadow; the violet's longing to be close to her bosom—these and other moments in the little drama are beautifully transformed into music by Mozart, the dramatist-composer. How different from the settings by several other composers (including Reichardt). There is a "Veilchen" by Steffan (or Stepan, 1779), perhaps known to Mozart, which is strophic, so that the gay little piano interlude, appropriate after "Es war ein herzig Veilchen," is also

Title page of the collection in which Friberth's *Veilchen* appeared. In the Preface it is specifically pointed out that in Friberth's songs "the music fits the words specially well." Austrian National Library.

Music (used for all three verses) and first verse of text for Friberth's *Das Veilchen auf der Wiese*. Austrian National Library.

heard after "[Das Mädchen] ertrat das arme Veilchen." ("[The girl] crushed the poor little violet")[8]

Style elements of Italian canzonettas, French *opéra comique*, German sacred music, and of Mozart's operas (especially German operas) all appear in his songs. Such variety need not surprise us, given the international musical world in which he lived and his eagerness to make a name for himself.

BIBLIOGRAPHICAL NOTES

Several surveys of song history include chapters on the Classic period, among them *A History of Song*, ed. D. Stevens (New York: Norton, 1960; "Germany and Austria" by Philip Radcliffe); J. Stein, *Poem and Music in the German Lied from Gluck to Hugo Wolf* (Cambridge, 1971); D. Ivey, *Song: Anatomy, Imagery and Styles* (New York: Free Press, 1970). A basic study in German, originally published in 1902, is Max Friedländer's *Das deutsche Lied im 18. Jahrhundert*, 3 volumes (reprint edition, Hildesheim, 1962). There are chapters on solo song in *NOHM* VII (R. Hughes) and VIII (L. Orrey). Classic-period songs are treated in *Grove 6*, especially in the article "Lied (iii)," by R. Barr. Reichardt's Goethe songs have been published in *Das Erbe deutscher Musik*, 58 (1964) and 59 (1970). There are editions of songs by Zelter (*Ausgewählte Lieder*, Mainz, 1932) and Zumsteeg (*Kleine Balladen und Lieder*, reprint New York: Gregg International Publishers, 1969). *MC* has a chapter on Mozart's concert arias but ignores the songs.

---

[8]Friedländer, *Das deutsche Lied*, II: 163f, lists settings of Goethe's poem by other composers.

ELEVEN

OPERA IN
THE CLASSIC ERA

Our present-day standard operatic repertory begins with works from the Classic era; of these, Mozart's operas—(and Beethoven's only opera, *Fidelio*)—are the only ones performed with regularity. Stylistically, Classic opera reflects the complex situation found in the late eighteenth century, with many currents and crosscurrents, with various operatic genres in existence and influencing each other. The international aspect of Classic music is once more brought into focus through the operatic careers of Gluck, Mozart, and others.

During this age, a gradual decline of *opera seria* is shown by various attempts at reform, by the rising popularity of other genres, and by the disappearance of the castrato. Among other things *opera seria* had been an expression of the social and economic structure of the Baroque age. It glorified the ruling prince through its splendor: elaborate sets and costumes, a beautiful hall, its representation of strong, virtuous, and magnanimous characters, and through the customary *licenza* or prologue addressed directly to the attending ruler. From its early years, *opera seria* had flourished in Vienna, represented by Marc Antonio Cesti (1623–69) and other Italians. Somewhat later the literary atmosphere of the Austrian capital was colored by the appointments as court poets of Zeno and Metastasio. The Metastasian kind of libretto, with virtue always triumphant in the end and with its many stereotyped complications and solutions of plot, may seem rigid to us, yet it represented an improvement over earlier texts. In this kind of opera the action was carried on in recitative, both *secco* and accompanied; the aria that followed a recitative contained reflection and expression of feelings about what had happened. This distinction continued to be observed in most Italian opera of the later eighteenth century. Metastasio's texts were set by many composers of the mid-eighteenth century and beyond. Two operas by John Christian Bach belong here, *Alessandro nell' Indie* (Naples, 1762) and *Temistocle* (Mannheim, 1772).[1] Some poets, including Ranieri da Calzabigi (1714–95), formulated other dramatic concepts and brought about a lessening of functional distinction between recitative, aria, and chorus.

The mid-eighteenth-century *opéra comique,* another important genre, has been referred to earlier. (See p. 18). Plots and style were simple; there was spoken dialogue and the music consisted of simple *ariettes.* Works of this kind were popular outside France as well; their influence was felt in the Viennese theater. Comparable to them was the German *Singspiel,* also dealing with ordinary mortals and everyday subjects, set to music in a simple style at times close to folk song. These genres also are represented in Gluck's work.

Christoph Willibald Gluck (1714–87) was born in the Palatinate. His father soon moved to Bohemia, and the young musician may have pursued some university studies in Prague. In 1736, after a brief stay in Vienna, he went to Milan and studied for four years with Sammartini. He absorbed the reigning operatic idiom and, beginning with his *Artaserse* of 1741, brought out a series of Italian operas that proved successful and opened the way to an engagement in London in 1745. Several subsequent years were spent traveling, some of them with a theatrical road company. By 1750, Gluck once more had reached Vienna. Several works from the following years show his involvement with *opéra comique;* in *L'ivrogne corrigé* (1760) and *Le cadi dupé* (1761) he uses both popular melodies *(vaudevilles)* and simple airs of his own. In the *Cadi* as well as in *La rencontre imprévue* (1764) the fondness of the age for oriental subjects reveals itself, a fashion or fad better known to us from Mozart's *Entführung.*

---

[1]See Loewenberg, *Annals of Opera, 1597–1940* (rev. ed., Geneva, 1955,) column 1657, for a list of Metastasian librettos set by late-eighteenth-century composers.

Scene from the Ballet-Pantomime *Le turc genereux*, performed in Vienna April 26, 1758. Engraving by Bernardo Bellotto, called Canaletto. Museum of the City of Vienna.

Gluck's collaboration with Calzabigi began with *Orfeo ed Euridice* of 1762. The Italian poet had spent several years in Paris, where heated arguments about the merits of French and Italian opera were still going on, arguments that were to influence his own librettos. His meeting with Gluck proved to be of greatest importance; later the composer freely admitted Calzabigi's significant role in shaping the reform concepts for which Gluck often had been given exclusive credit. However, similar ideas about desirable dramatic qualities in an opera must have occurred to Gluck some years before. *Orfeo* is considered the first "reform opera," but in his earlier Italian works he had already paid careful attention to *secco* recitatives and condensed the dialogue by cutting many lines in Metastasian librettos, a procedure that caused the Italian poet to refer to him as *pazzo* ("fool") in a letter to the famous castrato Farinelli.

Gluck's textual and musical reforms reflect certain beliefs of the age, especially his championing of the reasonable and the natural. In the preface to his pantomine *Don Juan* (1761), this belief had already been spelled out with regard to ballet: that it must be convincing *(vraisemblable)* and, therefore, more than decoration, with the dancing to be related to both drama and music. Other representatives of the enlightenment voiced similar demands for a return to the natural in drama, including music drama. Less importance should be attached to *le merveilleux*—to demons, monsters, shipwreck scenes, and the like—and a more central place should be given to the dramatic conflicts involving human beings.

Calzabigi's version of the Orpheus legend attained this objective at least in part. The action is reduced to the basic conflicts. The two principal characters are convincingly drawn; their actions and reactions are such that the audience would feel involved on a human level, would understand and feel compassion. In general, the libretto avoids the *accidenti*, the complications and subplots, so frequent in *opera seria*, and concentrates on the essential story; yet even Calzabigi felt called upon to supply a happy ending, brought about by the interference of Amor, a *deus ex machina* who once more returns Eurydice to the living.

The most significant musical reforms of Calzabigi and Gluck can likewise be related to the objective on which both poet and composer agreed: to bring out the essential dramatic qualities of the subject. Concentration on these, on the inner action, made it possible to eliminate long, narrative passages in *secco* recitative; these were abolished in favor of an expressive, accompanied recitative in which the prosody and meaning of

Gluck, *Orpheus and Eurydice*, Act II. A modern staging of this Classic subject. (Metropolitan Opera Guild, Inc. Reproduced by permission.)

text were carefully observed. Just as the recitative became more musical, the arias, for their part, moved closer to declamation. With few exceptions florid writing, pure vocal display, are avoided; instead the arias exhibit what Gluck called "beautiful simplicity." A homogeneous musical texture is thus provided by recitatives and arias. The chorus scenes further contribute to this, since they are made part of the action to a larger extent than before. Orfeo's pleading with the chorus of Furies to let him enter the underworld is a famous example of such a dramatic choral scene. Gluck carefully chooses the musical means by which the Furies' relentless "No!" gradually becomes softened, a change of heart brought about by Orfeo's pleading, which becomes increasingly human and persuasive.

Le vraisemblable was Gluck's concern in many details. He insisted that the Furies' reply be delivered in a wild, raucous tone at first. Only after they had been placated were they to sing in a more musical manner. Singers and audiences both in Vienna and in Paris objected to such unheard-of realism.[2]

Orfeo was followed by several operas in traditional style before *Alceste* appeared in 1767. Here again Calzabigi showed his concern with dramatic unity by eliminating from the ancient plot scenes and characters that were not essential to the main action. In his celebrated preface to the printed score of *Alceste*, Gluck provided a summary of his objectives and views:[3] All elements must contribute to the requirements of the drama. Neither vocal virtuosity nor elaborate orchestral ritornellos must interrupt or delay the dramatic action. The dancing likewise must contribute to the central theme rather than exist as an unrelated *divertissement*, and the overture should also be related to the drama (a requirement not yet observed in *Orfeo*). Again "reason and good sense" are invoked as the arbiters of operatic reform; a few years later (in the *Mercure de France* of 1773) Gluck stated that "Imitation of nature must be the chief aim of an artist. . . . I have always endeavored to have my music enhance the text in a simple and natural manner, through forceful expression and appropriate declamation."

Opera, then, in Gluck's view, was to be true drama, not a concert in costume. Drama, true to the models of antiquity, had to have lofty purposes. When various rulers of the past,

---

[2]Concern with realism did not extend to costuming, which continued to be stylized throughout the eighteenth century, so that a Greek goddess or medieval sorceress would appear in hoop skirt and eighteenth-century coiffure.

[3]A facsimile of the Italian preface to the first edition of *Alceste*, and a translation of the most significant portions, are included in *Grove 6*, "Gluck." Burney considered this preface sufficiently important to publish an English translation in *The Present State . . . Germany*, I: 265ff.

following the example of the Greeks, welcomed and sustained the arts, their objective was a more important one than to provide mere pleasures and amusements. . . . They knew that the arts alone can soften the hearts of men without corrupting them.[4]

Such beliefs inspired Gluck's first reform operas written for Vienna (including *Paride ed Elena*, 1770) and continued to guide him in the works written for Paris, notably *Iphigénie en Aulide* (1774) and *Iphigénie en Tauride* (1779). In the Viennese works the insertion of chorus and ballet scenes had served to reduce the preponderance of the aria. But in French opera, ballet had traditionally been important, so that Gluck's reforms dealt more with the removal of excessive spectacle and of secondary plots. In his Paris operas, dramatic continuity and persuasiveness are achieved to an even greater extent. Recitatives are free and flexible; far from being routine, they reflect subtle differences in temperament or changes in emotional states. Gluck's orchestra likewise is enlisted for dramatic purposes. A famous instance of psychological characterization occurs in *Iphigénie en Tauride*. Orestes, to reassure himself, sings that calm has returned to his heart. The vocal line expresses this sentiment, but the restless accompaniment reveals his true state of mind to the listener. In his use of the orchestra, especially, Gluck builds on the work of his Parisian predecessor Rameau.

Gluck's success in Paris was initially marred by involvement, apparently against his will, in an operatic "war" in which the opposing camp consisted of the champions of Italian opera as represented by Puccinni. Queen Marie Antoinette, Gluck's former pupil, actively took his side in this quarrel, and by the time *Iphigénie en Tauride* appeared Gluck's success seemed assured. But his next Paris opera, *Echo et Narcisse*, failed completely, causing the composer to return to Vienna.

When Nicolai described the musical life of Vienna in 1781, he could say that "The *chevalier* Gluck is the most famous musician in Vienna. Although highly praised there, as elsewhere, he has, to my knowledge, not exerted any very marked influence on the city's musical taste."[5] It may seem strange that the celebrated composer's views found no more tangible reflection in the operas of his younger contemporaries and immediate successors. The explanation in part can be found in the continued Italian orientation of operatic life in Vienna, at the Esterházy court, and elsewhere in Austria. Gluck's views were closer to the spirit of French tragedy than to Italian drama of the eighteenth century. It is characteristic of the traditional operatic outlook of Christian Bach, the Italianized German, that he should

---

[4]Dedicatory preface to *Iphigénie en Aulide*, reproduced in the full score (Paris, 1873).
[5]Friedrich Nicolai, *Beschreibung einer Reise . . . im Jahre 1781 . . .*, IV (Berlin, 1783–84), 527.

have felt free to compose additional arias for a London production of *Orfeo*, showing no concern for the dramatic unity that was so important to Gluck.

Through his insistence that the subject of an opera have ethical significance and express lofty emotions, and through the musical means by which he expressed the "majesty and energy" of the poem, Gluck became one of the foremost representatives of the Classic spirit in music.

Gluck: engraving based on painting by Duplessis. The verse under the portrait pays homage to Gluck, who, "among many rivals, was the only one to charm his own country, Italy, and France." Austrian National Library.

Around the mid-eighteenth century various attempts were made in Germany to establish opera with a distinctly national character. In the field of serious opera these attempts failed, partly because of the lack of enthusiasm of the better poets. The movement received official endorsement from some quarters. Karl Theodor's interest in developing a national theater in Mannheim stimulated some operatic activity; yet the works which it produced, especially those by Ignaz Holzbauer (1711–83), remained too close to the style of Italian *opera seria* to be a successful new departure. Also in Mannheim, Anton Schweitzer (1735–87), a typical *Sturm und Drang* composer, achieved some popularity, particularly with his *Alceste* (1773); but here, too, the proximity to Italian models, especially in the recitatives, prevented the movement for national opera from gathering momentum. The belief that recitative formed the main obstacle to the growth of a German operatic style caused Georg Benda (1722–95) and others to turn to the *Singspiel* as a more suitable medium.[6] Based on a light, frequently sentimental plot, containing spoken dialogue and songs in a simple, melodious style, the German *Singspiel* rose from lowly origins in the *Stegreifkomödie*—the partly improvised farce so popular on the Viennese suburban stage—to respectability and acceptance at court. The famous *Beggar's Opera* (1728) had been widely imitated in Germany. Works in a comparable style resulted, some based on other English models. J. C. Standfuss (died ca. 1756), Johann Adam Hiller (1728–1804), and Johann Friedrich Reichardt (1752–1814) are among the composers; Haydn, Mozart, and Dittersdorf also made successful contributions to the genre, with the latter's *Doktor und Apotheker* (1786) enjoying special popularity in Vienna, at the expense of Mozart's Italian *Figaro*. These works smoothed the way for German opera there, a movement to which Emperor Joseph II had already given at least sporadic support.

The Esterházy court, both at Eisenstadt and at Esterháza, was the scene of vigorous operatic activity during the period of Haydn's employment there. From 1776 to 1790, Esterháza had a leading position in the operatic life of Europe; the excellence of the productions there was acknowledged by many, including the empress herself (see p. 86). During this period Haydn conducted over a hundred operas. Besides producing his own works, he carefully adapted operas by other composers to the requirements and resources of his local ensemble. From 1780 to 1790, no less than 1,038 opera performances were given, not only with the live performers of the resident Italian troupe but also with puppets. The puppet operas, in German, included some by Haydn himself; these also delighted the empress on her visit to Esterháza.[7]

In spite of these successes then at the court for which they were written, and in spite of new discoveries and revivals in our century, Haydn's operas have not found a lasting place in the repertory. True, they

[6]His experiments with melodrama (spoken dialogue with orchestral accompaniment) in *Ariadne auf Naxos* (1775) were of limited significance for the future development of German opera.

[7]H. C. R. Landon, "Haydn und die Oper," *Oesterreichische Musikzeitschrift*, 22 (1967), 253ff. For further discussion of Haydn's operas, see Landon's *Essays on the Viennese Classical Style* (London, 1970), p. 37, and his "Haydn's Marionette Operas and the Repertoire of the Marionette Theatre at Esterhàz Castle," *Haydn Yearbook*, I (1962), 111–97.

were written with local conditions in mind—but so were Mozart's most successful operas. In Haydn's case the conditions were not unfavorable: a prince who was fond of opera, especially *opera buffa,* and a fairly stable musical establishment. More likely some of the reasons are to be found in the composer himself. When he approached the medium of opera—perhaps the most complex of all art forms—Haydn was less given to experimentation, less sure of himself than in other media. Individual arias may be forceful and dramatic; effective characterization is found in both serious and comic parts, as in the *dramma eroicomico, Orlando Paladino* (1782). But, as G. Feder reflects, "Since Gluck's time the music of an opera was expected to express the overall dramatic situation, not merely the text of an aria."[8]

Haydn often expressed a wish to go to Italy, realizing the many advantages he might derive from firsthand contact with that country's operatic life, but the wish never found fulfillment. Eventually he freely acknowledged Mozart's superiority in the operatic field. When, in 1787, an admirer in Prague suggested that he write an opera for performance there, Haydn replied that this would have to be an entirely new work, suitable for local conditions, but that "even that would be a daring thing for me to do, for there hardly is room for someone else next to the great Mozart." He continued by saying that if every lover of music were as impressed and moved by Mozart's musical knowledge as he, Haydn, was, "all nations would vie with each other to count such a treasure as their own."[9]

MOZART'S ITALIAN OPERAS

The remarkably varied international influences to which the young Mozart was exposed can be traced in his operatic writing. In this medium Italian impressions proved to be especially deep—understandably so, since Italy still was very much *the* land of opera when father and son undertook several journeys there. In Italy they are likely to have heard works by Jommelli, Tommaso Traëtta (1727–79). Francesco de Majo (1732–70), and other successful composers of the day. The young Mozart's Italian operas show his remarkable understanding and competent handling, not without individuality, of the conventional idiom and the accepted operatic forms. Competence had to be shown clearly by the very young composer since, with each work, he had to prove himself to influential *maestri,* singers, audi-

---

[8]Georg Feder, "Einige Thesen zu dem Thema: Haydn als Dramatiker," *Haydn-Studien,* II (1969), 127. See also "Haydn as an Opera Composer," panel discussion in *Haydn Studies* (1981), pp. 253ff.

[9]Quoted, among other places, in *Mozart, die Dokumente seines Lebens . . .,* ed. O. E. Deutsch, (Kassel, 1961), p. 271.

ences, and to himself. His *opere serie Mitridate* and *Lucio Silla* were produced in Milan in 1770 and 1772; earlier still he had demonstrated similar understanding of *opera buffa* (*La finta semplice*, 1768; followed in 1775 by *La finta giardiniera*.) Some acquaintance with French models is shown in *Bastien und Bastienne*, also written by the twelve-year-old. Though set to a German text, it is based on a French libretto which, in turn, goes back to Rousseau's *Le devin du village*. In general, French opera proved to have less attraction for Mozart than Italian. As for the German *Singspiel*, there seems to have been no further call for Mozart to compose one until *Zaide* of 1779, a work that remained unfinished.

After his extensive journeys abroad Mozart was most anxious to establish himself at home as a writer of Italian operas, this still being one of the usual avenues to a desirable court position. *Idomeneo* (1781) was the result of a commission to write an *opera seria* for Munich, an opportunity that Mozart welcomed with open arms, since Munich offered a good orchestra which he could use to good advantage. *Idomeneo* represents the beginning of Mozart's maturity as a composer of operas. With imaginative use of accompanied recitative and chorus, better dramatic continuity was achieved. Though in many ways the conventions of *opera seria* were observed in it, *Idomeneo* rises above its models because of Mozart's characteristic concern with portraying believable human beings. His letters from Munich, written during the rehearsals, show how much he was occupied with the dramatic aspects of the opera, for example, his demand to eliminate "asides" from arias and to omit arias altogether in dramatically inappropriate situations.

Mozart's only other *opera seria*, *La Clemenza di Tito* of 1791, was written in great haste, on a Metastasian libretto that had been assigned to him—early Metastasio at that. This kind of drama must have seemed very restrictive to the composer in the last year of his life, even though the libretto was modified in several ways, particularly through the introduction of ensemble scenes. By 1791, Mozart's talent for these must have been widely known; yet even with these modifications and with Mozart's music, *Tito* remained *opera seria*, a genre which had lost much of its appeal for late-eighteenth-century audiences, especially outside of Italy. With the social changes of the age, the courtly environment and standardized sentiments of *opera seria* had less to offer the growing operatic public than did *opera buffa*, which dealt with everyday sentiments and situations, with characters that were human and plausible. Mozart's interest in people and his keen powers of observation, so evident in his letters, must have instinctively led him to this genre, to which he contributed some of the most lastingly successful examples: *Le Nozze di Figaro* (1786), *Don Giovanni* (1787), and *Così fan tutte* (1790), all in collaboration with the poet Lorenzo da Ponte. In these works, once more, Mozart did not overthrow tradition.

Open-air theater in the garden of Mirabell Castle, Salzburg, ca. 1730. Engraving by Danreiter. Museum Salzburg.

Early nineteenth-century stage set for Mozart's *La Clemenza di Tito*. Austrian National Library.

Without considering himself a reformer he reformed the category from within, while retaining many of the traditional ingredients.

The stories on which Da Ponte and Mozart collaborated were not new. Many dramatizations of the Don Juan legend were known at the time; one of these, a libretto by Bertati with music by Giuseppe Gazzaniga (1743–1818), came out in Venice only a few months before Mozart's opera.

There are many traditional qualities in Da Ponte's librettos. Many of the stock characters—the comic types that had been in vogue for generations in the *commedia dell'arte*—are still present on Mozart's stage: the worldly-wise chamber maid (Despina in *Così fan tutte*); the lazy, cowardly, and generally comical servant (Leporello in *Don Giovanni*); and the crotchety old doctor (Bartolo in *Figaro*). We also find the traditional lack of realism in the solution of dramatic conflicts—the ridiculous disguises, resulting in numerous cases of mistaken identity; the last-minute revelation that someone is someone else's long-lost mother. The "outer action" frequently seems unconcerned with logic or realism, or at least leaves many details unexplained: Where does Don Ottavio come from in the middle of the night? Why does Donna Elvira appear "in traveling costume," singing about Don Giovanni? Nevertheless, these operas are realistic in a higher sense. The individual characters are humanly, believably drawn. Mozart often insisted on changes in the text to accomplish this, but he succeeded in the first place through musical means, confronting us with living people, complicated and fascinating. They change their minds; they give in; they are sorry. Since the emphasis is on people rather than on plot or setting (there is very little Spanish color in *Figaro* or *Don Giovanni*), Mozart's *opera buffe* have remained alive and meaningful to this day, thus again fitting the definition of "classic" as having meaning on a level that is universal rather than particular.

Many traditional musical devices were likewise taken over by Mozart. Most of the action continues to unfold in *secco* recitative, with accompanied recitative serving for more intensely dramatic moments. At times (but by no means always) Mozart treats the *secco* with greater care than his predecessors or contemporaries did. His choruses are relatively unimportant, as they traditionally had been in eighteenth-century Italian opera. The overtures are not yet programmatically related to the opera itself; yet, although they do not furnish a musical synopsis of the plot in the manner of some nineteenth-century overtures, they do occasionally introduce important themes from the work to follow. The *Don Giovanni* overture's opening anticipates the spectacular entrance of the statue in the last act, even to the music of Leporello's anguished exclamation "Ah padron! siam tutti morti." On a smaller scale Mozart introduces, in the overture to *Così fan tutte*, the music which, in the opera's finale, brings the "theme song" for the entire work (Example 11–1).

EXAMPLE 11–1. Mozart, Così *fan tutte, finale.*

To some eighteenth-century reformers the da capo aria had appeared unsatisfactory because of its retrogressive dramatic nature: a thought presented in the aria's first section is amplified or contrasted in the second part (also musically contrasting), only to be restated, text and music, in the da capo section. Here again Mozart and his librettist did not altogether break with tradition; they continued to employ the da capo aria, though less frequently. Opportunities were also provided for other traditional musical structures: the "comparison aria" (e.g., Fiordiligi's "Come scoglio immoto resta" in *Così fan tutte*), the military aria and chorus ("Non più andrai," *Figaro;* "Bella vita militar," *Così*). Unlike Gluck, Mozart did not hesitate to include coloratura writing where it suited his dramatic purposes and where it might serve to show off the voice of a certain singer. In a letter to his father Mozart once commented on an aria he had written for the tenor Raff: "A man like that deserves special treatment." Raff liked the aria but, no longer being able to sustain a long line as he could in younger years requested a few changes. Mozart was glad to oblige: "I like an aria to fit a singer perfectly, like a well-tailored suit." Another aria, he determined, was too high for Raff and seemed better suited for a soprano; "So I decided to write it to be just right for Mlle. Weber. It now is her best aria."[10] Occasionally, Mozart was not above interpolating additional arias (as in *Don Giovanni* for the Vienna performances of 1788) in order to accommodate a singer, even though it might be detrimental to the drama. This attitude may be more understandable when one reads in the Mozart correspondence about the many intrigues, real or imagined, involving singers, which created obstacles to the composer's operatic success in Munich, Vienna, Prague, and elsewhere.

While Mozart was quite willing to preserve those aspects of *opera buffa* which suited his purposes, his works, both dramatically and musically, contain much that is his own. *Don Giovanni* he called a *dramma giocoso*, a term that had been previously used for Haydn's opera *Il mondo della luna*, 1777) but was particularly apt for Mozart's opera, which incorporates such a remarkable mixture of the serious and the comical. Da Ponte, perhaps with Mozart's participation, fashioned a drama with an essentially serious theme, omitting many slapstick episodes included in earlier dramatizations of the story.[11] Its principal characters, especially Donna Anna and Don Giovanni, have been interpreted in a variety of ways, but they certainly are no mere *buffa* types. The curious mixture of the serious and the *giocoso* reminds one of Shakespeare. Moments of comedy, slapstick, and farce occur in many serious scenes. The mixture is most evident in the characterization of Donna Elvira, a serious, pathetic figure who, upon each appearance, becomes the subject of humorous or devastating remarks, some of them "asides" addressed to the audience. The famous "catalog aria" in which Leporello, in order to "console" her, gives a detailed account of his master's many affairs with women, is one of many examples. Even when the forces of hell are about to pull the Don into the abyss, Leporello's behavior and remarks are comical.

This mixture may be one of the causes for the lasting appeal of *Don Giovanni*. *Così fan tutte*, on the other hand, is all *giocoso*—a delightful comedy in which nothing can be taken seriously and in which the characters are far less subtly and convincingly drawn.

On the musical side, Mozart's individuality shows itself in many ways. Different types of aria serve different dramatic requirements. In *Don Giovanni* purely lyrical arias are given only to Don Ottavio, to most spectator-listeners the least convincing character in the opera. Of greater interest are the dramatic arias of all shades: here Mozart may portray great agitation (Donna Anna's "Or sai, chi l'onore") or conflicting emotions (Elvira's "Mi tradì quell'alma ingrata"). At times an aria or duet is not entirely reflective or static but represents a dramatic development. In the last part of "Batti, batti" the pace changes from andante, 2/4 to allegro, 6/8. Zerlina has achieved her objective: Masetto is no longer pouting. Likewise, in Zerlina's duet with Don Giovanni ("La ci darem la mano") her change of heart—from

[10]Letter of February 28, 1778.
[11]Strangely enough, Mozart allowed some of these to be reintroduced in the Vienna version of 1788.

"vorrei e non vorrei" to "andiam"—finds similar musical expression. Mozart is careful to distinguish musically between characters of differing social status: Donna Anna and Elvira, as aristocratic ladies, are given suitably florid music while Zerlina and Masetto, simple country folk, are given simple melodies. Don Giovanni, though the central character, has no characteristic arias to himself. In the duet with Zerlina he operates on Zerlina's level and has appropriately simple music.

In some important scenes the dramatic pace is maintained by continuous recitative-aria structures. The conversation between Don Ottavio and Donna Anna (following the cemetery scene in Act II), carried on in the customary *secco* recitative, flows without break into accompanied recitative which, after two measures, gives way to a brief orchestral larghetto in which the theme of the following aria is anticipated. The aria itself brings a da capo which is modified by expressive modulations. This is not the end: a final section of about the length of the entire aria thus far brings a change in meter and a faster tempo. This final section, as so often with Mozart, is most effective; all the fireworks occur here.

In the accompanied recitatives Mozart's dramatic treatment is masterfully subtle and expressive. Elvira's great scene "In quali eccessi" represents her conflicting emotions: "Che contrasto d'affetti in sen ti nasce!" Musically this is characterized in the opening measures, through contrast in dynamics (Example 11–2). Later her sighs are eloquently expressed in the orchestra, with careful dynamics indicated for each sigh (Example 11–3).

EXAMPLE 11–2. Mozart, *Don Giovanni*, Act II, Scene 2.

EXAMPLE 11–3. Mozart, *Don Giovanni*, Act II, Scene 2.

Mozart's vocal style generally reflects his perfection of symphonic technique which, applied to opera, means more thematic work, closer relations between voice and orchestra and, above all, more counterpoint, especially in the ensemble scenes. The importance of the latter represents perhaps Mozart's most significant departure from Italian models, in which ensemble writing was either nonexistent or treated in the manner of an aria for two or more persons, all expressing similar sentiments and often singing alternately rather than in true ensemble. With Mozart, the ensembles became important enough to take up substantial portions of each act—almost half of Act II in *Figaro*. They contain some of the most important dramatic developments, as in the quartet (No. 9, Act I) of *Don Giovanni*, in which Anna and Ottavio gradually realize that Don Giovanni is the villain and that Elvira is not mad or imagining things; or in the sextet (No. 19), with the participants commenting on the unexpected turn of events.

To bring all characters back on stage was customary in an *opera buffa* finale. Da Ponte, well aware of this convention, described it once in satirical terms: If an opera includes three, six, or sixty parts, in the finale they must all appear together and sing trios, sextets, or sessantets, whether or not the plot makes their simultaneous appearance likely. He implies that this convention serves to show off the composer's skill at writing ensembles. If the drama suffers from it—too bad for the librettist. Mozart had no hesitation about taking over this convention for the finale's last part, but its main portion is inevitably lively and dramatically convincing. Things happen continually in the ensemble finales, which are long, complex structures. They are the opera's essential supports; more so than the arias in which, as has been said, Mozart was willing to make substitutions and other adjustments.

What sets these ensembles apart from conventional finales is the masterly part-writing. This is not counterpoint for its own sake but a means by which each character, singing different words to different music, preserves his individuality. Here Mozart created a device that accomplishes something impossible to achieve in spoken drama: the simultaneous expression of different sentiments by characters involved in a dramatically complex situation. Many of Mozart's ensembles, particularly the act finales in *Figaro* and *Don Giovanni*, furnish fascinating examples of the successful collaboration of librettist and composer.

MOZART'S GERMAN OPERAS

Mozart's mature operas set to German librettos—*Die Entführung aus dem Serail* ("The Abduction from the Seraglio," 1782) and *Die Zauberflöte* ("The Magic Flute," 1791)—both show that his concept of the *Singspiel* went beyond tradition. The age's fondness for Turkish subjects manifested itself in many ways. There was general fascination with exotic people—their appearance, art, costumes. The Chinese rooms and pavilions in Schönbrunn, Esterháza, and other palaces testify to this. On another level, Eastern religion and philosophy interested many during the Age of Enlightenment. Books such as Jean Terrasson's novel *Séthos*,[12] dealing with ancient Egypt, had wide circulation. In plays and opera librettos, Eastern rulers tended to be characterized as wise, magnanimous, and forgiving. Mozart's German operas furnish the best-known examples.

Mozart's long letter of September 26, 1781, deals with the *Entführung;* from it we know that in German opera he was also concerned with the creation of psychologically convincing characters, and that he insisted on changes in the libretto to accomplish this. Again he accommodated specific singers: the aria "Martern aller Arten" was a concession to the virtuosity of Caterina Cavalieri and, with its coloratura passages, lifts the work out of the earlier *Singspiel* class. About Herr Fischer, his first Osmin, Mozart said that such an excellent singer should be given more music, and appropriate changes were made in the libretto. This seems to bear out Mozart's often-quoted statement that, in opera, poetry should be the obedient daughter of music; but it would be a mistake to generalize from this that Mozart was not concerned with text or drama. Other passages in the same letter make this quite clear: it was his purpose to write Osmin's part in such a way that it would best express his character. When the old harem overseer is in a towering rage, Mozart has him sing an almost incoherent series of imprecations ("Erst geköpft, dann gehangen . . .") admirably supported by the accompaniment, which at this point also "forgets itself."

If the *Entführung* contains more substantial music than had been customary in the *Singspiel,* this may in part be due to the Emperor's desire to place the *Nationalsingspiel* on a higher plane—to have its personnel composed of "nothing but musical virtuosos"—whereas elsewhere a *Singspiel* frequently was performed by actors from the legitimate stage who had no vocal training. Still, much of the *Entführung* is written in a simple style, utilizing song forms (as in Petrillo's *Romanze*) and concluding with the customary *vaudeville,* a finale in the form of a *rondeau* in which each participant sings a stanza, followed each time by a refrain sung by all. But here, too, Mozart shows himself above routine and conventional form: after each character has sung his or her verse, Osmin once more becomes so enraged that he forgets all about the *vaudeville* stanza and bursts out with his "vengeance music" of Act I—an excellent, realistic, and amusing touch.

What kind of an opera shall we call *The Magic Flute?* Much has been written about its complex history and its symbolism. Certainly it is a work that lends itself to interpretation on many levels. Its fairy-tale aspects relate it to many of the Viennese *Stegreifkomödien,* in vogue all through the eighteenth century. Works with titles such as *Die Zaubertrommel* or *Die magische Violine* were ever popular on the suburban stage, offering many things to delight the eye of the unsophisticated spectator and containing much slapstick, particularly for the comic person called Hanswurst or Kasperl. Similar themes involving some kind of magic continued to be

[12]Published in 1731 and soon translated into English, German, and Italian. See Dent, *Mozart's Operas,* pp. 224ff.

dramatized after Mozart's time as well, particularly in the comedies of Ferdinand Raimund (1790–1836; *Moisasurs Zauberfluch: Der Barometermacher auf der Zauberinsel*). Mozart's opera, in a sense, is such a "machine opera": doors open by themselves, a richly set table appears out of the ground, animals dance to the sound of Tamino's flute, and the Queen of the Night appears among thunder and lightning. Papageno is a *Hanswurst*, here disguised as a birdlike creature; like his predecessors he lives in a world of the senses in which food, drink, and beautiful girls matter the most. His simplicity is, of course, reflected in his music, beginning with the introductory song that soon achieved popularity throughout Germany. But other dramatic and musical qualities take *The Magic Flute* out of the *Singspiel* realm. In essence the work extols the virtues of love, forgiveness, tolerance, and the brotherhood of men—concepts central to the creed of the Masonic order of which both Mozart and his librettist Schikaneder were active members. A great deal of Masonic symbolism pervades the action[13] including the emphasis on the number three: the three temples of Reason, Wisdom, and Nature; the three doors which Tamino tries; the three repeated chords in the temple scenes. Tamino's manly silence is one of the Masonic virtues; the general distrust of women likewise goes back to Masonic beliefs. Even the preference for certain keys, especially E♭ major, and for wind instruments conforms to Masonic practices in Vienna. Thus the style of several compositions that Mozart wrote for occasions in his lodge reminds one strongly of the Masonic scenes in *The Magic Flute*.

On the original playbill the work was called "grosse Oper," a designation that reminds us of its great arias, among them the Queen's "Der Hölle Rache" with its taxing coloratura passages and dramatic orchestral writing. But the scenes with an affinity for Italian opera are few, while the spoken dialogue and the simple music sung by Papageno, Tamino, and others suggest German and, to a lesser extent, French models. Other musical ingredients—the use of a Lutheran chorale *cantus firmus*, the ceremonial music with the priests' chorus, Sarastro's hymnlike song—show the futility of attempts to classify the work: it is a unique opera. Once more one can point to aspects that make it representative of Classicism and that inspired Goethe to write a sequel to the text: it deals far more than Mozart's other operas with human and universal ethical concepts. The characters have symbolic significance and therefore are not drawn in the psychologically subtle and realistic way found in *Figaro* and *Don Giovanni*. This difference is most apparent in the ensemble scenes where greater simplicity and less character-drawing prevails.

The Magic Flute, then, was many things to many people. Its immediate success may have helped to widen the appeal of Mozart's music in

[13]The Masonic implications can hardly have been secret, since Masonic symbols appeared on the cover of the printed libretto.

general.[14] With its success, the undisputed reign of Italian opera was seriously challenged in Austria and Germany. The challenge was to lead to the eventual triumph of national opera in the Romantic era, beginning with Weber's *Der Freischütz*, first performed, with great success, in Berlin in 1821.

Mozart's operas never achieved complete success in Italy; yet there, too, the more humanized *opera buffa*, represented by Giovanni Paisiello (1740–1816) and Domenico Cimarosa (1749–1801), contributed to the decline of *opera seria*. The latter saw a gradual change in subject matter from the heroic and classic—still found in some works of Cherubini (1760–1842: *Il quinto Fabio*, 1779; *Olimpiade*, about 1783) and Spontini (1774–1851: *La vestale*, 1807)—to medieval and later historic subjects, often treated in a Romantic manner.

BIBLIOGRAPHICAL NOTES

D. J. Grout's *Short History of Opera*, 2nd ed. (New York: Norton, 1965) has several chapters relevant to this period. The article "Gluck" in *Grove 6* is thorough and includes an extensive, up-to-date bibliography. Thoughtful observations on Gluck's *Orfeo* are contained in J. Kerman's *Opera as Drama* (New York: Knopf, 1956). Kerman's chapter IV ("Mozart,") stresses the structure and meaning of the complex finales of *Figaro* and *Don Giovanni*. *Mozart's Operas* by E. Dent (London: Oxford University Press, 1947; originally published in 1913) covers the librettos and their history in great detail, as well as the music. Other important specialized studies are W. Mann, *The Operas of Mozart* (New York: Oxford University Press, 1977) and H. C. R. Landon, "The Operas of Haydn," *NOHM* VII (1973), 172ff. Eric Weimer, *"Opera Seria" and the Evolution of Classical Musical Style, 1755–1772* (Ann Arbor: UMI Research Press, 1984) traces this evolution by examining arias from operas by Hasse, Jommelli, and J. C. Bach. Several selections in *SMH* deal with Gluck's reforms and operatic thought in eighteenth-century France. See also R. Pauly's *Music and the Theater* (Englewood Cliffs, NJ: Prentice-Hall, 1970), especially chapter 4.

Several major reprint series, recently published or forthcoming, now make it possible to investigate operatic developments through the scores themselves: *Italian Opera, 1640–1770* (97 volumes, New York: Garland, 1985—); *Early Romantic Opera* (44 volumes, New York: Garland, 1984); *French Opera in the 17th and 18th Centuries* (75 volumes, New York: Pendragon, 1984); *German Opera, 1770–1800* (22 volumes, New York: Garland, 1986.)

[14]G. Gruber, *Mozart und die Nachwelt* (Salzburg, 1985), p. 50.

TWELVE

SACRED MUSIC
OF THE CLASSIC ERA

In the field of church music our attention in this chapter is focused primarily on developments in Southern Germany and in Austria, the region that produced so many other examples of the Classic style in music. Classic church music therefore is largely Catholic church music. Northern Protestantism, which had produced such a wealth of liturgical music during the Baroque era, culminating in Bach's cantatas, Passions, and organ works, failed to continue this distinguished tradition. The explanations usually advanced for this decline are complex and not altogether convincing. With the great diversity of Protestant denominations and sects there was no widely accepted, uniform ritual or an established sacred text. In general, rationalistic thought had made stronger inroads in the north and had brought to Protestantism greater emphasis on the spoken word, on instruction, and on the central position of the sermon.

PROTESTANT CHURCH MUSIC

Protestant church music of the age presents a complex picture, with many conflicting crosscurrents. There is continued concern with individual, subjective aspects of devotion, with the expression of personal religious thought and feeling rather than with established, generally observed liturgies. Singing, by the congregation in church and by the individual in the home, is stressed. Much of the religious poetry set to music by northern composers was *empfindsam*—for example, the texts by Christian F. Gellert (1715–69) which were set to music by C. P. E. Bach and others, including Haydn and Beethoven. Sacred music of this age represents a reaction to the complexity of Baroque contrapuntal writing (see p. 24); the preference now was for simplicity, for music that appealed to all. Reichardt, among others called for simplicity in church music: It should have solemn, noble qualities but above all it should (once more) "speak to the heart."

Nevertheless, J. S. Bach's influence continued to be felt. Johann Friedrich Doles (1715–97), cantor at St. Thomas's Church in Leipzig after 1755, acknowledged his indebtedness to Bach's instruction in contrapuntal writing, but in his own composing preferred a "gentle and touching melodious style." In setting Gellert's texts to music Doles's avowed purpose was to create "gentle and artless chorale melodies."[1] A text such as No. 22 in Doles's collection typifies the subjective, introspective nature of pietistic hymns; here is the first of twenty verses:

> Wer bin ich von Natur, wenn ich mein Innres prüfe?
> O wieviel Greul lässt mich mein Herze sehn!
> (What is my real nature, when I examine myself?
> O how much horror does my heart reveal to me!)

Doles's successor, Johann Adam Hiller (1728–1804), expressed similar views. In the preface to his *Allgemeines Choral-Melodienbuch* (1793) Hiller voices his dissatisfaction with the "improper rhythmic extensions of unimportant syllables, which have no place in our chorales." The rhythmic "improvements" in his hymnal seem to result in blandness compared to earlier versions, such as those familiar to us in harmonizations by Buxtehude, Bach, and others.

Chorales continued to be sung by congregations; choirs often sang four-part harmonizations which tended to be simpler than Bach's. Works in which a chorale melody serves as a cantus firmus also were sung, continuing the earlier tradition of chorale motets and chorale variations. Settings

---

[1]Doles, preface to *Melodien zu . . . Gellerts Geistlichen Oden und Liedern* (1758).

by Karl Fasch (1736–1800) represent this style. Active at the court of Frederick the Great, he was also the founder of the Berlin *Singakademie*, a choral society which, under Fasch's direction, included works by J. S. Bach in its repertory. In the motet for five voices "Was mein Gott will," Fasch uses the well-known chorale melody prominently, for solo and choral combinations, with melodic variations in several verses (Examples 12a, 12b, and 12c).

Gottfried August Homilius (1714–85), one of the major Protestant composers in Germany, also wrote motets using chorale melodies as cantus firmi. Reichardt considered Homilius "without a doubt the best composer for the church, and also the greatest organist."[2]

Cantata and oratorio, including Passion and Resurrection oratorios, continued to be cultivated in the North; they are represented by several major works by C. P. E. Bach, especially from his Hamburg years. Carl Heinrich Graun's *Der Tod Jesu* (1755) achieved lasting success. But in many churches the trend was moving away from concerted, soloistic music; instead, simple music for both congregation and choir was favored.

No clear division exists between songs intended for devotional use in the home and the religious folk (or folk-like) song, a repertory that flourished with the coming of literary and musical Romanticism. Matthias Claudius's "Der Mond ist aufgegangen" was mentioned above in connection with the solo song; others, still widely sung today, include the Christmas song "Ihr Kinderlein kommet" (music by J. A. P. Schulz) and, above all, "Stille Nacht" (J. F. Mohr and F. X. Gruber, 1818). Though written, according to the well-known story, for use in a Catholic country church, "Stille Nacht" has transcended all barriers of denomination, langauge, and place.

CATHOLIC CHURCH MUSIC

The sacred music of the Catholic church, the faith almost universally embraced in the south, had different, less complicated aspects. There, a strong Church representing spiritual, political, and financial power offered, through its many institutions, a stable environment in which the function of music was established by tradition.

The term "sacred music" includes both liturgical and devotional music, along with borderline categories—musical observances that had become locally sanctioned as liturgical in those places. Most important were the Mass (including the Requiem Mass), the motet (especially for the Offertory), vesper psalms and the Magnificat, the Te Deum, and litanies. Poly-

---

[2]*Briefe eines aufmerksamen Reisenden . . .,* II: 109ff.

EXAMPLE 12–1. Fasch, motet "Was mein Gott will."

phonic as well as Gregorian music was heard in all of these, with the style of the music (length, instrumental participation, and so forth) depending on the nature and solemnity of the occasion. In countries where Catholicism was universally accepted, religious holidays were public holidays. Their general observation required much special music, not only for High Mass on Sunday, but for the numerous saints' days, including those of local patron saints, and for other holidays. The sumptuous architecture and the large libraries of many Austrian monasteries still testify to their importance as patrons of the arts and sciences in the eighteenth century, with the Benedictine order being particularly active in the field of music. Various special religious events, among them processions, pilgrimages, and other outdoor ceremonies, called for special sacred music as did events of state like the births of princes, coronations, and installations of public or religious dignitaries. The celebration of the Feast of Saint Cecilia, the patron saint of music, understandably was the occasion for outstanding musical efforts, in which the leading musicians of the time were eager to participate. Veneration of the Virgin Mary gave rise to numerous settings of litanies (e.g., Mozart's *Litaniae Lauretanae*) and Marian antiphons; also to devotional songs in the vernacular. The celebration of commemorative Masses and litanies was frequently privately endowed, with some funds earmarked for musical expenses.

Through the ages church music has tended to be conservative. For the eighteenth century this meant that some style features of Classicism were slow to find their way into the sacred field, while certain aspects of Baroque style, particularly the inclusion of a figured bass, maintained themselves longer in this field than in other kinds of music. Formal conventions that continued to be observed in Classic sacred music, and into the nineteenth century, are the fugal endings of the Gloria and the Credo in the Mass, of the Te Deum, and of certain litany movements. Traditional also was the inclusion of an organ obbligato (if found at all) in the Benedictus, and the distribution of solo and tutti writing in the Mass (discussed in this chapter). Some of the conservative aspects of Classic sacred music stem from the continued official favoring of the *stile antico*, with the polyphonic style of Palestrina serving as the model. Throughout the seventeenth and eighteenth centuries, compositions in a strict, imitative style were deemed most suitable for the Church, especially during Advent and Lent; yet the composer who wrote a *missa in contrapuncto* for a Sunday in Advent might revert to an entirely different style, with florid arias and vigorous accompaniment, for other occasions. Many Masses from the late eighteenth century include music in both *stile antico* and *moderno;* even if the writing is contrapuntal it may still include orchestral accompaniment doubling the voice lines consistently. In Vienna the imperial Kapellmeister Johann Joseph Fux (1660–1741) had written numerous Masses and motets in the *stile antico,* including some canonic Masses. Through these and particularly through his famed treatise on counterpoint, the *Gradus ad Parnassum* (1725), Fux exerted considerable influence. Both Haydn and Mozart studied the *Gradus;* even Padre Martini, another champion of the strict style, is said to have based his system of counterpoint on Fux's precepts.

In spite of the conservative nature of church music, compositions entirely in strict, contrapuntal style were in the minority during the Classic era: Most works employed the musical vocabulary—melodic, harmonic, rhythmic—found in other categories of music. To the nineteenth and twentieth centuries the vocal style of the Classic era is best known from opera; this, in part, accounts for the frequent accusation that Classic church music is operatic, and for its virtual exclusion from liturgical performance today. Today the Masses of the Classic composers are performed in Austrian churches, as part of the religious ceremony, while elsewhere they are normally heard only in the concert hall or in extraliturgical performances, as a sacred concert.

According to the musical treatment we distinguish between the Missa Brevis and Missa Longa or Solemnis. In the former the five parts of the "Ordinary" text—Kyrie, Gloria, Credo, Sanctus, and Agnus Dei—are each treated as one short and continuous musical movement; in the latter, numerous subdivisions occur, especially in the textually longer Gloria and Credo. To Classic composers the text of the Kyrie *(Kyrie eleison, Christe eleison, Kyrie eleison)* at times suggested sonata form; other parts of the Mass were similarly treated. Symphonic procedure is brought to mind by the slow introduction found in many Kyrie settings. The serious text sometimes received contrapuntal treatment; at others, neither the briskly moving voice parts nor the accompaniment seem to express the text meaning, "Lord, have mercy upon us!" (Example 12–2). The long texts of the Gloria

EXAMPLE 12–2. Haydn, *Paukenmesse*, Hob. XXII:9

Allegro moderato   Violins

Ky - ri - e   e - lei - son,e - lei-son   Ky - ri - e

and the Credo presented problems to Classic composers, especially to Mozart, whose Archbishop insisted that an entire Mass, including musical and spoken portions, should not last more than forty-five minutes. Occasionally, composers resorted to the simultaneous singing of different parts of the text, a device that was eventually frowned upon by Church authorities. In a Missa Longa these problems did not arise; here composers felt free to repeat words or text phrases where it seemed musically desirable.

The texts of the Gloria and Credo are not always composed in their entirety: the Quoniam tu solus may bring back or "recapitulate" the opening of the Gloria. The Benedictus may call for one or several solo voices, often forming a separate section or movement, even in a Missa Brevis. In the Agnus Dei any solo-writing normally occurs at the opening, adagio or andante, leading into a contrasting, choral Dona nobis pacem. The extensive use of solo-writing in Masses from the early Classic period points to Italian influences, which, as we know, were strong in Vienna. Italian musicians were strongly represented in Salzburg as well, though German composers including Karl Heinrich Biber (1681–1749), Johann Ernst Eberlin (1702–62), and Leopold Mozart had exerted their own influence.

When Mozart, in 1790, applied for the position of second Kapellmeister in Vienna, he stated that since his childhood he had been familiar with the church style. This was no exaggeration: some shorter sacred works even antedate Mozart's first Mass, probably written at the age of twelve. This work (K. 139 in C minor) shows amazing maturity and familiarity with the church style. After the slow introduction the Kyrie continues allegro, C major, in a vigorous style with typical busy accompaniment in the violins. The Christe forms a contrasting middle movement for solo voices; at its end "Kyrie allegro da capo" is indicated. The Gloria contains many sections, with solos or duets in the customary places (Laudamus te; Domine Deus). The Cum sancto spiritu fugue that ends the Gloria is long in relation to the preceding movements. Traditional are the predominantly syllabic setting of the long Credo text, the solo-writing for Et in Spiritum Sanctum, and the Et vitam fugue (here a double fugue) at the end. In the Sanctus we have the customary tempo change from adagio to allegro at the words "Pleni sunt coeli." The Benedictus is unusual in that the soprano solo is periodically interrupted by the choral interjection "Osanna in excelsis."

Most of Mozart's later Salzburg Masses observe the same general formal conventions. Individual movements are at times expanded and show their relation to Classic instrumental forms. The Dona nobis of K. 275, with its refrain structure, suggests a rondo, as do some of the Credo settings. In these unity may be achieved by repeating music to different portions of the text (K. 258), or by treating the word *Credo* in the manner of a short, characteristic motif which recurs throughout the movement, as in the "Credo Mass," K. 257 (Example 12–3.)

EXAMPLE 12–3. Mozart, "Credo Mass," K. 257.

Best known among Mozart's Salzburg Masses is K. 317, the "Coronation Mass." The assumption that it was written in 1779 for the small pilgrimage church of Maria Plain near Salzburg has been refuted.[3] Its relatively long Credo has the quality of a briskly moving rondo, with a return of the opening words at the end. Expressive, lyrical writing for solo quartet distinguishes the Benedictus; parts of it are repeated after the choral Osanna in excelsis. A soprano solo opens the Agnus Dei; its melody, as has often been noted, bears a strong resemblance to the aria "Dove sono" from *Figaro*. For the concluding Dona nobis, Mozart returns to the più andante section of the opening Kyrie, eventually increasing the tempo to allegro con spirito.

The brevity of this and other Salzburg Masses stands in contrast to the great C Minor Mass of 1782–83, K. 427. In planning this, Mozart did not consider the limitations imposed by the Archbishop for the Salzburg cathedral. The work, which would have been his most extensive, varied, and profound setting, remained incomplete, perhaps for the very reason that it was not written for an employer, Mozart and the Archbishop by then having parted ways. It was performed in the monastery church of St. Peter's in Salzburg with Mozart's wife Konstanze singing the soprano solo part. Only the Kyrie, Gloria, and Sanctus were completed, all conceived on the large scale of a true "cantata Mass," with many self-contained movements. Most of these are composed in a manner that seems more serious and profound than that of Mozart's earlier sacred works, a manner that represents a changed concept of the Church style. He draws on larger vocal and instrumental resources, including five-part and eight-part choir. Counterpoint is much in evidence, as it is in many instrumental works from this time (during which the composer occupied himself intensively with Bach's and Handel's music). This is not the learned counterpoint of the *stile antico:* the orchestral accompaniment is frequently independent of the voice lines.

In a number of movements (the Laudamus te and the Domine Deus, for instance) Mozart turned to the kind of florid coloratura writing that to him seemed a suitable interpretation of the jubilant text (Example 12–4). Passages of this kind, with trills and cadenzas, have often been cited

EXAMPLE 12–4. Mozart, *C Minor Mass,* K. 427.

Glo - ri - fi - ca - - - - - - - mus te

[3]See Karl Pfannhauser, "Mozarts Krönungsmesse" in *Mitteilungen der internationalen Stiftung Mozarteum,* 11, Heft 3–4 (August 1963), 3–11, and E. Hintermaier, "Die Familie Mozart und Maria Plain," *Oesterreichische Musikzeitschrift,* 29 (1974), 350–56.

Salzburg: monastery and church of St. Peter's in 1769. (From the author's collection.)

to lend weight to the accusation that Classic church music in general is secular and operatic. In most of the work, however, the prevailing mood is serious and austere. The opening Kyrie sets such a mood; the textual meaning of the supplication is interpreted far more conscientiously than in most of Mozart's earlier Masses. Some sections are conceived in an elaborately contrapuntal manner (the Quoniam for two sopranos and tenor), culminating in fugal writing of grandiose design in the Cum sancto spiritu.

In this Mass, then, Mozart draws on a great variety of musical traditions, resources, and styles, according to the text's requirements as he interpreted them. In modern performances (and, presumably, at the first performance), movements from other Mozart Masses are usually substituted for the missing portions. The dimensions of the work remind us of Bach's great B Minor Mass, the length of which also precludes liturgical performance and which, in its final form, also incorporated music originally intended for other occasions.

Aside from Mass, Vespers traditionally called for special music. As in an eighteenth-century Missa Longa, the long text (five psalms followed by a hymn, the Magnificat, and often a Marian antiphon) offered opportunities for musical variety and display. Mozart's liturgical music from the Salzburg years includes two settings: *Vesperae de Dominica*, K. 321 (1779), and

Vesperae solennes de confessore, K. 339 (1780). The latter work in particular demonstrates great variety, showing, in two successive movements, Mozart's mastery of both the *stile antico* and *stile moderno:* "Laudate Pueri," a stern, rigorously contrapuntal movement, is followed by "Laudate Dominum," a beautiful, gentle soprano solo to which a subdued, homophonic refrain is added at the end.

Mozart's years in Vienna coincided with the era of Josephinism—the decade during which Joseph II, through legislation and imperial decrees, substantially curtailed the political and financial power of the Church. The number of Masses and other rites to be celebrated was sharply curtailed, as was the veneration of miraculous images, statues, and shrines. Some holidays were abolished; monasteries were dissolved. These conditions understandably discouraged the composing of elaborate church music.[4] In Mozart's case only two sacred works were to follow the C Minor Mass: the Ave Verum, K. 618, and the Requiem Mass, K. 626, on which he worked to the last day of his life and which was completed by his pupil Franz X. Süssmayr (1766–1803). To this day there is uncertainty about the exact extent of Süssmayr's collaboration, but with his additions the Requiem has remained the best known of Mozart's sacred works. Its substantial choral movements range from the double fugue of the Kyrie to the massive chordal texture of the Dies Irae. Solos are few and for the most part restricted to incidental passages in a choral movement. In solos and ensembles alike, the vocal lines are cantabile and simple; nowhere do we find display or virtuosity for its own sake. Clearly the terrible struggles and disappointments of the composer's last years, his rapidly declining health, and his preoccupation with death caused him to find a musical language that was intensely personal and yet, as a sincere interpretation of the sacred text, one far more widely understood than that of any other sacred work of the Classic era.[5]

Haydn's early Masses vary in length and resources. The *Grosse Orgelmesse* of about 1768 is a fairly extensive work, a Missa Solemnis calling for an orchestra that includes English and French horns. Its popular name derives from the importance of the organ part, especially in the Benedictus. In this and other Masses by Haydn before the 1790s, however, the orchestra seldom moves to the foreground. At times, too, he shows a lack of concern with text meaning: the Dona nobis which concludes the *Grosse Orgelmesse,* in rapid 6/8 time, seems jubilant rather than imploring. Extended fugal movements occur in the *Missa Sanctae Ceciliae* (about 1770)

[4]In a letter to his father (December 16, 1780), Mozart uses strong language to express his dissatisfaction with the new Church decrees.

[5]A little known Requiem in C minor by Michael Haydn, composed in 1771, may well have been known to Mozart. The two works correspond in a remarkable number of structural details, especially in the Introit (Requiem), Sequence (Dies Irae), and Offertory (Domine Jesu Christe).

along with equally extensive solos. The *Missa Brevis Sancti Joannis de Deo* (about 1775) is conceived on a smaller scale since it was written for the small church of an Eisenstadt monastery. Once more we find the simultaneous singing of different parts of the Credo text. Here the accompaniment consists only of the "church trio"—two violins and figured bass.

After the *Missa Cellensis* of 1782, partly because of the reform decrees mentioned above, Haydn did not write any Masses for fourteen years, a period that saw his rise to greatest fame. His last six Masses, beginning with the *Missa in tempore belli* or *Paukenmesse*, of 1796, owe their existence largely to the interest in sacred music of Prince Nicholas II. Conceived on a large and impressive scale, these works could not have been written before Haydn's London journeys. The majesty of Handel's oratorios speaks from them; the choruses, including the fugal movements, are weightier, and vocal solos are largely eliminated in favor of ensembles, especially the vocal quartet. In instrumentation Haydn applied what had proved to be successful in the London symphonies: more consistent and prominent use of woodwind instruments. (The *Harmoniemesse* of 1802 owes its name to such prominent use.) The prevailing tone in these Masses is serious and weighty, particularly in the "Nelson" Mass of 1798, today one of the more frequently performed Classic Masses.

The Mass, especially the unchanging part or Ordinary of the Mass, was the service that most often allowed or even required polyphonic music during this period; accordingly it received most attention from composers. Introit, Gradual, and Communion were normally chanted, while an Offertory, not necessarily based on the correct liturgical text, might be sung by a soloist, by the choir, or both. Soloistic motets, consisting of recitatives and arias with perhaps a short concluding chorus, were widely performed in the late eighteenth century. Mozart's motet *Exsultate, jubilate*, K. 165, ending with the well-known *Alleluia*, represents the purely soloistic type (Example 12–5). Mozart wrote it in Milan, in January 1773, for the castrato Venanzio Rauzzini. Dr. Burney, who had heard Rauzzini the previous year, was impressed by his brilliant voice and good musical taste.

EXAMPLE 12–5. Mozart, Motet, *Exsultate, jubilate*, K. 165.

[Allegro]

Al - le - lu - ja, al - le - lu - ja,_____

Among Haydn's other sacred works the *Stabat Mater* (about 1770) and the *Te Deum* in C (about 1799) should be mentioned as particularly rewarding. Unlike Haydn, Mozart wrote a fair number of smaller sacred works which show masterly handling of contrapuntal texture effectively contrasted, at times, within one and the same work, with chordal portions (*Misericordias Domini*, K. 222; *Venite populi*, K. 260).

The performance of an instrumental composition during Mass was widespread, going back at least to the early seventeenth century. Organ compositions, or pieces for organ and other instruments, were played at various points during the service, as indicated by titles such as *Concerto per l'elevatione* and *Sinfonia alla communione*. Later eighteenth-century orchestral works, such as movements from symphonies or violin concertos, were at least occasionally heard during Mass.[6] In Italy and Austria instrumental compositions often took the place of a sung Gradual—that is, between the readings of Epistle and Gospel—a custom to which Mozart's "Epistle Sonatas" owe their existence. Because of Archbishop Colloredo's insistence on brevity these are all short, one-movement compositions; those by Karl Heinrich Biber and other Salzburg predecessors were closer to the Baroque church sonata in length. Mozart's sonatas are brief orchestral movements; only a few of them contain significant organ parts (K. 336, for instance, with organ cadenza). In some instances the instrumentation gives a clue as to the Mozart Mass for which the sonata was intended.[7]

Around 1782, in line with the reforms of Josephinism, these instrumental pieces were suppressed and choral settings of the Gradual text were substituted. Michael Haydn composed such Graduals for most Sundays and holidays; in doing so he paved the way for a return to greater liturgical propriety than had been customary in the eighteenth century.

Most modern listeners never hear the instrumentally accompanied sacred music of this period as part of a religious service, and the issue of its propriety for church may never have occupied them. But attacks had set in already during Haydn's and Mozart's lifetimes; not long thereafter, the view that was to be typical in the nineteenth century was expressed by E. T. A. Hoffman in a series of essays entitled "Old and New Church Music" (1814). The sacred works of Haydn and Mozart were considered to be contaminated by "excessive sweetness which banned all seriousness and dignity. . . . Even Masses, vespers, etc. displayed a character that would have been undignified and too superficial in an *opera seria*." While Hoffmann uses words of glowing praise for the Requiem, he condemns Mozart's Masses as among his weakest works. He finds similar faults in Haydn's masses, though he concedes that musically they are far superior to the shallow imitations of Hoffmann's own time. He finds words of high praise for Michael Haydn's sacred music, which, because of its serious tone, fre-

---

[6]S. Bonta, "The Uses of the Sonata da Chiesa," *JAMS*, 22 (1969), 54ff.

[7]H. Dennerlein, "Zur Problematik von Mozarts Kirchensonaten," *Mozart-Jahrbuch* (1953), pp. 100ff.

quently surpasses that of his brother Joseph. On the other hand, he deplores the fact that serious works such as Mozart's Requiem have moved from the churches into the concert halls: They are out of place there—"like the appearance of a saint at a ball. . . . A Mass performed in a concert is like a sermon given in a theater."

How can the modern listener come to terms with the "happy" sound of so much Classic church music? One approach might be to understand these works as expressions of the religious outlook of their time. In the eighteenth-century view, sacred music, and religious art in general, were to provide a frame, a beautiful setting for the divine ceremony—this in spite of the fact that Mass, whether spoken or sung, *is* itself a ceremony, an act of worship. The beauty of the house of God and the music that filled it were to be artistic expressions of praise for His goodness and mercy. If one accepts such a view, the exuberant, jubilant mood of Baroque and Rococo architecture seems appropriate, and so does the music, which exudes a joyful, hopeful, often simple and childlike spirit rather than asceticism or austerity. To many an eighteenth-century Catholic worshiper, the stately ritual suggested brilliance and magnificence. The festive music with its apparently theatrical display was there for the same purpose as the brightly colored vestments, the gold and silver vessels, the many candles, the abundance of statues, paintings, decoration, and the incense. Whether or not Classic church music impresses us as secular may also depend on the setting in which we listen to it. A Mozart Mass heard in a small Austrian church with the congregation present may sound proper and liturgical; performed during the Salzburg Festival in the presence of dressed-up, admission-paying tourists, it may sound worldly. Yet even under the latter circumstances the listener who can reconstruct for himself the setting for which the music was conceived will not fail to be moved by its sincerity.

THE ORATORIO

The Catholic sacred music discussed so far is liturgical music. As in the north, Austrian and South German music also accorded a place of importance to the oratorio. Here the conventions established in Italy earlier in the century continued to prevail, as they did in opera. Italian poets held leading positions at the Austrian court (see p. 192), furnishing librettos for operas and oratorios. Oratorio texts by Metastasio and Zeno had been set to music by resident Italians (by Caldara, in *Joaz*, 1726) and Austrians (by Reutter, in *La Betulia liberata*, 1734). The same texts continued to serve composers later in the century. The Vienna-born Giuseppe Bonno (1711–88) set two oratorio texts by Metastasio. Florian Gassmann (1729–74), like

Bonno a court composer, contributed another *Betulia liberata* (1772). The Italian tradition is still reflected in Paisiello's *La passione di Gesù Cristo* of 1782, a widely performed oratorio with text by Metastasio.

Haydn's first oratorio, *Il ritorno di Tobia*, was successful when first performed in Vienna in 1775. Consisting of two parts, both of them long, the work required two days for its performance. Its grand dimensions are evident at once: a very substantial overture is followed by an equally extensive opening chorus. Later, a dramatic accompanied recitative (for one singer or several) may precede an elaborate coloratura aria in da capo form, or a long, complex finale may involve soloists and chorus. *Tobia* was given again in 1784, with cuts in the arias and with additional choruses. Another revival in 1808 was less well received. By then Haydn's two German oratorios had generated great enthusiasm: *Tobia* seemed old-fashioned by comparison. In general, "a new era of musical taste had dawned during which the rule of neither Italian oratorio nor *opera seria* could be maintained."[8]

The great popularity of the oratorio in the nineteenth century, which has lasted, particularly in English-speaking countries, to the present day, is in part due to Haydn's late works, *The Creation* (1798) and *The Seasons* (1801). In England Handel's oratorios continued to be widely heard after his death; the massed performances that Haydn heard there impressed him profoundly. These performances continued well into the nineteenth century, at times involving 150 to 200 musicians. Handel's oratorios were also heard, in similarly massive presentations, in the Vienna of Haydn's and Beethoven's time, largely owing to the initiative of Baron van Swieten (see p. 90). Until fairly recently, *Messiah* was generally given with Mozart's augmented orchestration.

The subjects of both *The Creation* and *The Seasons* must have held a strong fascination for Haydn, with their many opportunities for vivid imagery, for arias of a lyrical, contemplative nature, for the expression of simple and devout religious feelings, for rousing choruses with suitably brilliant accompaniment by a large orchestra. Haydn's talent for descriptive writing is displayed in the orchestral introduction to *The Creation*, the famous "Representation of Chaos," and throughout this oratorio and the later one Haydn seldom let an opportunity for tone painting go by. Some contemporaries, including his biographer Dies, criticized him for this with surprising severity, putting some of the blame on the text which "forced" Haydn to do this, "to the detriment of art."

Haydn's musical interpretation of nature is, for the most part, realistic and descriptive, lacking the sentimental and subjective approach of the Romantic era, but this did not prevent both works from finding enthusiastic

---

[8]E. F. Schmid, preface to *Haydn: Werke*, XXVIII/1¹, p. vii.

acceptance in the early nineteenth century. A Paris performance of *The Creation* in 1800, in the presence of Napoleon, was so great a success that it was soon repeated. In 1808, Haydn received the medal of honor of the St. Petersburg Philharmonic Society; the letter of transmittal mentioned specifically only the last two oratorios, along with "so many other great works." The success of these oratorios, with German texts, helped the attempts then being made in Germany to revive choral singing on a large scale. The famous Berlin *Singakademie* was founded in 1790, and a musical journal of 1807 could refer to a choral concert there as the first attempt to have a public concert consist of vocal music exclusively. Massed performances of *The Creation* by then had taken place in many cities, including performances with scenery, as *tableaux* or "living pictures." Both works, *The Creation* in particular, did much to stimulate the growth and popularity of oratorio societies, the kind of amateur music-making that was to hold such an important place in nineteenth-century musical life.

MOZART'S ORATORIOS

In the Salzburg of Mozart's youth, oratorios in the reigning Italian style could be heard, along with works in German that represented a local tradition. The sacred *Singspiel*—dramatizations of Bible stories, usually with strongly didactic, moralizing intent—was cultivated by Eberlin and others. Mozart made contributions to both Italian and German types, beginning with the remarkable *Die Schuldigkeit des ersten Gebotes* ("The Duty of the First Commandment," K. 35), performed in 1767. The printed libretto's title-page points out that act I was composed by "Herr Wolfgang Motzard, ten years old"; acts II and III were written by Michael Haydn and Adlgasser respectively. Even assuming that father Leopold lent a helping hand, the long first act is a remarkable achievement. Text meaning is closely observed: a dramatic, rising unison passage in the orchestra underscores the words "arising from the grave." There are other passages that are quite imaginative and go beyond routine, such as the accompanied recitative "Wie, er erwecket mich?" with its brief quotation from the preceding aria.

Metastasio's *Betulia liberata* was set by Mozart in 1771. Of its fifteen numbers only three are choruses, and of these only the last one, concluding the oratorio, is substantial. It presents a Gregorian cantus firmus in the soprano—the same melody *(Te decet hymnus)* that Mozart was to use again in his Requiem Mass.[9]

[9]See M. E. Bonds, "Gregorian Chant in the Works of Mozart," *Mozart-Jahrbuch* (1980–83), p. 306.

In Vienna, Mozart once more turned to oratorio. He was asked, on short notice, to provide one for a concert in 1785. Under constraints of time, he made use of his incomplete Mass in C Minor, substituting an Italian text (perhaps by Da Ponte) and writing two new arias. The resulting oratorio, *Davidde penitente,* K. 469, achieved remarkable success at the time.

One of the arias of *Davidde,* "Fra l'oscure ombre funeste" for soprano, serves well to illustrate a point made earlier about the nature of Classic sacred music—the lack of clear distinction between sacred and secular style. This oratorio aria sounds very much like an aria from an opera by Mozart—say, *The Abduction from the Seraglio;* in fact, Mozart wrote the aria for Caterina Cavalieri, for whom he had also written the role of Konstanze in that opera. Vocal writing, treatment of accompaniment, and other features may seem "operatic"—but what about the text?

> Fra l'oscure ombre funeste
> Splende al giusto il ciel sereno,
> Serva ancor nelle tempeste
> La sua pace un fido cor.

The words of the first two lines—"through menacing, dark shadows the righteous will see the serene sky"—express feelings of confidence, using images of darkness and brightness, just as in an operatic "comparison aria." But such feelings are neither exclusively religious or exclusively worldly; they are universal. To the composer of Mozart's time they suggested musical means equally apt for opera or for oratorio or for other sacred music. The same applies to the concluding pair of lines, contrasting the tempest with the peace felt by a faithful heart. The words, the similes, and the musical style are best known to us from eighteenth-century opera, but they are not solely "operatic."

ORGANS AND ORGAN MUSIC

Given the flourishing of organ music during the age of Bach and Handel, its small part in the repertory of the Classic period is surprising. There is no simple explanation; it seems that many factors contributed to a complex situation.

To begin with, the ideas of the Enlightenment produced in many places suspicion and hostility to church and clergy. Though the Catholic church continued to be a powerful institution, its liturgical and musical practices were often questioned and sometimes revised. Near the end of the century these revisions affected the use of instruments in particular. (see p. 219.)

In France, leaders of the Revolution, violently opposed to the Catholic church as an institution, destroyed churches and monasteries—along with their organs—and brought death or exile to countless members of the clergy.

But even before the 1780s, composers who wrote many Masses and other sacred vocal music contributed little to the organ repertory. Here an attitude of liturgical laxness may have brought about a seemingly contradictory state of affairs: Instrumental compositions were frequently heard during Mass, replacing vocal settings of liturgical texts, but significant, substantial works for organ were few. It appears that in the south of Europe (South Germany, Austria, Italy) the organ served for accompaniment and brief preludes and interludes rather than for solo performance. For such purposes short and simple pieces sufficed, giving rise to publications such as Vanhal's *Praeambula für Stadt- und Landorganisten.* One must also remember that in the north the chorale, for over a century, had held a place of paramount musical importance, especially in Lutheran church music. This importance is reflected in the vast repertory of Baroque chorale-based organ music.

Finally one might point to characteristics of the instrument itself. The organ as treated by J. S. Bach and other Baroque-era composers was a medium for polyphony—but mid-eighteenth-century composers, as we have seen, shied away from polyphonic complexity. The clavichord and, in time, the fortepiano, capable of expressing delicate dynamic nuances, were more suited to the aesthetic concepts of the age of *Empfindsamkeit.* Only in the nineteenth century did new concepts of organ building produce instruments with the appropriate new tonal qualities. These organs could also imitate the instrumental timbres and volume of the growing symphony orchestra. Such concepts had already occupied Georg Joseph Vogler, the "Abbé Vogler" (1749–1814). Given to experimentation and considered a crackpot by many, Vogler, as organ builder, designed and added new ranks of pipes that approximated various orchestral timbres. He went on concert tours with his own organ, which he called an "Orchestrion."[10] But in general one can say that organs, being large, complex, and expensive instruments, were slow to keep pace with style changes.

These considerations may at least in part account for the state of organ music at the time of Haydn and Mozart. For Mozart it is indeed a puzzling (to us) state of affairs. His official position in Salzburg included duties

---

[10]The introduction of mechanical organs that imitate the sound of an orchestra might also be mentioned here, among them the "Panharmonicon" invented by J. N. Maelzel, the instrument for which Beethoven originally wrote his "Battle" symphony (*Wellington's Victory,* Op. 91, 1813). See also p. 78. Vogler's work is further discussed by P. Rummenhöller, *Die musikalische Vorklassik* (Kassel, 1983), pp. 140ff.

as cathedral organist. He was fond of the instrument and was praised for his organ playing, including his skillful improvising. He played on fine organs wherever he went. Schlichtegroll (see above, p. 194) records that as early as 1763 Mozart played the organ at Versailles, with the royal family in attendance. A year later, in England, "everyone esteemed his organ playing even higher than his harpsichord playing," and soon after, during a trip through the Netherlands, he often played on organs in monasteries and cathedrals.[11] In 1789 he visited Leipzig and played on the organ in St. Thomas Church in the presence of Bach's successor, J. F. Doles.

Nevertheless, Mozart wrote little that was specifically designated as organ music. The seventeen "Epistle Sonatas" mentioned earlier are symphonic movements rather than organ sonatas. Occasionally Mozart included an organ solo or obbligato in a Mass, usually in the Benedictus. His Mass in C., K. 259, is such a work; it is significant that even this fairly simple organ part led to the work's becoming known as the "Organ Solo" Mass (Example 12–6).

Quite likely a number of other keyboard works were intended for the organ, though not labeled as such in the sources. The fugue K. 401 is among these; it was first published as "for harpsichord or organ." Other works were assumed to be harpsichord compositions because of the absence of pedal parts, among them the "Adagio in B Minor," K. 540.

To a lesser extent Haydn also was active as organist, in his early Vienna years and in Eisenstadt. His "Great Organ" Mass (about 1768) has extended organ passages in the Kyrie and Benedictus, but much of the time the organ has the continuo function that it usually does in Classic church music. Haydn's "Little Organ Mass" (*Missa Brevis Sancti Joannis de Deo*, about 1775) features an extended organ solo in the Benedictus—a real solo, with other instruments providing a discreet accompaniment. Here we find a texture characteristic of much Classic organ music: The solo is entirely a melody for the right hand while the left hand provides simple harmonic support; there is no distinct pedal part. This texture suggests that much Classic "organ" music in reality is "two-hand" music that could be (and often was) performed on a harpsichord.

Haydn's concerto of 1756, Hob. XVIII:1, is such a work. Although in the autograph it is labeled "per l'Organo," the composer's own *Entwurfskatalog* lists it as "per il clavicembalo." There are at least two other organ concertos by Haydn, possibly more.[12] Few organ concertos by other Austrian composers need be mentioned here. Michael Haydn's concerto for or-

---

[11]H. Dennerlein discusses Mozart keyboard works intended for organ rather than piano, and gives detailed documentation, in "Mozarts europäische Orgelerfahrung," *Mozart-Jahrbuch* (1978–79), 269–75. Some of Mozart's own letters provide information about what was expected of an organist during Mass (letter of November 9, 1777).

[12]G. Feder, "Wieviel Orgelkonzerte hat Haydn geschrieben?," *Die Musikforschung*, 23 (1970), 440–44. See also A. P. Brown, *Joseph Haydn's Keyboard Music* (Bloomington, 1986), 134ff; 160.

EXAMPLE 12–6. Mozart, *Mass in C*, K. 259, excerpt.

gan, viola, and strings is an attractive work, offering challenges to both soloists. Johann Georg Albrechtsberger (1736–1809) was organist at Melk and
later court organist in Vienna. Known best for his theoretical writings, and
as a teacher of Beethoven, he also wrote much sacred music including a
concerto (1762) and preludes and fugues for organ. Lack of idiomatic writing characterizes the six concertos by the Spanish Padre Antonio Soler
(1729–83), written for two chamber organs and requiring no pedals. The
term "concerto" may seem misleading today, as there is no orchestra.
These works are in two or three short movements, each concerto including
a minuet. The style in general is light and *galant*.

All things considered, the most likely explanation for the lack of liturgical organ music from the Classic period is the strong tradition of organ
improvisation—a tradition that required an organist to develop the necessary skills to enable him to provide music of the exact length required at
any given moment in a service.[13] Such skills were admired in the organ-
playing of Wilhelm Friedemann Bach (1710–84). As late as 1829, in a letter
to Goethe, Zelter recalled Friedemann's playing:

> He was the most accomplished organist I have known. . . . His organ impro-
> visations (when he was in the mood for improvising) were admired by men
> such as Marpurg, Kirnberger, Benda . . ., most of them outstanding organists
> themselves. They realized that he was far ahead of them.[14]

Another type of "organ" music, found chiefly in Austria and Germany at this time, was that written for various mechanical instruments or
automatons. Maelzel's Panharmonicon was described in 1808: "It plays the
most difficult compositions with full harmony, as beautifully as the best orchestra could perform them."[15] Maelzel, the writer continues, took it to
Paris, where he and his invention were much admired. Its repertory included a Mozart overture, the finale of a Haydn symphony, and much else,
"all rendered with the finest nuances of forte and piano." Some of these
inventions, because of the manner of tone production, are properly called
organs and can still be heard today in eighteenth-century castles and
palaces. Mozart contributed to the genre: his Fantasies K. 594 and 608
were written for a *Flötenuhr*—an automaton consisting of a miniature organ
with one rank of pipes. Haydn also wrote pieces for musical clocks (Hob.
XIX; see also the preface to *Haydn: Werke*, XXI.) Conventional organs with
tonal properties similar to these mechanical instruments existed in church-

---

[13]R. Freeman, "The Role of Organ Improvisation in Haydn's Church Music," *Haydn
Studies* (New York: Norton, 1981), pp. 192ff.
[14]Quoted by Rummenhöller, *Die musikalische Vorklassik*, pp. 83f.
[15]"Maelzel und seine musikalischen Kunstwerke," *Vaterländische Blätter für den österreichischen Kaiserstaat*, I (1808), 112ff.

(Top) Interior of the
Salzburg cathedral,
showing the lofts
with organs and
musicians.
Engraving by
Melchior Küsel, ca.
1680. Museum
Salzburg.

(Bottom) Detail of
above, in front of
the main altar,
showing *(l)* singers
(in front of clergy)
and *(r)* singers,
organist, and other
instrumentalists.
Museum Salzburg.

es as well,[16] as in the Kajetanerkirche in Salzburg, built by J. C. Eged-acher, who also built—or, rather, added to—the large organ in the Salzburg cathedral. Most Austrian cathedrals and many monastery churches had large organs. In the Salzburg cathedral, several additional small organs were located near the main altar (see illustration) while the main organ was and is located in the loft, above the portals. Today such small organs, in the small lofts on the pillars, are again being built.

A detailed discussion of organs and organ music in other parts of Europe is beyond the scope of this study. A few major composers in the Protestant north carried on traditions of the great past, among them Johann Ludwig Krebs (1713–80), a pupil of Bach in Leipzig. The decline of organ composition in France has been related to the secular orientation of the age.[17] Charles Burney, during his extensive travels, visited churches in Paris and other French cities. He was surprised to hear an organist play, between verses of the Magnificat, "minuets, fugues, imitations, and every species of music, even to hunting pieces and jigs, without surprising or offending the congregation."[18] He regretted that the fine organs at Notre Dame and in Lille were little used, but he admired the new organ at St. Roque in Paris which had four manuals and a pedal keyboard.

A popular genre of French organ music throughout the eighteenth century was the *noël* for organ. These were based on both sacred and secular tunes that were well known to the congregations. Composers of organ *noëls* included Louis-Claude Daquin (1694–1772), Michel Corrette (1709–95), and Claude Balbastre (1727–99).

BIBLIOGRAPHICAL NOTES

Both Einstein's and Blom's books on Mozart include chapters on his sacred music. Geiringer's coverage is not concentrated in one chapter; he also contributed an essay on Mozart's church music to *MC*. Relevant chapters in *NOHM* are volume VII, chapter 4 ("Classic Church Music and Oratorio"), and volume VIII, chapter 13 ("Choral Music"), with much material on Beethoven and French contemporaries. The complex story of Mozart's *Requiem*, including its completion after the composer's death, is related in the preface to *NMA* I:1/2 (L. Nowak) and discussed by F. Blume ("Requiem But No Peace") in *The Creative World of Mozart* (New York, 1963; previously published in *MQ*, 47 [1961]).

[16]Peter Williams describes the organ at Weingarten with its "toy stops": cuckoo and other bird sounds, drum, Zimbelstern. "The effect it gives is of a huge rococo cinema organ, built to delight all who saw and heard it." *The European Organ 1450–1850* (London: Batsford, 1966), p. 79.

[17]C. A. Arnold, *Organ Literature: A Comprehensive Survey*, (2nd ed.; Metuchen, NJ: Scarecrow Press, 1984), I: 132f.

[18]*The Present State of Music in France and Italy* (London, 1773), p. 38.

Restrictions on church music in Austria are discussed in Pauly's "The Reforms of Church Music under Joseph II," *MQ*, 43 (1957). A. Hanson's *Musical Life in Biedermeier Vienna* (Cambridge: Cambridge Univ. Press, 1985), though dealing chiefly with a later period, surveys traditions and practices of church music around 1800.

Volume 3 of H. Smither's *History of the Oratorio* includes the Classic period (Chapel Hill, NC: Univ. of North Carolina Press, 1987). G. Feder's chapter "Decline and Restoration" in F. Blume's *Protestant Church Music* (New York: Norton, 1974) gives detailed information about this period. Blume's volume also includes a chapter on sacred music in North America during the colonial and federal periods. In addition to sources cited in the text, a specialized study by F. Douglass should be mentioned: *The Language of the Classical French Organ* (New Haven: Yale University Press, 1969).

Examples of the sacred music of Adlgasser, Biber, Eberlin, and Michael Haydn can be found in several volumes of *DTO* and in more recent practical editions. Many scores which previously have not been easily accessible will be included in the series *The Latin Mass, 1720–50* (New York: Garland, 1987–   ; 22 volumes planned) and *The Italian Oratorio, 1650–1800* (New York: Garland, 1986–   ; 31 volumes planned).

THIRTEEN
FROM CLASSICISM
TO ROMANTICISM

MUSIC AND THE FRENCH REVOLUTION

French music of the late eighteenth and early nineteenth centuries understandably reflected the stormy political events of the age. With the overthrow of the monarchy and with the abolition, at least temporarily and officially, of organized Christian religion, music had been deprived of areas in which it had filled an important need. Political leaders, however, were well aware that music could become a powerful tool of the new state. As on other subjects, their views on the function of music resembled those held by philosophers of antiquity, in this instance ancient Greece rather than Rome. Music no longer existed for the entertainment of a privileged class of society but was to have higher purposes: to arouse patriotism, to serve the state and, ultimately, humanity. In place of traditional religion an elaborate official cult was set up in honor of a supreme being, along with

233

special holidays in honor of nature, youth, marriage, agriculture, and other institutions. Musical compositions held an important place in these celebrations and had to be approved by the French legislature. Among officials concerned with education there was a similar awareness that music might accomplish much; consequently, detailed instructions were contained in new curriculum directives. Hymns in honor of country, liberty, and mankind were to be sung regularly. The singing of such hymns was to contribute to the development of virtuous and loyal citizens—a view close to that expressed in Plato's *Republic*.

As a result of political events a large amount of music was rather suddenly needed for patriotic and civic functions, and for education. Many of France's leading composers contributed to the cause, among them Luigi Cherubini (1760–1842), Gossec, André Ernest Modeste Grétry (1741–1813), François Lesueur (1760–1837), and Etienne Méhul (1763–1817). Much of this Revolutionary music was destined for outdoor ceremonies, with massed choruses and monstrous bands or orchestras, and with refrains sung by the people. The interest in Greek and Roman antiquities also gave rise to the construction of brass instruments similar to those represented on ancient columns and pictures. A ceremony on the first anniversary of the Revolution included a large procession and an open-air religious service said to have been attended by two hundred thousand. In 1789, Gossec became *directeur de la musique des fêtes nationales;* in this capacity he wrote marches, choruses, and other works with titles such as *Hymne à l'Etre suprême* and *Offrande à la liberté*. The recently composed *Marseillaise* (1792) was included in some of these.[1]

Large-scale, grandiose works became very fashionable, causing Grétry to remark that composers would soon be "noisemakers" only, and that the taste of the public stood in danger of being corrupted by so much music with cannon shots. Music on a grand scale, colorful and pictorial, appealed to Lesueur (the teacher of Berlioz!) and to Méhul, some of whose hymns came close to achieving the popularity of the *Marseillaise*. Liberty had also come to the theater with a public decree proclaiming the "freedom of the stage."

Ideas and events of the Revolution found reflection in many plays and operas. The "horror-and-rescue opera" in which justice triumphs over tyranny became a genre that strongly appealed to a public with vivid memories of violence and acts of oppression. J. N. Bouilly's *Léonore*, based on actual happenings during the Reign of Terror was such a play. It was set to music by Pierre Gaveaux (1798); Beethoven's *Fidelio* was composed to a German translation of it. Cherubini's *Lodoïska* (1791) is a rescue opera; his *Les deux journées* (1800) may also be based on a real incident. Many of

---

[1]A proclamation signed by Gossec, Lesueur, Méhul, and others, pledging their participation in teaching patriotic songs to the people, is translated in Weiss and Taruskin, *Music in the Western World* (New York: Schirmer Books, 1984), pp. 319ff.

these highly dramatic, emotional operas employ the orchestra (especially in the overtures) and chorus in conspicuous, forceful ways more familiar to us from symphonies and operas of nineteenth-century Romanticism. Lesueur's *La Caverne* (1793) contains these dramatic qualities in both text and music. Typically violent emotion is expressed in one of the accompanied recitatives, with changes in tempo and mood and with short arioso interpolations. The recitative leads into a heroic aria expressing great courage and determination. This scene and others, such as the concluding chorus, strongly suggest moods of Beethoven's *Fidelio*. In such operas

> The world of pastoral make-believe has gone; instead we may be confronted by political agitators, passport inspections and resistance movements, and nearly always by inflamed passions and an atmosphere of violence and terror. The plots are full of spectacular catastrophes—earthquakes, avalanches, shipwrecks . . . the collapse of caverns—with a happy end supervening just in time, generally the rescue of innocence from a grisly or unjust fate by an act of heroic human courage.[2]

In general, then, the mood of French music during and after the Revolution was serious and stern, incorporating a classic-heroic outlook comparable to the neoclassic paintings of David and Ingres. These qualities found their way into purely instrumental music also—the symphonies of Méhul, the violin concertos of Viotti. Méhul achieved some success with his symphonies, but in general French symphonic music of the early nineteenth century was overshadowed by the popularity of Haydn and, eventually, Beethoven. Napoleon's preference for Italian music was an additional handicap; he made no secret of his preference for the music of Paisiello and Cimarosa to that of Méhul. Not until Paisiello had returned to Italy did Napoleon offer Méhul the position of *maître de la chapelle*. At Napoleon's coronation in Notre Dame (December 2, 1804), a Mass and Te Deum by Paisiello were performed, as well as motets by LeSueur. Méhul had composed a Mass for this event but it was not performed at this time.[3]

LUDWIG VAN BEETHOVEN (1770–1827)

Beethoven's position in relation to both Classicism and Romanticism has been mentioned before. His music shows many characteristics familiar to us from the mature Haydn and Mozart; yet, especially in his later works, typical qualities of Romanticism appear clearly and frequently.

[2]Winton Dean, "Opera under the French Revolution," *Proceedings of the Royal Musical Association*, 94 (1967–68), 82.
[3]Jean Mongrédien, "La musique du sacre de Napoléon 1," *Revue de musicologie*, 2 (1967), 154.

His birthplace, Bonn, was the capital of a church state. Both his father and grandfather had served in the court chapel. The sacred repertory that young Beethoven came to know included Caldara and Pergolesi. In the instrumental field the Mannheim composers were represented, along with Dittersdorf, Haydn, Gossec, and Boccherini. Both *opera buffa* (Galuppi, Piccinni) and *opéra comique* were staged; performances of Gluck's operas took place in the years just before Beethoven left Bonn, after having played in the opera orchestra for four years. The ruler at this time, Maximilian Franz, youngest son of Austrian Empress Maria Theresa, was a great lover of Mozart's music. Both the *Entführung* and *Don Giovanni* were given in Bonn in 1789, and *Figaro* followed the next year.

In addition to the flourishing official musical life there was much informal music-making. In the home of the von Breuning family, Beethoven found warmth and friendship, both sadly lacking in his own home, and met educated people from all walks of life—painters, musicians, aristocratic enthusiasts of music. The friendship with Count Waldstein, who was to do so much for the young composer, in all likelihood also began in the von Breuning home.

A set of nine variations for piano, on a march in C minor by Dressler, was published in 1782; it may be Beethoven's earliest preserved work. Piano variations were generally popular with Classic composers and especially so with Beethoven, who wrote many variations movements in sonatas, symphonies, and other multiple-movement genres, aside from over twenty separate sets of variations on original or borrowed themes, culminating in the great Diabelli Variations of 1823. Marches also attracted Beethoven throughout his life, as did the key of C minor; so the Dressler variations by the twelve-year-old are in several ways a significant beginning. Other early works include a set of piano sonatas (published in 1783), three piano quartets (1785), and fragments of a violin concerto. Two cantatas, on the death of Joseph II and the coronation of Leopold II, are among the few early vocal works. In fact, Beethoven wrote little vocal music of importance before *Fidelio*, thereby demonstrating, at least in the opinion of some biographers, that it was to be his mission to overcome the dominant position of vocal music.

In a farewell note to Beethoven, about to depart for Vienna, Count Waldstein expressed the belief and hope that there Beethoven would receive "the spirit of Mozart from Haydn's hands." Undoubtedly Beethoven felt sure that Vienna more than any other city could offer all that a young, serious, and ambitious musician might ask for.[4]

Haydn, then at the height of his fame, agreed to give him lessons, but the pupil—young, impatient, demanding, and suspicious—felt that the master did not devote sufficient care to the assignments. Behind Haydn's

[4]Parts of Reichardt's glowing description of Vienna as a center of music are quoted in *SMH*, pp. 728ff.

back he sought other instruction. The great differences of their personalities further contributed to a parting of ways; yet Beethoven continued to respect Haydn the composer and dedicated to him the three piano sonatas, Op. 2, of 1795.[5] The documentary evidence published by Landon points to a complex, ambivalent relationship—a mixture, on Beethoven's part, of reverence for the older master and jealousy, often aroused by petty incidents. By the time of the *Eroica* (1804) Beethoven no longer felt threatened by the aged Haydn.[6]

Like Mozart, Beethoven first established himself in Vienna as a pianist.

> For the last two years he has chosen Vienna as his residence. His great dexterity at the keyboard causes general admiration, also the ease of execution of unusual difficulties. . . . We already have several fine sonatas composed by him.[7]

He gained the admiration and friendship of Prince Lychnowski and his family; through him he met other members of the music-loving nobility, including the Russian ambassador, Count Rasoumowski. These and other noble patrons helped the young composer most generously. Rasoumowski maintained a private string quartet, an excellent ensemble that was always at Beethoven's disposal for experimentation, to give an immediate hearing to his compositions.

Among other important works from the early years in Vienna are the piano trios Op. 1 (1795), other piano sonatas including Op. 13, the famous *Pathétique* (1798–99); the First Symphony (1799–1800), the C Minor Piano Concerto (1800), the Septet (1799–1800), and the six quartets Op. 18 (1798–1800). Many of these works show clear and organic ties to the Classicism of the preceding generation. In the trio Op. 1, No. 1, for instance, the range of the piano part is conventional and the violin and cello parts still lie fairly low; Beethoven gives them far less thematic material or elaborate passagework than he gives to the piano, which traditionally had been dominant in this combination of instruments. The cello still sometimes doubles the left-hand piano part. The development is approximately half as long as the exposition—a fairly conventional proportion, in contrast to the more extensive development sections in many later works. Nor does the development in this trio reach very remote keys. Cadential progressions are traditional, as is some of the figuration in the violin part. Yet there is much in this trio and in the other two of Op. 1 that is new and characteristic of Beethoven.

---

[5]See also D. Johnson, "1794–95: Decisive Years in Beethoven's Early Development," *Beethoven Studies*, 3 (Cambridge, England: Cambridge University Press, 1982), 16ff.

[6]Landon, *Chronicle and Works*, IV: 269f; V: 238, 258, 356, 358ff.

[7]*Jahrbuch der Tonkunst von Wien und Prag* (1796), 7f. The writer continues that Beethoven's choice of Haydn for a teacher is proof of his love of music.

Chromaticism is used for its own sake—for color rather than modulation. A wider dynamic range includes such favorite Beethoven effects as a sudden pianissimo after a fortissimo. The third movement is a scherzo, simple and regular in form but with the characteristic drive and the light, humorous quality that the name implies. (The third movement of Op. 1, No. 3 is again a minuet.)

The early piano sonatas likewise contain much that is new and characteristic. In the adagio of Op. 2, No. 1, marked cantabile, the sonorities of the low register are explored in a manner that one meets again in many later works. The prestissimo finale of this sonata, with its persistent triplet motion, displays an intensity that goes beyond the eighteenth-century manner. At other times it is a slow movement that shows the greatest originality and depth, as in the piano sonata Op. 7 (largo, con gran espressione). The tonal qualities and expressive characteristics of the piano suited Beethoven's personality, and therefore his musical style, especially well. Changes in his style often appeared first in his piano sonatas. In a letter of 1796 Beethoven said: "The pianoforte is still the least studied and developed of all instruments; often one thinks that one is merely listening to a harp. . . . Provided one can feel the music, one can also make the pianoforte sing."[8]

During these years, Beethoven moved freely from conventional to new paths: he wrote minuets and other dances for orchestra when asked for them in 1795; only four years later the *Pathétique* Sonata was published. At about the same time another work of chamber music was finished: the delightful, unproblematic Septet for strings and winds, Op. 20, a work close to the eighteenth-century serenade tradition. That the Septet should for a long time have been one of Beethoven's most popular works shows how the conservative facet of his musical personality was understood, while many later and, to us, more typical compositions were considered bizarre, cacophonous, and unintelligible.

Only after much experimentation and many sketches did Beethoven venture before the public with his first symphony. Undoubtedly he considered it difficult to follow Haydn and Mozart in this field. (Schubert was to feel the same way about Beethoven's symphonies.) Originality is found here, within the conventional symphonic idiom. To begin the work with a seventh chord was an original touch; to write a slow introduction for the last movement also was unusual. Though in general mood and dimensions the First Symphony built on the immediate past, it also established precedents for Beethoven's later symphonies. The third movement, though labeled minuet, is in effect a scherzo—a worthy forerunner of the scherzos in the Third, Fourth, and Seventh Symphonies. The orchestra of the First

[8]E. Anderson, ed., *The Letters of Beethoven*, I (New York: St. Martin Press, 1961), 25f. Concerning the instrument for which Beethoven wrote his piano music see below, p. 257.

is the usual one for Beethoven; he made only a few additions to it in some later works.

The general tone and especially the melodic style of much of Beethoven's music has been characterized as heroic. To an extent this already applies to the First Symphony but far more so to the Third, the *Sinfonia eroica*, finished early in 1804. Six years before, Count Bernadotte, the French Ambassador in Vienna, had suggested that Beethoven write a symphony in honor of Napoleon, a suggestion that was not unreasonable during an age of Napoleon-worship. Beethoven, as a great champion of liberty and as an admirer of Bonaparte—a man who had risen through the ranks, by virtue of superior ability—intended the Third Symphony to be his homage to the First Consul of the Republic. His disappointment must have been profound when Napoleon made himself Emperor, for he erased the name "Bonaparte" from the score that was ready to be sent to Paris. The printed edition (1806) carried a subtitle, in Italian, "to celebrate the memory of a great man"—the Napoleon that *had been.* Yet a few years later, Beethoven (according to Thayer) said to Czerny: "In earlier days I couldn't bear him. Now I think quite differently."[9]

Beethoven "Eroica" Symphony. Title page with erased dedication to Bonaparte. Austrian National Library.

[9]Thayer, *Life of Ludwig van Beethoven,* V: 135.

The "Eroica's" length, the nature of the thematic material and its manipulation, the emotional depth and range, the harmonic daring, and the handling of the orchestra—all these set it apart from any earlier symphonies. The formal construction of the first movement has been the subject of countless analyses, most of which point to the extensive development, introducing a new theme, as the most significant expansion of traditional first-movement form. Here the Classic technique of thematic fragmentation is carried to new heights. Accented harmonic clashes occur in several places and the recapitulation is prepared in a startling manner, with the French horn anticipating the main theme in the tonic against a dissonant tremolo (still on the dominant) in the strings. A funeral march forms the second movement. Its original significance is not known, but when Beethoven learned in 1821 of Napoleon's death, he said that he had written the music for this event twenty years before. Beethoven's piano sonata Op. 26 also contains a "Marcia funebre sulla morte d'un Eroe," but it seems less related in character to the other movements than is true in the "Eroica." In the latter, neither the powerful scherzo nor the stormy finale contradict the mood of the opening movements.

Beethoven's concertos also represent a continuation and intensification of earlier classic concertos. Mozart's piano concertos, much admired by the younger composer, exerted a strong influence, but there are substantial differences in form and in expressive content. All of Beethoven's concertos, especially the Third, Fourth, and Fifth piano concertos and the Violin Concerto, have the dimensions and musical substance found in other Beethoven works in larger forms; they contain qualities of seriousness and serenity rather than *galanterie*. There is nobility of line and a lack of virtuosity for its own sake. For the Violin Concerto, works by G. B. Viotti (1753–1824), Rodolphe Kreutzer (1766–1831), and Pierre Rode (1774–1830) may have served as models. Beethoven's orchestral tuttis are long and symphonic in character, so much so that the Violin Concerto has been called a "symphony with violin obbligato." Yet the relation between solo and tutti is one of Classic balance and proportion—whereas in many virtuoso concertos of the later nineteenth century the orchestral accompaniment provides but a flimsy backdrop in front of which the performer may shine.

With the six quartets of Op. 18, Beethoven for the first time entered that category of chamber music which Haydn and Mozart had made one of the foremost media of instrumental music. The quartet continued to hold a significant position throughout Beethoven's career: his last and, in the opinion of many his most profound, compositions were string quartets. Far from being "early" works or social music in the manner of the septet or some of his string trios, the Op. 18 quartets, while based on the mature chamber music of Haydn and Mozart, in every movement reveal Beethoven's individuality and personal style. Neither of the two earlier masters could have written a movement with the sustained tension, energy, and pathos of the opening allegro of Op. 18, No. 4, with its relentless eighth-note motion in the bass, its sforzatos and violent chords. This opening theme is long; elsewhere (as in the opening of Op. 18, No. 1) Beethoven works with extremely concise material—a conciseness that was the product of much experimentation, as is demonstrated by numerous sketches.

The superscription of the second movement of Op. 18, No. 1, *adagio affettuoso ed appassionato*, expresses well the mood of that piece, said to have been inspired by the tomb scene of *Romeo and Juliet*. In such movements Beethoven achieves an intensity and profundity of expression often associated with Romanticism. These quartets make considerable demands on each instrument, not only the first violin. Difficulties are related to the complexity of melodic line, to intricate rhythmic divisions, and to the high register (especially for the cello) rather than to bravura passagework.

Aside from the musical qualities just discussed, there are aspects of Beethoven's personality that show his affinity for the spirit of Classicism. Popular biography has represented him as the stormy revolutionary, but this picture is only partially true. While he embraced the ideas of the Enlightenment wholeheartedly, he was not an outspoken opponent of monarchy, and he abhorred the extremes of the French Revolution. He thought highly of Joseph II as an enlightened ruler, but few monarchs lived up to his idealistic concepts. He took no position against Catholicism as a religion or as an institution, though he was frequently critical of its clergy.

Beethoven's friendship with Archduke Rudolph, brother of the Austrian emperor, was mentioned earlier. Rudolph, one of the composer's important patrons, was made cardinal in 1819 and soon after installed as archbishop of Olmütz. Beethoven was eager to make an appropriate musical contribution. The *Missa Solemnis* (though not completed in time) became his most substantial sacred composition.

In his study of Greek and Roman philosophers, the moral concepts in their works impressed Beethoven most strongly. Other moral philosophers, among them Kant, also shaped his thinking. To Beethoven, the purpose of art was not entertainment but man's moral improvement. Much as he admired Mozart, the subject of *Don Giovanni* (even more so, one would think, of *Così fan tutte*) seemed improper to him, while the story of *Fidelio*, highly ethical in its praise of conjugal love and heroic self-sacrifice, attracted him strongly and led him to look for equally suitable subjects, without success. Such a lofty view of the purpose of art does suggest Platonic concepts; at the same time it points to the attitude of so many Romantics, to whom the mission of an artist was quasi-religious, his function in society being comparable to that of a high priest.

Beethoven's manner of composing, involving high standards of craftsmanship, constant polishing and improving, can also be related to the Classic tradition. He acknowledged the importance of inspiration, but said that after an idea had appeared "I change and reject much [of the idea or theme] and try again until I am satisfied with it. Then the working out in depth begins." This is not dreamy inspiration, the self-conscious Romantic cherishing of the first spark. E. T. A. Hoffmann, in a review of Beethoven's Fifth Symphony, showed fine insight when he took issue with the already popular view of the composer as one who relied on the spark of momentary inspiration, saying that "in his deliberateness Beethoven must be put next to Mozart and Haydn. He detaches his personality from the inner realm of music over which he reigns as undisputed master." Beethoven's own statements about his process of composition at times also reveal a matter-of-fact attitude, as when he referred once to his works as "products of the human brain." Many of Beethoven's sketches have been preserved and studied. Thus we know a good deal about this creative process, often slow and torturous, with constant self-criticism and—when a work was about to appear in print—with changes even during the proof-reading stage.

BEETHOVEN'S SONGS

> Herr van Beethoven, a genius, not tied to rules and conventions as is proper for a genius, has not been altogether successful in the larger vocal forms. In a number of shorter arias and songs, however, he has displayed true and profound feelings.[10]

Condescending as it may sound to us, this report reflects fairly widespread opinion of the time. Certainly Lieder held a significant place in Beethoven's life, though his songs are far less well known to today's audiences than his works in most other categories.

Over sixty Beethoven songs exist, varying greatly in style. Some are simple and light, if not trivial; others are substantial and beautiful in traditional ways, while some contain emotional qualities we associate with the composer's great and well-known instrumental works.

Examples of the first kind can be found among the songs published as Op. 52, all of which stem from the Bonn years. Some are still notated on two staves—true *Klavierlieder* in which the singer might also be the accompanist. Op. 52, No. 1, "Wenn jemand eine Reise tut," is believed to be one of Beethoven's first compositions; along with Nos. 7 and 8 it has the characteristics discussed in connection with Lieder by Schulz and others (see above, p. 29).

---

[10]Übersicht des gegenwärtigen Zustandes . . ." in *Vaterländische Blätter für den Österreichischen Kaiserstaat* VII (Vienna, 1808), p. 42.

Another spirit speaks from the *Six Lieder to Texts by Gellert* (Op. 48, composed in 1803). Their hymn-like, dignified, and strong music well suits Gellert's devotional texts. Op. 48, No. 4, is representative and perhaps the best known of the set (Example 13–1).

EXAMPLE 13–1. Beethoven, "Die Ehre Gottes aus der Natur" (Op. 48, No. 4), ending.

EXAMPLE 3–1. *Continued.*

läuft   den   Weg,   gleich   als   ein   Held.

"Adelaide" (Op. 46, 1795), aria-like and sectional in construction, was called a "cantata" when first published. Though conventional in some ways, it has a surging, Romantic quality. A substantial piano part includes detailed dynamic markings (including a crescendo leading to a sudden piano) and a modulation to the key of the lowered sixth (F to D♭), both characteristic of many later works.

Beethoven's keen interest in German Classic poetry gave rise to some of his best, and best-known, vocal writing. Schiller's "An die Freude" had inspired other composers to write songs, all forgotten today, before Beethoven set portions of the *Ode to Joy* in his Ninth Symphony. But Goethe's poetry exerted an even stronger influence. Beethoven venerated him, corresponded with him, and spent several days with him in 1812. A good number of Lieder to lyrics by Goethe were written before and after that year. There is incidental music for Goethe's play *Egmont,* but plans for music for *Faust* were never realized. Differences in their personalities and Goethe's generally conservative tastes are the likely reasons that no close friendship developed between these great men.

Beethoven was attracted, too, to Goethe's *Wilhelm Meister* poems and set two of them. Four versions of "Nur wer die Sehnsucht kennt" were written in close succession (1807 and 1808), the fourth being more ambitious than the others (which are strophic). All four are short and fairly simple. As Stein points out,[11] they appear all the more traditional when one recalls that 1808 was the year of the Sixth Symphony and two years after the *Leonore Overture* No. 3. Given Goethe's preference for simple settings in a folk-like style, these songs may well have received his approval. "Kennst du das Land" (Op. 75, No. 1, 1809) goes beyond these, in harmonic inventiveness and in attention to text-music relationships in general. A short setting of Goethe's "Wonne der Wehmut" (1810), andante espressivo, includes elaborate phrases for the piano, completing and imitating vocal phrases. Here, too, a great range of dynamics reflects the emotions of the text.

---

[11]J. M. Stein, *Poem and Music in the German Lied* (Cambridge, MA: Harvard University Press, 1971), p. 53.

Two versions of "An die Hoffnung" (text by Christian August Tiedge [1752–1841]) serve well to demonstrate different approaches to Lieder composition at this time: they were written within ten years of each other. Op. 32 (1805) uses identical music for the three stanzas, with a perfunctory piano introduction and postlude. The music captures the basic underlying elegiac mood but no more; there is no attempt to express qualities of individual words or concepts. The much longer, complex version of Op. 94 (1815) consists of three basic sections corresponding to the three verses of the poem—all very different, with close observation of the text. The song (like "Adelaide," it has also been called a cantata, and with more justification) opens with a short, intensely chromatic keyboard introduction which leads into a recitative, *accompagnato* style; following the dramatic conclusion of the recitative, the song proper begins. Near the end Beethoven repeats the first verse and then concludes by bringing back the two words that are central to the poem's message: "O Hoffnung!"

Often considered the first (and certainly the first significant) song cycle, *An die ferne Geliebte* (Op. 98; 1815–16), is literally a *Liederkreis:* Its first song is repeated at the end, the whole thus forming a circle. Unlike most nineteenth-century song cycles it forms a continuous musical whole: Each song, without a break, leads into the next, through a keyboard interlude. For example, the melody of No. 4, in A♭ major, ends on B♮, leading-into the C major of No. 5. Likewise, the adagio ending of No. 5 leads to a new key by way of a characteristically Romantic repetition in the minor mode of an idea first stated in major (Example 13–2):

EXAMPLE 13–2. Beethoven, "An die ferne Geliebte," conclusion of No. 5.

The entire work exudes a Romantic spirit, through the emotions expressed and in the way nature is portrayed. We "see" moving clouds, rippling brooks, barren trees of autumn, the sun's last rays, the return of spring. With this cycle we have reached, in time and in style, the age of Schubert's great Lieder, such as "Gretchen am Spinnrad" (1814) and "Erlkönig" (1815).

BEETHOVEN AND ROMANTICISM

Other facets of Beethoven's personality—those that are usually dwelled upon by biographers—correspond more closely to nineteenth-century views. His moodiness, his brooding, his famous fits of temper belong here; often they were due to the early deterioration of his hearing which made him shun crowds and seek peace and consolation in nature. His sensitivity to the beauties of the countryside, leading him to take long, solitary walks in the environs of Vienna, was understood and shared by many Romantic poets, painters, and musicians.

Liberté, égalité, fraternité—Beethoven welcomed these tenets of the French Revolution. For him, as for the nineteenth century in general, they led to a changed view of the artist as one who, by virtue of ability and genius, belonged to the highest order of society, equal if not superior to kings and princes. That Beethoven had strong feelings on this subject is evident from his relations to his noble patrons. He seems to have accepted much of the help he received from them, financial and otherwise, as something that society owed to him as an artist. Certainly he did not show himself overly thankful. At times he could be downright insulting, as in a note to Prince Lychnowski, one of his most faithful supporters: "What you are, you are by accident of birth; what I am, I am by myself. There are and will be thousands of princes; there is only one Beethoven."

In general, Beethoven's attitude toward the Romantic movement in literature and other fields—a movement that was much in evidence in the Vienna of his later years—was one of suspicion and rejection. Arnold Schmitz[12] has thoroughly investigated Beethoven's relation to Romanticism. In his opinion the nineteenth-century view of Beethoven as a Romantic is distorted, an opinion he documents with many statements by Beethoven about the purpose and nature of music and with musical examples demonstrating that Beethoven followed an approach to composition that, in many ways, reflected and grew out of Classic ideas.

Sentimentality in particular was repugnant to him. When his own improvising at the keyboard brought tears to the eyes of his listeners, he laughed at them noisily: "Fools! They are not artists. Artists are made of

[12]Arnold Schmitz, *Das romantische Beethovenbild* (Berlin, 1927; reprinted Bonn, 1978).

fire; they do not weep."[13] Still, in spite of his disassociation from the Romantic movement, his music—especially that of the middle and late periods—displays traits that came to be characteristic of Romanticism. While their study would lead beyond the scope of this volume, we may list some of the more important ones: unifying a multiple-movement work by avoiding breaks between movements (e.g., the scherzo of the Fifth Symphony, which leads directly into the finale) and by reintroducing in a later movement one or more themes from an earlier one (Fifth, Ninth symphonies); introducing the human voice into symphonic music (Ninth Symphony); extending the dimensions of the sonata, and at the same time increasing its complexities and technical difficulties (many late piano sonatas; the "Kreutzer" Violin Sonata); cultivating smaller forms, especially in keyboard music (the Bagatelles); displaying greater variety in form and sequence of movements, frequently with subtle thematic interrelationships (the late string quartets); showing some concern for tone painting and program music (the "Battle" Symphony, for which there were precedents; the "Pastoral" Symphony); exploring extensively the coloristic qualities of the piano, including its highest and lowest registers; and paying careful attention to a wide range of dynamics.

THE CHANGING GUITAR AND ITS REPERTORY

Plucked-string instruments enjoyed widespread popularity during the Renaissance and Baroque periods. Lute, theorbo and chitarrone frequently played continuo parts; there was also much solo repertory. Preferences for particular instruments varied from country to country. The guitar was popular in France at the time of Louis XIV. The king, instructed by the Italian guitarist Francesco Corbetta (died in 1681), was an enthusiastic player, as was Charles II of England. Many eighteenth-century paintings by Watteau and other French artists show guitar-playing aristocrats in *fêtes galantes* settings. But the lute continued to be preferred by many, especially in Germany, where Sylvius Leopold Weiss (1686–1750) composed for it, as did J. S. Bach. Mattheson preferred the lute to the guitar: After a long discussion of lute and theorbo, he urges his countrymen to "leave the flat guitars with their eternal 'strump strump' to the Spaniards while they feast on garlic," but he admits that lutes have the disadvantage of needing constant tuning: "If a lute player lives to be eighty years old he surely spent sixty years tuning."[14] The delicate tonal properties of the lute may also have contributed to its declining popularity, along with that of other soft instruments of the Baroque period (recorder, viola da gamba).

[13]A. Thayer, *The Life of Ludwig van Beethoven* (London, 1960), I: 195f.
[14]J. Mattheson, *Das neu-eröffnete Orchestre* (Hamburg, 1713), pp. 275ff.

Changes in the guitar's construction and stringing took place in the late eighteenth century. Five double courses (ten strings, two for each pitch) had been usual in Baroque guitars. These were gradually replaced by six single strings in Italy and France, and somewhat later in Germany and Spain. Single-stringing facilitated good intonation and fluent technique; it reflected and accommodated the gradual reemergence of the guitar as a solo and virtuoso instrument in the nineteenth century. Fan-strutting and other ways of strengthening the body of the instrument increased its resonance. These changes are similar to those found in instruments of the violin family at the same time. A larger body, and hence longer strings, and the adoption of a larger, open sound-hole were other changes that led, in the early nineteenth century, to the appearance and sound of the guitar as we know it today.

While earlier guitar music was written in tablature or "finger notation," the familiar pitch notation was now adopted. Fernando Ferandiere's *Arte de tocar la Guitarra española por Musica* (1799) is an instruction book representing the change. The author explains the greater usefulness of pitch notation: the player who can read it will also be able to play music written originally for other instruments, such as keyboard accompaniments for singers.[15]

It took time for the guitar to establish itself as an instrument for professional players to display their artistry before appreciative audiences. The musical world of the mid-eighteenth century (especially in northern Europe) viewed the guitar chiefly as a social instrument for amateurs, suitable mainly for simple, strumming accompaniments. Changes in this attitude reflect changes in late eighteenth- and early nineteenth-century society, especially in music patronage. As public concerts became frequent, the virtuoso performer assumed greater significance. For the guitar this meant (in addition to the structural changes of the instrument itself) the need for suitable repertory. Some of this development took place in Austria, especially in Vienna, the capital that attracted musicians of many nationalities.

Simon Molitor (1766–1848) was an Austrian composer and performer who in both capacities contributed to this development, providing repertory (solo, chamber music, and a guitar method) that took into account the instrument's enhanced capabilities. Other Austrians who wrote for the guitar, especially as an ensemble instrument, were Leonhard von Call (1769–1815), who also wrote songs with guitar accompaniment, and Anton Diabelli (1781–1858), who as an editor, also contributed to the availability of guitar music. His collection *L'Ape musicale per chitarra* (1806–7) contained arrangements of popular selections from ballets and operas for one or two guitars, and for guitar with voice or with other instruments. The *Notturno*, op. 21, for flute, viola, and guitar of Vaclav (Wenzel) Matiegka (1773–1830)

[15]V. Grunfeld, *The Art and Times of the Guitar* (New York: Macmillan, 1969), p. 140.

was arranged (with an added cello part) by Schubert. J. N. Hummel also composed chamber music with guitar, along with the inevitable arrangements and potpourris based on operatic airs.

Best known to guitarists today is Mauro Giuliani (1781–1829), an Italian who lived in Vienna for some years after 1806. He knew Beethoven and Hummel; his music was published by Diabelli. Contemporary chroniclers who still had reservations about the instrument were full of praise for Giuliani's composing and playing. Thus Reichardt (". . . perfection on such an imperfect instrument") and the correspondent of the *Vaterländische Blätter:* "Giuliani has brought this instrument to a height never reached before. He alone causes us to forget that its true function is that of accompanying and that its real character disappears when it tackles solos, sonatas or concertos."[16]

Giuliani was among the first guitar virtuosos to tour extensively. Among his compositions are guitar etudes (including 120 short arpeggios), several concertos, much chamber music, and songs with guitar accompaniment. A *Sonata Eroica,* a guitar method, and various potpourris contributed to his considerable fame, which extended to England where *The Giulianiad, Or Guitarist's Magazine* began a short-lived existence in 1833. His Concerto for Guitar and Orchestra in A Major, first performed in 1808, is an attractive work. Its general layout and much of its melodic material resemble Paganini's violin concertos, also composed by a virtuoso performer. The guitar is prominently featured in idiomatic and technically challenging passages and in a cadenza. A Siciliano (pastorale) in the minor mode provides contrast in the second movement; it leads into an *Alla polacca* finale.

Outstanding among Spanish guitarists was Fernando Sor (1778–1839), whose reputation rested on both his playing (he toured extensively, including Russia) and composing. Sor's works include much dance music but also sonatas, arrangements of operatic airs, and sets of variations on themes by Mozart, Paisiello, and others. His *Méthode pour la guitare* (1830) was widely used; his etudes still are, today.

Luigi Boccherini arrived in Spain in the 1760s. He became court composer to the king's brother and to the guitar-playing Marquis of Benavente. A *Sinfonia a grande orchestra* (Op. 21, No. 3; Gérard 523), really a *sinfonia concertante,* includes a part for *chitarra obligata.* The work is an arrangement, by the composer, of his string quintet Op. 10, no. 4 (Gérard 268). As in Boccherini's guitar quintets (also arrangements of other chamber works), the guitar-writing consists largely of accompaniment patterns.[17] The composer, a cellist, writes cello parts that are far more challenging than the guitar parts. A fandango contributes Spanish flavor to the last

---

[16]*Vaterländische Blätter für den österreichischen Kaiserstaat,* I (Vienna, 1808), 53.

[17]See Example 13–3, the only guitar solo in this movement, and Example 13–4, showing the typical guitar treatment.

EXAMPLE 13–3. Boccherini, *Sinfonia*, Op. 21, No. 3, *Grave* (Gérard 523).

EXAMPLE 13–4. Boccherini, *Sinfonia*, Op. 21, No. 3 (Gérard 523) Allegro.

movement of one quintet (Gérard 448).

Given the increasing popularity of the guitar in the nineteenth century one wonders why major composers contributed so little to the repertory. Schubert played the guitar but (in spite of claims to the contrary) did not write guitar accompaniments to any of his songs. Nor, it seems, did Beethoven, though his songs of Op. 52 were soon published with guitar accompaniment. Weber and Rossini played the instrument but did not add to its literature. The same is true of Berlioz who discusses the guitar in his *Grand traité d'instrumentation* (1844) and reflects on the difficulty of writing for it. Perhaps the spectacular rise of the modern piano, with its great variety of volume and timbres, made the guitar less competitive in public concerts and hence less attractive to composers.

BIBLIOGRAPHICAL NOTES

Good discussions of the French Revolution and music are found in *NOHM* VIII ("The Age of Beethoven"), Introduction and pp. 650ff; there also is good coverage of French opera on pp. 26ff.

The first major Beethoven biography, written by an American over one hundred years ago, is still a basic resource: Thayer's *Life of Ludwig van Beet-*

hoven, ed. E. Forbes (Princeton, 1964; rev. ed. 1967). Thayer does not, however, discuss the music. G. Pestelli's *The Age of Mozart and Beethoven* (Cambridge, England: Cambridge University Press 1984) contains a fine summary ("Beethoven's language") of the chief style characteristics of his music. M. Solomon, *Beethoven* (New York: Schirmer Books 1977) is recommended as a recent general study. *Ludwig van Beethoven,* J. Schmidt-Görg and H. Schmidt, eds. (New York: Praeger, 1969), contains essays on his life and the principal categories of his music; it is copiously illustrated. Schindler's recollections, though unreliable, are of interest, as they are based on years of personal acquaintance with the composer; they have been published in an annotated English edition by D. McArdle as *Beethoven as I Knew Him* (Chapel Hill, NC: University of North Carolina Press, 1966). William Newman's *Performance Practices in Beethoven's Piano Sonatas: an Introduction* (New York: Norton, 1971) is scheduled for publication in revised and greatly enlarged form.

Major reference works are the thematic catalog *Des Werk Beethovens,* G. Kinsky and H. Halm, eds. (Munich, 1955), and *The Letters of Beethoven,* trans. and ed. E. Anderson (London, 1961). A new complete edition of Beethoven's works is in process of publication (Munich, 1961–).

Lesueur's *La Caverne* has been reissued in a facsimile edition (New York: Pendragon, 1986). See also the bibliographical notes at the end of Chapter 11.

CONCLUSION
CLASSIC MUSIC
AND TODAY'S LISTENER

To the reader of this book one need hardly point out that Haydn's and Mozart's music today is performed and enjoyed everywhere. That it was widely accepted soon after their deaths is less obvious; nevertheless, its almost uninterrupted cultivation sets it apart from music before the Classic era. Few, if any, earlier musicians had risen to such international fame and were so popularly admired as was Haydn during his old age. To be sure, this admiration rested on only a small part of his work, especially the late quartets and symphonies. As for Mozart, little attention was paid to him in his home town if the Salzburg newspapers of the time are accurate as indicators: For twenty years after 1798 his name is not mentioned once. To be sure, these were turbulent years in Salzburg history.[1] Mozart's late operas soon did acquire a permanent place in the repertory. *The Magic Flute* was played everywhere soon after his death; by 1795 Schikaneder had

---

[1]F. Zaisberger, "Mozart im Spiegel der Salzburger Presse um 1800," *Mozart-Jahrbuch* (1980–83), p. 137.

Heute Montag den 4 Jäner 1802

Wird in dem kaiserl. königl. priv. Theater an der Wien unter der Direktion des Emanuel Schikaneders gegeben:

Der erste Theil
der

Zauberflöte.

Eine große Oper in 2 Aufzügen, von Emanuel Schikaneder.
Die Musik ist von Herrn Wolfgang Amade Mozart, weil. Kapellmeister, und k. k. Kammerkompositeur.

Personen.

Sarastro		Hr. Trimer.	Papageno,		Hr. Schikaneder
Tamino		Hr. Simoni, Sänger	Ein altes Weib,		Mad. Gsur
		der k. k. Hofkapelle.	Monostatos ein Mohr,		Hr. Schmidtmann
Sprecher		Hr. Reif	Erster		Hr. Reerat
Erster		Hr. Pfeifer.	Zweyter) Sklav.		Hr. Helmböl
Zweyter) Priester.		Hr. Weiß.	Dritter)		Hr. Segatta.
Dritter)		Hr. Hartmann.	Erster)		Frd. Neukäufler
Königin der Nacht.		Mad. Campi.	Zweyter) Genius		Kl. Ruck.
Pamina, ihre Tochter		Mad. Willmann.	Dritter)		Kl. Appel.
Erste)		Mad. Pfeiffer.	Priester, Sklaven, Gefolge.		
Zweyte) Dame.		Mlle. Constantin.			
Dritte)		Mlle. Wipfel			

Die hiezu durchaus neuen Dekorationen sind theils von Herrn Vinzenz
Sachetti, theils von Herrn Gail dem jüngern gemalt.

Da ich so glücklich war, Mozarts Freundschaft zu besitzen, und er aus wahrer
Bruderliebe zu mir, auf mein originelles Werk seine Meistertöne setzte, so werde
ich heute das verehrungswürdige Publikum mit zwey mir allein hinterlassenen Musik-
stücken von Mozarts Komposition vielleicht angenehm überraschen. Da übrigens das
gute Kind heute wieder zum erstenmal, nicht nur im neuen Hause, sondern auch mit
neuen Kleidern erscheint, so nahm ich als Vater mir die Freyheit, solchem hie und da
einige neue Worte in den Mund zu legen; ob sie wohlklingen, das überläßt dem Ur-
theil eines gnädigen und verehrungswürdigen Publikums
                    Dero
                    unterthänigster Diener
                    Emanuel Schikaneder,
                    k. k. priv. Schauspiel-Unternehmer.

Der Anfang ist halb 7 Uhr.

Playbill for performance on 4 January 1802 of "The First Part of The Magic Flute,"
produced by Schikaneder who, in 1798, had written a sequel to Mozart's opera, with
music by Winter. By this time Mozart's opera had been performed several hundred
times. Austrian National Library.

performed it two hundred times. By 1860, when the new opera house (today's Vienna State Opera) was built, scenes from Mozart operas were chosen for many of the paintings decorating its public areas. The building was inaugurated in 1869 with a performance of *Don Giovanni*. By 1830 approximately two-thirds of Mozart's music had reached print and several publishers had planned and begun complete editions. The interest in Mozart's music taken in the nineteenth century led to several early attempts at drawing up lists of his works and eventually made possible the publication of Köchel's catalog in 1862. Systematic publication of Haydn's works proceeded more slowly; a complete edition is still in progress at the time of this writing. Yet the twentieth-century interest in both composers has produced a wealth of editions, recordings, and scholarly writing. In 1982 Haydn's 250th birthday was observed worldwide with performances of both well-known and less well known works and with international congresses in Europe, America, and Australia. Recordings of the complete symphonies were issued by not one but two companies, who expected to sell more than three million copies.[2]

To explain why Classic music appeals so strongly to today's listener is an intriguing and difficult task in which many tempting oversimplifications present themselves. Serious music of *all* kinds and periods—from Gregorian chant to the latest trends, including complete serialization, minimalism, and others—today reaches a large public, so that much of what we may interpret as a special fondness for late-eighteenth-century music is merely part of this catholicity of taste. But the special attraction of Haydn's and Mozart's music for today's concertgoer and high-fidelity enthusiast may have some causes of its own. Probably more so than Romantic music, it can be experienced on many levels. Some listeners (St. Foix) may find "contorted, demonic force" or "paroxysms of exaltation" in Mozart's symphonies, but many others will derive complete satisfaction on a less intense emotional level. For them the music has meaning and gives pleasure because of its well-balanced, well-ordered nature. This, of course, is not to imply that Classic music lacks emotional intensity. Listening to a great deal of music discussed in these pages should confirm this—keyboard music by C. P. E. Bach, much of *Don Giovanni*, many slow movements from Haydn symphonies and quartets, along with much else. While being far from superficial, music of this kind nevertheless incorporates aesthetic and emotional qualities that stand in welcome contrast to the stresses and conflicts of our everyday lives.

Mozart, noting that certain violin sonatas by Schuster had pleased a large public, decided to write some in the same style. Much Classic music

[2]O. Biba, "Haydn after the Haydn-Year," *Haydn Yearbook*, 14 (1983), 212ff.

was written to please—to provide spontaneous, immediate enjoyment. Such music may well be profound without being self-consciously and introspectively so, without intending to represent or symbolize violent struggle, exaltation, or apotheoses of various kinds. To say of a conductor that he makes Haydn sound like Tchaikovsky is a criticism heard more frequently today than two generations ago. This may merely reflect our greater consciousness of style differences between Classic and Romantic music, but it may also imply a preference for the qualities of restraint and serenity with which, subtly yet persuasively, so much Classic music speaks to us today.

THE "EARLY MUSIC" MOVEMENT
AND THE CLASSIC PERIOD

We noted earlier that most music performed at the time of Mozart and Beethoven was "contemporary"—literally of their own time—and that consequently Burney could refer to some sacred music of the preceding generation as "admirable old music" (see p. 8). For twentieth-century listeners the terms "old music" and "early music" have a different meaning, for today we are exposed to a wealth of music of all periods, from the Middle Ages to the present, including the new and vast dimension of non-Western music.

Today's listener, through live performances and a vast selection of recordings, has easy access to two thousand years of music: Gregorian chant, *trecento* madrigals, late Renaissance Masses and lute songs, to say nothing of virtually all major works of the Baroque era, from Monteverdi and Schütz to Bach and Handel. This is a drastic change, largely brought about during the last half-century. Credit for it is appropriately given to the work of music historians—to the emergence of musicology as a scholarly discipline. Increasingly since the late nineteenth century music researchers have located the musical source material and—a precondition for editing and publishing—have found ways to decipher its often problematic, previously unintelligible notation.

The editions resulting from such musicological research represent, however, only the first step—though probably the most important one—on the road to musical performance. Many questions have still to be addressed about how music of a particular period was sung and played at that time. Solving these questions has become the objective of a special field of investigation: the study of "performance practice"—a field to which increasing attention has been paid since the 1950s. It has provided a welcome meeting ground for scholars and performers, and it has been the ground from which an "early-music movement" grew. Its flourishing today is apparent. Few colleges and universities are without a *Collegium Musicum*—a group in which students and others experience early music, singing it and playing it, preferably under the leadership of well-trained musicians. Many of the larger institutions offer degree programs in early music, and there are countless workshops, in the United States and in Europe, offering instruction through master classes, lectures, and faculty recitals.

Instruments of the period, or modern replicas, have become essential. General interest in the harpsichord was stimulated by the playing and teaching of Wanda Landowska (1879–1959); gradually the interest extended to other instruments. Concerts in which "authentic" or "period" instruments are used are common today. A random sampling of the concert offerings in New York in one recent week included four different ensembles giving concerts on period instruments: one Renaissance program, one all-Mozart concert using the fortepiano (see below), another program featuring early nineteenth-century brass instruments, and one of Classic-period string quartets played on original instruments. When performing eighteenth-century orchestral music today, using an appropriate number of instruments is a matter of concern. There may also be a preference for a hall with acoustics similar to those of an eighteenth-century performance space.[3]

Given the rapidly growing interest in early-music performance, it is not surprising that at times excessive claims are made. As Joseph Kerman views it, " 'Authentic' has now acquired the same cult value when applied to music as 'natural' or 'organic' when applied to food."[4] Of course, the term "authentic performance" needs to be used with caution, for in spite of all possible research no one can claim to know—in the absence of recordings—how, in every detail, a work such as a Monteverdi opera was performed, let alone how it was heard through seventeenth-century ears.

Music of the Classic period has been late in being taken up by the early-music movement. One reason is the general assumption, widely held, that there has been an uninterrupted musical tradition from the late eighteenth century to the present—that sources were never lost and that there have been no changes in musical notation, the make-up of performing groups, or other aspects of performing practice. These assumptions have, however, been scrutinized and revised. As we have become familiar with the sounds of eighteenth-century instruments we have often found them attractive and preferable in actual performances: Couperin's and Scarlatti's music played on a harpsichord rather than a modern piano; a *Brandenburg*

---

[3]See, among other sources, the articles by Biba and Zaslaw cited at the end of this chapter.

[4]As he puts it in the chapter "The Historical Performance Movement," in his *Contemplating Music* (Cambridge MA: Harvard University Press, 1985), p. 192.

Concerto played by a group that uses the number of performers and the instruments characteristic of Bach's own day.

For the late eighteenth and early nineteenth centuries similar considerations have brought back the fortepiano as the appropriate keyboard instrument for much of the Mozart-Beethoven-Schubert repertory, both for solo and for accompaniment use (see p. 125). Some performers today, at home in Baroque and Classic keyboard music, may choose different instruments for different composers: an appropriate harpsichord (Flemish, Italian, or French) for Baroque music; a German or Viennese fortepiano of about 1780 for Mozart; for Beethoven and Schubert, an instrument by a later Viennese maker such as Joseph Böhm or Konrad Graf.[5] Players may prefer a pitch somewhat higher than A = 415 (generally in use today for Baroque music) but lower than modern pitch (A = 440). Tunings other than equal temperament may be used. String players may play with bows of the time, which have less tension of the bow hair and a narrower band of hair. The string section of a Haydn-Mozart orchestra had a softer sound; bassoons, oboes, and clarinets, on the other hand, were apt to be louder, though the (wooden) eighteenth-century flute was much softer than its modern counterpart. The valveless horns, in orchestral writing, were soft, as were trumpets, which were seldom required to play the high (clarino) parts of Baroque music.[6]

But aside from matters of instrument construction and tuning, performers now concern themselves with musical interpretation, trying to recreate, to the extent possible, performance styles of the period and—a complex and controversial issue—generally to express the composer's intentions. Proper phrasing, articulation, improvisation (including cadenzas), ornamentation,[7] dynamics, vibrato, tempo choices, and other aspects of vocal and instrumental interpretation—many performers are interested in studying these. Those who are serious about the subject should not underestimate the difficulties that stand in the way of acquiring the necessary vocal and instrumental techniques; they are quite different from what has traditionally been taught in our schools and conservatories. Much enthusiasm has been kindled by recent performances, live and recorded, of eminent soloists and ensembles. Well known (to mention just a few) are Malcolm Bilson, Kenneth Drake, and Igor Kipnis (fortepiano), the Esterházy Quartet (which performs Haydn and Mozart string quartets), and the Academy of Ancient Music, especially its recordings of Mozart symphonies.

[5]Concerning Beethoven's instruments, see also Derek Melville, "Beethoven's Pianos," in *The Beethoven Reader* (New York: Norton, 1971), pp. 41–67.

[6]E. Badura-Skoda, "Performance Conventions in Beethoven's Early Works," in *Beethoven, Performers and Critics* (Detroit, 1980), p. 73.

[7]Badura-Skoda, "Performance Conventions," p. 57f., quotes from a 1796 source in which solo performers are advised that they must know how to add ornamentation—gracefully, appropriately, not to excess.

BIBLIOGRAPHICAL NOTES

For a summary of Haydn's place in nineteenth- and twentieth-century musical life, see the last chapter ("Epilogue: The Haydn Renaissance") of H. E. Jacob's *Joseph Haydn* (London, 1950). A. Hyatt King's *Mozart in Retrospect* gives a thorough account of the fate of Mozart's music, the compilation of Köchel's catalog, and the various attempts at a complete edition; the latter are also discussed in Köchel's catalog (6th ed.; Wiesbaden, 1964), pp. 915ff. In the chapter "The Clavier in Mozart's Life," King is one of the early advocates of a return to the fortepiano. A detailed account of attitudes toward Mozart and his music, from his death to Schaffer's *Amadeus*, is G. Gruber's *Mozart und die Nachwelt* (Salzburg, 1985).

The periodical *Early Music* is an important, ongoing resource. Its November 1984 and February 1985 issues are devoted to early piano-makers and performance practices. J. Montagu's *The World of Baroque and Classical Musical Instruments* (Woodstock, NY: Overlook Press, 1979) contains a chapter "The Classic Era" which is amply illustrated. *The New Grove Dictionary of Musical Instruments* (3 volumes, London, 1984), a magnificent reference work, includes many articles on eighteenth-century instruments. Among other articles with up-to-date bibliography are "Performance Practice," "Ornamentation," "Improvisation," "Cadenza," "Tempo," and "Expression Marks." A *New Grove Handbook of Performance Practice* is in preparation. Contemporary sources are cited in C. MacClintock's *Readings in the History of Music in Performance* (Bloomington, IN: Indiana University Press, 1979) and W. Newman's *Performance Practices in Beethoven's Piano Sonatas: an Introduction* (New York: Norton, 1971). Other aspects of performance practice are treated by Otto Biba, "Concert Life in Beethoven's Vienna," in *Beethoven, Performers and Critics* (Detroit, 1980), pp. 77ff, and by N. Zaslaw, "Toward the Revival of the Classical Orchestra," in *Proceedings of the Royal Musical Association*, CIII (1976–77), 158–87.

More general questions about "authentic" performances are raised by R. Taruskin, "The Musicologist and the Performer," in *Musicology in the 1980s*, ed. K. Holoman and C. Palisca (New York: Da Capo Press, 1982), pp. 101ff; by L. Dreyfus, "Early Music Defended against Its Devotees: A Theory of Historical Performance in the Twentieth Century," *MQ*, 49 (1983), 297–322; and by R. Dipert, "The Composer's Intentions: An Examination of their Relevance for Performance," *MQ*, 66 (1980), 205–18. The literature is growing rapidly.

F. Grunfeld's *The Art and Times of the Guitar* (New York: Macmillan, 1969) deals chiefly with the instrument and its changes and the role of the guitar in different societies. H. Turnbull's *The Guitar from the Renaissance to the Present Day* (New York: Scribner's Sons, 1974) contains some discussion of music for guitar and includes a few musical examples. A. Bellow's *The Illustrated History of the Guitar* (New York: Colombo Publications, 1970) has a chapter on the eighteenth-century guitar. There is a facsimile edition of F. Sor's complete works for guitar (New York: Ariel Publications, 1977).

INDEX